Managing Information Systems Security and Privacy

Denis Trček

Managing Information Systems Security and Privacy

 Springer

Assoc. Prof. Denis Trček, Ph. D.

Department of Communication Systems
Jožef Stefan Institute
Jamova 39
1000 Ljubljana
Slovenia
E-mail: denis.trcek@ijs.si

Cataloging-in-Publication Data
Library of Congress Control Number: 2005934656

ISBN-10 3-540-28103-7   Springer Berlin Heidelberg New York
ISBN-13 978-3-540-28103-0   Springer Berlin Heidelberg New York

Springer is a part of Springer Science+Business Media
springeronline.com

© Springer-Verlag Berlin Heidelberg 2006
Printed in Germany

Cover design: Erich Kirchner
Production: Helmut Petri
Printing: Strauss Offsetdruck

SPIN 11381846   Printed on acid-free paper – 43/3153 – 5 4 3 2 1 0

To my family and parents

Preface

Strong penetration of information technologies into all segments of our lives has significantly influenced numerous issues that were of a minor importance only some ten years back. The game has changed, and among the most affected areas are the areas of security and privacy in information systems. No wonder, because organizations are getting tightly coupled with modern information technology based information systems, individuals are dependent on e-services, and even various infrastructures of nations are backed by information systems that deploy sophisticated technologies.

Before the era of globally interconnected networks (and consequently information systems), an entity's security and privacy could be managed within the physical perimeter, in which this entity was living. With the emergence of globally interconnected information systems, this perimeter has been enlarged enormously. Information systems and our dependence on them have increased threats to our security and privacy and resulted in new vulnerabilities. The only answer to counter this situation is to be armed with appropriate knowledge, because predators were, are, and will remain a fact of life.

The area of management of information systems security and privacy is now a multidisciplinary area. To cope with it, this book provides a focused umbrella methodology that covers relevant areas: technology, organization and legislation. Although the emphasis is on management of information systems security and privacy in organizations, individuals are also considered and should benefit from this book.

The first chapter presents the scope and methodology that this book is based upon. In the second chapter, organization related issues are discussed with emphasis on security policies. In the third chapter information technology concepts are presented in a way in which technical and mathematical details are completely omitted. Thus readers that are not of mathematics or technology origin should be able to understand the basic tools of trade. In the fourth chapter, the most relevant international legislation and legal frameworks in this area are given. The fifth chapter presents conclusions with anticipation of future trends. Finally, there is an appendix with explanation of mathematical principles and research (methodologies), which are promising to improve management of security and privacy through computer simulation.

What is the targeted population of this book? As mentioned, the area is now multidisciplinary, meaning that it includes various profiles - these profiles are the targeted population. Besides, the book is intended also to bridge the gaps between these profiles. Non-technical profiles are supposed to become more familiar with the domain of technical profiles, and understand their way of thinking, including the limitations of the world that they are dealing with. On the other hand, technical profiles are supposed to be able to look upwards to stay with an organization's strategy and objectives while taking care of information systems security and privacy.

Last but not least, the book bridges the gap between pure science and its results in a form of contemporary solutions that can be already applied in production environments.

We will do our best to accomplish these goals and to present the reader with a focused and properly structured approach. This approach should enable the reader to get a detailed understanding of information systems security and privacy management. Further, the reader should be able to find a solution for specific problems in this field by anticipating future developments and grasping the big picture perspective.

And thank you for choosing this book.[1]

Ljubljana,   *Denis Trček*

September 2005

---

[1]Every effort has been made to provide accurate information in this book. Nevertheless, please send errata suggestions and related questions through e-mail to dtbooks.errata@gmail.com.

Acknowledgements

Each scientific and professional book is the product of knowledge that has often been gathered over many generations. Consequently, each such book presents just one contribution that is added to the existing mosaic of knowledge, and handed over to the larger community, often also to future generations. This book is no exception.

From a wider perspective, each book is also the product of numerous interactions with people that have influenced the author's life - starting with parents, family, friends, teachers, university professors, professional colleagues... And even this list is far from being exhaustive.

Therefore, I should list here names of a few hundred persons to whom I wish to express my gratitude. But this is almost impossible, so I want to offer a word of thanks to all those people mentioned above. However, those persons that are directly related to the birth of this book, be it with professional discussions, general support or because of their work - they should be listed explicitly. With some of these persons I was in touch only for a day or two, with some of them for months, and with the rest of them for a few years. So here are their names ordered alphabetically. And please excuse me, because I will omit their academic and professional titles - the majority hold high academic and professional titles:

T. Bates, P. Bertema, A. Brodnik, H.G. Hegering, G. Hödel, T. Javornik, D.M. Johnson, T. Kalin, G. Kandus, G. Klemenčič, T. Lenggenhager, J. Lühe, S. Micalli, R. Novak, R. Pain, N. Pavešić, H. Reiser, M. Roe, R. Rüppel, J.F. Tasič, M. Terpstra, S. Tomažič, R. Trobec, V. Turk, M. Wiget, and K. Žontar.

Many thanks go to my main employer, "Jožef Stafan" Institute.

Special thanks go to the people at Springer Verlag, particularly M. Bihn, with whom I was in touch during recent months. You are great partners and great professionals. No wonder why Springer remains among the top ranking scientific and professional publishers.

Nothing happens without funds. There are five main sources that are directly linked to this work. These are the former Ministry of Science and Technology of the Republic of Slovenia, the former Ministry of Information Society of the Republic of Slovenia, the Ministry of Higher Education, Science and Technology of the Republic of Slovenia, and Slovenian Research Agency. In addition, thanks go to Deutscher Akademischer Austausch Dienst - DAAD (German Academic Exchange Service). Finally, a small but important contribution from the Internet Society has to be mentioned. It has enabled the attendance of one of its biggest events, which has influenced certain parts of this monograph.

Denis Trček

Contents

1

Introduction - The Scope of the Work and its Methodology

Felix qui potuit rerum cognoscere causas.[1]

Not so long ago, one could relate security in information systems (ISs)[2] more or less only to cryptography, and it was a common understanding that this was all about it. But some ten, fifteen years ago security issues started to explode and they became very extensive. Cryptography became just one among many areas of the whole game. A variety of profiles are now engaged in the area of ISs security and privacy, and the situation is becoming complicated for an increasing number of information technology (IT) users. Practically every individual is becoming affected by the above mentioned issues, because we are more and more dependent on ISs, professionally and personally. We are facing a complex world, which is full of strange sounding acronyms like X.509, XML Signature, SSL, ISO 17799 and others. Additionally, a picture that used to be clear is now becoming blurred because of the inter-dependence of numerous issues ranging from technology domain through organization domain to legislation domain.

And this is where this book comes in. To effectively realize its mission, the following has been taken into account:

- Certain profiles such as systems and network administrators, technologists and developers innately use a bottom-up approach. Their origins are typically in computer and information technology or mathematics. These profiles often overlook human factor details, organizational views and legal considerations. However, these factors are essential for ISs security and privacy. The majority of threats directly or indirectly involve the human factor, a lot of them program implementation, many of them also security protocol flaws, while almost no security incidents are caused by "faulty" mathematical algorithms.

---

[1]Happy the man who has been able to learn the cause of things.
[2]To denote one information system, IS will be used.

- Other profiles, whose origins are often in economics or management, use a top-down approach, e.g. general managers, ISs managers and ISs project leaders. But at the core of contemporary e-business services is technology, whether it is a digital payment system or a Web merchandise portal. Moreover, technology is becoming a driving factor, even at the strategic level, of organizations [192]. Thus it is vital for these profiles to have a conceptual understanding of the lower levels. Further, ISs security and privacy area is now regulated by a large number of standards, and one has to be aware of them, not to mention legislation.

The time has come when bridging gaps is essential. The first gap is the one between social sciences, and mathematics and technology sciences. The second is the gap between the top-down and bottom-up approaches. Consequently, the profiles that are involved (and targeted by the book) include ISs managers, project managers, ISs security officers, ISs developers, researchers and (post)graduate students, be it with social sciences, or mathematics, or technology backgrounds.

The book is structured top-down, from managerial concepts of ISs security and privacy downwards to the technical details. Thus the reader can get as deep into details as needed. The book will not teach the reader how to configure a device, shift bits in a program code, etc. Rather, it will assist the reader in grasping "the big picture", together with an understanding of the principles, regardless of a particular technology or organization. Further, it will enable the reader to match these principles to actual needs, taking into account important technological and organizational standards, as well as legislative demands.

Despite our decision to adopt a top-down approach, it should not be forgotten that knowing and understanding technical issues is important, otherwise one easily runs into a situation where certain kinds of security and privacy issues become inapplicable or unimplementable. This happens often with security when policy makers overlook "techies" issues [357]. Understanding these issues, the way of reasoning of these people, and the grounds for their reasoning are important factors. That is why the book gets more and more down to the detailed technical and mathematical issues towards the end.

1.1 Defining Security and Privacy

It is necessary firstly to devote some efforts to define the basic notions, while the remaining important definitions will be given throughout the book.

The first question is: Security and privacy for what kind of systems? According to [216], an information system is a system of interrelated components working together to collect, process, disseminate and store information to support decision making, coordination, control and analysis in an organization. Thus, information systems are clearly more than just computers, they comprise not only information technology, but also management and organization. While this is only implicit in the above definition, we will use the following one, which is more expressive and exact [8]: *An information system is a system, whether automated or manual, that comprises people, machines, and/or methods organized to collect, process, transmit, and disseminate data that represent user information.* This definition also depends on two important notions, data and information [216]: *Information is data that have been shaped into a form that is meaningful and useful to human beings,* while *data are raw facts representing events or physical environment.*

Now concentrating on information technology, a good definition can be found in the Cambridge Advanced Learner's Dictionary, which says that information technology is the science and activity of using computers and other electronic equipment to store and send information. We will again stick with a more precise definition, given in [8]: *Information technology is the branch of technology devoted to the study and application of data and the processing thereof; i.e., the automatic acquisition, storage, manipulation (including transformation), management, movement, control, display, switching, interchange, transmission and reception of data.*

The formulation of the above definitions is not a straightforward task. But it is even harder to define security in ISs. One of the oldest, but very accurate and useful definitions is that *security is a minimization of vulnerabilities of assets and resources* [168]. Another definition can be found in [178], where security means confidentiality, integrity and availability of resources. Additionally, it is frequently stated in the literature that security means processes of authentication, authorization and accountability (AAA). We will stick with the first definition of security, which effectively serves the purpose. Moreover, this definition implies an important fact that there is nothing like "one hundred percent security". One can get closer and closer to it, but it is not realizable even theoretically, as will be discussed at the end of this chapter.

The road is now paved for the definition of privacy, which is often confused with data protection. Generally, privacy can be seen as a way of drawing the line at how far a society can intrude into one's affairs [19]. And according to the Cambridge Advanced Learner's Dictionary, *privacy means someone's right to keep their personal matters and relationships secret.* And we will stick with this definition.

What is the relation of privacy to security? Security can be seen as a key to privacy, as a necessary condition to assure it [53]. Using technology for this purpose is of immense importance. However, technology alone cannot assure privacy, and it has to be adequately complemented by legislation.

Having defined the basic building blocks of the field, we have to point out that the terms information technology security and information systems security are often used interchangeably. It is important to clarify that *information technology security means security of systems that are based on computers, and is considered from a technological point of view,* while *information systems security means security of computer based systems that includes human factor*. Because the latter makes most sense in real life (or counts most in reality), we will concentrate throughout the book on information systems security, while information technology security will remain only its sub-part.

1.2 The Importance of Standards

The basic purpose of standardization is to support and harmonize trading. In the area of contemporary ISs standardization plays an additional role. The complex task of computer communications has to be divided somehow into smaller tasks that are realized by specialized entities implemented in a program code.[3] To enable communication, the separation and execution of tasks has to be well defined in terms of protocols and interfaces. This makes communication not only possible, but also meaningful. And this is the technological reason for the major involvement of standards. Of course, to improve flexibility of organizations and to stimulate free market competition, standards are also imperative for computer communications. Last but not least, a positive effect of standardization is that standards set norms, which make IT products or services comparable. This is also important when studying achieved and assured security levels of ISs.

But standardization in the area of ISs is not limited only to technological issues. Due to tight integration of ISs with business processes, standardization of the human factor and organization related issues is playing an increasingly important role.

Thus becoming familiar with standards is a must. The most important standardization bodies in the field of ISs security and privacy are briefly described below:

- ITU-T: The original name of this organization was International Telecommunication Union (ITU) until 1956. Later it was changed to CCITT (Comite Consultatif International Telegraphique et Telephonique), and finally, in 1993, to ITU-T (the last T stands for Telecommunications Standardization Sector). Its job is standardization of international telecommunications. At the beginning, this meant telegraphy, later telephony, and now computer communications. ITU-T has five classes of members: administrations, private operators, regional telecom organizations, telecom vendors, scientific organizations, and other interested partners. Only administrators may vote about recommendations. Recommendations are made by study groups, which consist of working parties of expert teams. ITU-T is financed by members with contributory units, which are proportional to the economic power of the member.
- The International Standards Organization (ISO) is a voluntary organization established in 1946. Its members are national standards organizations.

---

[3]The reason to mention standardization of computer communications is straightforward - computer communications are at the heart of contemporary ISs.

ISO is organized into Technical Committees (TCs), which are further divided into subcommittees (SCs) and these into working groups (WGs). There are 200 TCs, where TC97 deals with computer and information processing. ISO standardization procedure goes as follows:

- TCs play a central role in the process of standards development. Within TCs, national delegations of experts work on a subject, until a consensus is reached in the form of a draft agreement.
- This draft is circulated as a draft international standard (DIS) to all ISO members for comment and balloting.
- After successful voting, final modifications are included in the draft, which becomes a final draft international standard (FDIS).
- FDIS is circulated to members again and, if all goes well, it becomes an international standard and is published.

ISO is financed by members that pay in proportion to their GNP. Part of the financing comes from sales of standards. In the field of telecommunications, ISO and ITU-T cooperate - in fact ISO is an ITU-T member.

- The Internet Society (ISOC) is an international, non-profit organization that takes care of the Internet expansion. Under the ISOC operate the Internet Engineering Task Force (IETF) and the Internet Engineering Steering Group (IESG). These two are directly responsible for Internet standardization by publishing Requests for Comments (RFCs). More precisely, IETF works in working groups (WGs), which are dedicated to specific areas. The first published outcomes of WGs are Internet Drafts. These are made available for informal review, and may be changed, recommended for publication or dismissed. Recommendation for publication means that a draft becomes a candidate for becoming an RFC standard. First, it becomes a proposed standard. It may be then advanced to a draft standard, and finally, it may become an internet standard. Being labeled with "RFC" does not actually mean that a document is indeed an Internet standard. Because of archival reasons, some documents are retained as informational or experimental RFCs. In the final instance, all standards developed by the IETF are considered by the IESG, which is responsible for the technical management of IETF activities. So in fact, the IESG approves all advancements and publications of RFCs. There is another standards body within ISOC, the Internet Assigned Numbers Authority (IANA). IANA takes care of standardization of elements that are essential for proper functioning of applications, like types of e-mail messages to be recognized by programs, or address numbers for existing and new applications, etc.
- The American National Standards Institute (ANSI) was founded in 1918 by five engineering societies and three government agencies. ANSI is a private, non-governmental and non-profit US organization. Members are companies, organizations, government agencies, institutional and international members. Individual membership of US citizens is also possible. ANSI is the main US standardization and accreditation organization with over 70 employees. ANSI is the official US representative in ISO.

- The National Institute of Standards and Technology (NIST) is an agency of US Department of Commerce. It was founded in 1901 as the US first federal physical science research laboratory. NIST is not only active in many fields of research, it is also directly involved in specification of standards. The responsible body for these activities is the Standards Services Division (SSD). With relation to information technology, the majority of work is done by Information Technology Laboratory. In addition, NIST SSD provides test-beds for collaborators to improve standards evaluation.
- The Institute of Electrical and Electronics Engineers (IEEE) is the largest professional organization. Origins of IEEE date back in 1884 - its predecessor organizations were the American Institute of Electrical Engineers and the Institute of Radio Engineers. It is a non-profit organization that is mainly specialized in electrical engineering, computers and control technology. IEEE has almost 900 active standards, and some 700 are under development. Membership can be on an individual or corporate basis.
- The European Computer Manufacturing Association (ECMA) - this is now an international non-profit industry association that was founded in 1961. It is dedicated to standardization of information and communication technology systems. Membership includes ordinary members, associate members, small and medium-sized enterprises, small private companies, and non-profit members (their membership is free of charge). The General Assembly (GA) of the ordinary members is the highest authority. The work is done by Technical Committees (TCs) that are supervised by a Coordinating Committee. Drafts are produced by TCs and final drafts are submitted to GA for approval with voting. Among others, ECMA liaisons with ISO and ITU-T.
- The WWW Consortium (W3C) is a consortium created in 1994 to lead development of the World Wide Web and promote its evolution by ensuring its interoperability. It has around 400 member organizations. The Advisory Committee has one representative from each member organization. Representatives of member organizations take part in Working Groups (WGs), interest groups and coordination groups. WGs produce technical reports, which may be advanced to recommendations, i.e. W3C standards. The procedure for adoption of a standard is as follows: publication of the first public working draft is followed by a last call announcement. Next, a call for implementations is issued, and is followed by a call for review of the proposed recommendation. If all goes well, the document is published as a recommendation that constitutes a de jure W3C standard. W3C liaisons with IETF.
- The Object Management Group (OMG) was founded in 1989 by eleven companies as an independent, non-profit consortium. OMG is oriented towards the standardization of interoperable enterprise applications. Membership is open to any company, which gets the right to participate in a standards-setting procedure through "one company, one vote" policy. Standards are initiated with requests for proposals, which are available to

anyone, while the standardization process itself is restricted to members. OMG's de jure standards are called specifications, and some of them are recognized as standards by other standardization organizations like ISO and ANSI. Besides ISO and ANSI, OMG liaises also with W3C, IEEE and others.

- The Foundation for Intelligent Physical Agents (FIPA) was established in 1996 to foster standardization of agent-based systems. It has two kinds of members from commercial and research/academic environments: principal and associate members. Standardization activities are centered around Technical Committees and their Working Groups, which are supervised by the Architecture Board. Other supporting (managerial and administrative) activities are carried out by the Board of Directors, Image Committee and Secretariat. FIPA cooperates also with other standardization organizations, e.g. OMG.

- Organization for the Advancement of Structured Information Standards (OASIS) was established in 1993 and it is a non-profit, global consortium for development, convergence and adoption of e-business standards. OASIS is the main player in the field of Web services standardization, including security. It has a few thousand members, ranging from organizations to individuals who may choose different membership levels. Members join the OASIS Technical Committees (TCs), where they can choose to be observers or active voting members. TCs are formed by proposals of members and govern technical work on a vendor-neutral, open and democratic basis. Among others, OASIS liaises with W3C and ISO.

It can be seen that the business models of the above organizations differ considerably. This is also reflected in the accessibility of standards. The majority of these organizations provides standards on a royalty-free (or mostly royalty-free) basis, e.g. IETF, W3C, NIST, OASIS, ECMA, OMG. A minority charge for standards, e.g. ITU-T and ISO. In the case of ISO, some 30% of the total income comes from selling standards.

1.3 Technological Issues

The importance of security has been growing with the wider application and penetration of computer communications during the last decades. Therefore it should be no surprise that, until recently, the emphasis in the field of security and privacy has been on technology.

Before Internet took the lead and became the mainstream technology (Internet is based on TCP/IP technology), there was a sharp competition between various technologies in wide area networks (WANs). IBM promoted its Systems Network Architecture (SNA), which was the basis for BITNET WAN. Digital introduced its own DIGITAL Network Architecture (DNA) for DECNET networks. Novell tried to dominate with its SPX/IPX suite of protocols, while Microsoft bet on its own network technology... This created more or less isolated islands with no real global connectivity, at least not for ordinary users. In the end, the clear winner was TCP/IP technology that has its origins in the UNIX world, and things started to change radically.

The above facts are also reflected in the field of security. Roughly, it all started in the sixties and seventies with intensive work on cryptographic algorithms and secure operating systems. Later, with the introduction of computer communications, the research paradigms shifted towards cryptographic protocols. At the end of the eighties and beginning of the nineties, the emphasis shifted to formal methods and security engineering in general.

In the mid-nineties, it seemed that security technology was just about to solve all information security related problems. This attitude was also reflected in the literature of that time, e.g. [306]. But the reality started to show another face.

1.4 Organization and the Human Factor

The importance of the human factor became a major concern in the second half of the nineties, as noted in frequently cited literature of that time, e.g. [87, 307]. Today it is a known fact that human resources usually present the weakest link in the security of ISs. Some researches suggest that as many as eighty percent of major security failures are the result of poor security behavior and not poor security technology [217]. No wonder that these issues are being addressed even in standards like ISO 17799 [178], which is a successor of the widely accepted BS 7799 standard [43].

To achieve effective management of ISs security and privacy, security and privacy need to become an integral part of corporate culture. It has to start at the top with the dedication of management to security. This should be obvious nowadays since data constitute one of the key assets of each and every organization. This goes hand in hand with another key asset - people.[4]

As far as organizational issues are concerned, innovative approaches to human resources management have to be considered:

- Based on fact that learning through models and examples significantly improves the learning curve, business dynamics [326] and agent technologies [36] can be useful methodologies for security awareness with supporting tools for simulation.

---

[4]Although these two kinds of assets are known to be fundamental, they are not considered in balance sheets or financial reports. This valuation is a hard issue, because it includes a wide and diverse range of specific views - in the case of human resources even ethical issues. As a result, this will be a hard issue for managing ISs security as well. A complete risk analysis is tightly coupled with valuation of assets. In addition, vulnerability of human factor has to be estimated, where obtaining proper estimates is another problem.

- Inclusion of creative thinking techniques also needs to be considered. Research on how organizations plan their future shows that those that are better at long term planning have all used brainstorming [158, 243]. Inclusion of creative thinking in the security area is additionally backed by the fact that the very subtle ins and outs of a particular job function are usually best known to the employee who is in charge of this particular function.

Summing up, evolution in the field of ISs security has led to standardization of related organization management procedures. Security is thus no longer just a matter of technology, but also a matter of proper human factor management.

1.5 Legal Frameworks

The last important ingredient for effective orchestration of ISs security and privacy is legislation. Legislation usually lags behind the technological advances and this was also the case with ISs security and privacy. When computer systems were isolated, there was no need for a more "customized" legislation. Classical means provided a sufficient basis for proper handling of computer misuse. With a wide penetration of new services that have led to new paradigms, legislation had to address the technological specifics.

It is known that TCP/IP technology is a clear technological winner. It was developed for academic and research environments in line with the philosophy of cooperation and resource sharing. But the evolution of the Internet led to more and more people being connected, many of them having not only good intentions. Further, wide acceptance by businesses exposed issues of business secrets, proprietary use, charging, etc. Security turned out to be critical, and the situation was getting worse due to appearance of new specific threats. Intrusions, i.e. penetrations into systems, were just the beginning. Other threats appeared, like spamming and new ways of copyright infringements. We are now facing problems that were hardly imaginable twenty years ago, like spyware, identity thefts and the like.

Legislation is important for ISs security and privacy, not only to prevent unacceptable practices, but also to support and further stimulate development in this field (a positive attitude towards electronic documents, which are not discriminated a priori just because of their digital nature, is one such example).

The legislation that can be considered as a direct consequence of technological advances started to gain momentum some ten years ago. By now, it has become very complex, which is a major problem. Good news, however, is that there is a logical thread in this field based on historical perspective, which will be reflected in this book. Despite avoiding many details, the approach is aimed to arm the reader with an overview of the area that should pave the road for an effective orientation, and anticipation of future trends.

1.6 Before Proceeding Further

To summarize, ISs security and privacy can be viewed on three planes: technology, organization and legislation. Each plane can be analyzed from the safeguards perspective. The basis consists of assets and resources, which have to be protected by the use of physical and logical safeguards. Some risks are usually accepted without implementing the safeguards for them. In such cases appropriate safeguards may not actually exist, or may be impossible to implement, or too costly - this is a matter of risk management. Of course, also threats have to be identified, being in principle physical threats, logical threats and social threats. All these components are presented in the general model given in Fig. 1.1 (the ISs security and privacy cube).

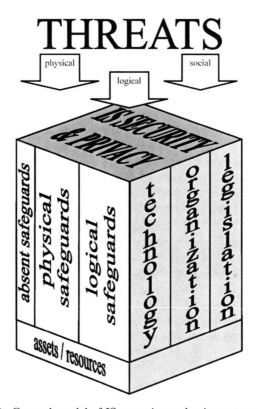

Fig. 1.1. General model of ISs security and privacy management

The general model is further elaborated by inclusion of standards, which bind technology and organization. Further, the safeguards plane is divided into layers (see Fig. 1.2). This is to reflect the technological reality of contemporary ISs that are built around cryptographic solutions. The protection of assets and resources starts at the second layer with cryptographic algorithms (security mechanisms) that are the basis for security services at the third layer. During regular operations, human to machine interactions are linked to this layer. Further, the fourth layer constitutes programs, i.e. actual implementations that are interfaced to human users. The highest layer is human to human interactions for the reasons already mentioned. In parallel to the second, third and fourth layers, there are physical mechanisms, which cannot be avoided entirely. By the use of cryptography one only reduces the amount of information that has to be protected, but in the end a small set of bits has to be physically secured (e.g. cryptographic keys).

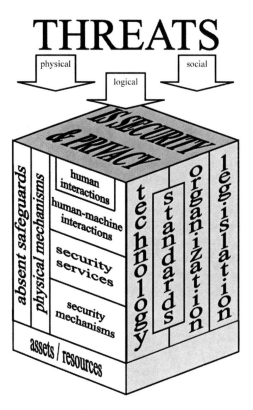

Fig. 1.2. Detailed model of ISs security and privacy for networks based ISs

This book follows the above concept of layered multi-plane ISs security and privacy. Its holistic methodology starts with the management of risks caused by threats in all three relevant domains: physical, logical and social. Based on this, ISs security and privacy is managed through appropriate safeguards, that are studied from technological, organizational and legal points of view. Further, with this methodology standards play a central role.

Before concluding this chapter, some words about total security. There is nothing like 100 % security. For cryptographic algorithms (also called crypto-primitives) one can identify the lack of some formal proofs, e.g. about the existence of bottom line time-computational complexities for certain problems. Put another way, it is not known whether more efficient algorithms for attacks than those currently known exist or not (see e.g. [6, 257] and [293, 94]).

A similar situation holds true for crypto-protocols. It is not possible to state watertight evidence that a particular protocol has no flaws. Formal techniques may strengthen such a belief, but they cannot provide complete assurance about it. As a result, wise protocol engineering practices have to be followed [1].

The third point relates to implementation. Security is also, and to a large extent, a matter of software correctness [131]. But things are getting worse for several reasons. Emerging technologies like wireless nomadic computing require handling of unpredictable application environments, emerging peer-to-peer networking inherently brings more entropy [268], etc. As far as 100 % software correctness is considered, this can be assured only for a certain range of inputs, which is almost impossible to predict with nomadic computing, where agents operate at their own will.

Now considering a human factor, 100% security is something that one can only imagine. Therefore it is important to address insurance to complement the organization's own measures and to compensate for damage in worst-case scenarios. It is a fact that most organizations never recover after a serious incident - in the UK, in the case of a major fire, over 80% of businesses never recover, despite insurance arrangements, which effectively cover only 30% to 50% of total losses [89]. It is also often stated that organizations are not insured to value, but the fact is that insurance companies know all of the rules better than majority of organizations and have the necessary experience [270].

In the end, 100% insurance coverage is very unlikely and it is wiser to prepare for proper handling of bad times as much as possible. Although one hundred percent security is unachievable, even theoretically, it is possible to do a lot to prevent many of the worst case scenarios.

*   *   *

When talking about security and privacy in ISs, the relevant literature usually starts with some statistical facts. We have avoided this practice. Nowadays, it is common to be aware of the extreme growth rate of ISs security and privacy incidents. To obtain the most up-to-date figures, a reader is advised to consult authoritative sources. Among these, some of the most notable are: Computer Security Institute with its CSI/FBI Computer Crime and Security Surveys (http://www.gocsi.com), Carnegie Mellon University's CERT Coordination Center with its reports (http://www.cert.org), and the SANS Institute with its news and articles (http://www.sans.org). All these sources are accessible on the Web.

2

Organization, Security and Privacy

Quis, quid, ubi, quibus auxiliis, cur, quomodo, quando.[1]

This chapter presents the main standards in this field and typical issues that they address. Further, it complements them by exploring additional issues that are not covered by these standards, or by presenting them in a different context. The reader will notice that the chapter is influenced mainly by relevant standards from ISO. The reason is that these standards cover a spectrum that should be broad enough for a large number of organizations. However, this chapter is by no means a substitute for the relevant standards.

Before starting with the central part of this book, it is probably the right time to state clearly what the managers do not like to hear, since this cuts right across the fundamentals of their concern. Managing ISs security and privacy inherently means costs. The only "profit" an organization can make is optimal protection, achieved through effective risk management. However, with ISs security some of an organization's most valuable assets are protected. Moreover, ISs security and privacy is not only a matter of questioning whether it is worth the investment or not. It is already becoming legally obligatory for many organizations in some countries. And this situation is not likely to become more relaxed. The opposite scenario is far more likely, because if money goes digital, criminals go digital, too.

2.1 Recent History of the Field

Organizational issues in the area of ISs security - and consequently privacy - became a subject of standardization in the nineties. To be more precise, human factors started to be addressed in standards already in the eighties with the most notable example being the US Department of Defense Orange Book [349]. But paying attention to human factors gained true importance in the nineties with the penetration of internet into the business environment.

---

[1]Who, what, where, with what, why, how, when.

As mentioned in the first chapter, experience shows that security problems rarely have their roots in cryptographic primitives (mathematical foundations level). More frequently their origin is in cryptographic protocols and software errors (design and implementations level). But most often, they are a result of improper human factor management (organizational level).

As a consequence, the emphasis has shifted towards organization and human resources related issues. It became clear that these elements are at least as important as the classical, technological ones. It has also become clear that even technologically superior solutions will be in vain without complementary organizational measures (this is reflected in the literature of the past decade [13, 87, 307]). Thus, risk management should address not only technological but also human resource management through organizational and, consequently, through legislative aspects.

According to the concept of this book (the ISs security and privacy cube from Fig. 1.2), this chapter will take into account ISO 13335 technical recommendations [173, 174, 175, 176, 177].[2] These recommendations do not focus on exact solutions for managing ISs security, but they support those that are responsible for ISs security and privacy. More precisely, these documents:

- define and describe the concepts related to the management of ISs security,
- identify the relationship between ISs security management and ISs management in general,
- introduce models for better explanations and understanding of ISs security,
- provide general approaches to the management of ISs security.

To fulfill the above goals, the reports are structured in five parts. The first part gives an overview of the basic concepts and models for security. The second describes management and planning aspects, while the third describes security techniques that can be applied within management activities during the whole IS life-cycle, from planning, designing, implementing, testing to operating. The fourth gives further details, providing guidance for selection of safeguards. Similarly, the fifth part concentrates on safeguards for outbound and inbound connections.

It is helpful to recognize that standards are often developed in hierarchies, i.e. in a stack-like manner. Such stacks typically consist of three levels that can be related to frequent reasoning in management. This is depicted in Fig. 2.1, and will be followed throughout this monograph.

---

[2]These documents are technical recommendations, which are collected data of a different kind, not a standard. They are about state-of-the-art methodologies, thus these recommendations remain valid until the data they provide is superceded.

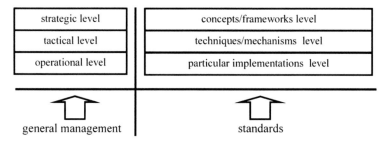

strategic level	concepts/frameworks level
tactical level	techniques/mechanisms level
operational level	particular implementations level

general management   standards

Fig. 2.1. A methodological approach to ISs security and privacy standardization through hierarchies

2.2 Frameworks Level[3]

Frameworks level forms the basis for guidance on ISs security management. This requires identification of concepts, their definitions, descriptions, and relationships between ISs security management and general ISs management. All these elements are then structured into models, a variety of which exists for management of ISs security. *Models cover security elements with their relationships, risk management relationships and the management of the ISs security process*, and they serve as a basis for deriving particular security solutions.

The core of the game comprises assets and threats. We define *assets* as *anything of a value to the organization*, while *threats* denote *any potential cause of an incident*. The first consequence of interaction between assets and threats is *risk*, which means *the potential of a given threat to exploit vulnerabilities of an asset and cause damage*. And *vulnerabilities* in this case mean *weakness(es) that may be exploited by a threat*.

In order to minimize risks, *risk analysis* is necessary, which means *identifying security risks, their magnitude and required safeguards*. As expected, *safeguards comprise practices, procedures or mechanisms that reduce risks*. Certainly, *residual risk, which means the remaining risk after the implementation of safeguards*, should be sufficiently low to be acceptable. The determined *minimal set of safeguards is referred to as baseline control*.

The sources of risks are manifold. Risks are related to *data integrity, meaning that the data have not been altered or destroyed without authorization*. From a wider perspective, *system integrity means the property that ensures the intended system functionality in an unimpaired manner*. This is directly related to *reliability, the property of ensuring intended behavior*, and to *availability*, which means *being accessible and usable as planned*. Certain risks are related to a break in *authenticity - the property that ensures that an entity is the one claimed*. Other risks are related to break in *confidentiality that*

---

[3]Definitions in this subsection are based on ISO 13335 documents [173, 174, 175, 176, 177].

denotes the property of preventing information disclosure to unauthorized entities. Risks should always be evaluated from these perspectives.

The above terms related to risks are commonly referred to as *risk management*, which means *the total process of identifying, controlling and minimizing (or eventually eliminating) events that may endanger resources* (see Fig. 2.2). Risk management is a trade-off oriented process, where the optimal solution is sought between the value of an asset and investments needed for its protection.

Finally, based on risk management, and aligned to the organization's mission and goals, *a security policy* is defined, which means *rules and practices that govern ISs' assets protection.* One of the main things that enables implementation of security policy is *accountability - this is the property of ensuring that the actions of a certain entity can be traced to this very entity.*

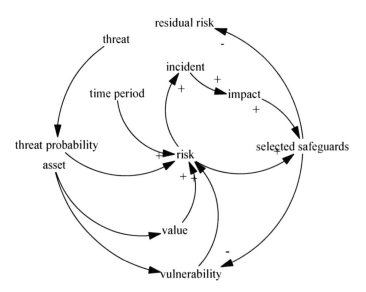

Fig. 2.2. Understanding risk management - the elements of risk management and their relationships

From the above definitions it follows that security (and consequently privacy) is not a state, but a process. This process, which is referred to as ISs security and privacy management, includes:

- determination of security and privacy objectives, based on strategies;
- determination of required safeguards, based on risk analysis;
- monitoring implementation and operation of safeguards;
- detecting incidents and reacting to these incidents;
- establishing security and privacy awareness culture.

IS security and privacy management is embodied in security policy, which covers in detail the following areas: organizational principles, risk management, system development, administration and monitoring, change and configuration management, contingency planning, incidents handling and disaster recovery, security awareness, and continuous review with compliance checking and auditing.

2.2.1 Assets

Identification of IS assets is the first step in establishing security policy. If one does not know what should be protected, or what the priorities are, then the whole process of risk management makes a little sense.

Asset identification usually starts with physical assets, and ends with assets that the e-business era has exposed, which are all kinds of non-tangible assets. In deriving security policy, identified assets are allocated to owners that get in charge of them. This assignment is usually done on the basis of roles.

2.2.2 Threats

The identification of threats is the second step. It is necessary to identify their basic attributes, which are the expected frequency, i.e. their likelihood of occurrence in relation to a particular asset, and (eventually) the motivation of a potential attacker. To deal effectively with threats, an appropriate *taxonomy, i.e. a system for naming and organizing things into groups that share similar qualities*, is of utmost importance. According to [11], a proper taxonomy has the following properties:

- its categories do not overlap;
- the categories together cover all possibilities;
- it is unambiguous and precise;
- it is repeatable, in the sense that whoever makes the classification, the results are the same;
- it is logical and intuitive;
- it is useful in terms of providing an insight into the field.

In the absence of a general and extensive taxonomy of threats, one can stay with the following grouping: threats of a human and environmental origin, accidental and deliberate threats, general threats and asset specific ones, and internal and external threats. It is also helpful to start with concerns and identify threats in a backward manner.

Security concerns typically include loss of authentication, confidentiality, integrity, availability, accountability and reliability [176].[4] Further, for particular needs and groupings, organizations can obtain threats lists from the

---

[4]Some definitions of security are based on concerns, stating that security means processes for assurance of authentication, confidentiality, integrity, availability, accountability and reliability.

literature and specialized organizations, like CERTs. Last but not least, organizations can improve the processes of identification of threats with a use of creative thinking methods, like brain-storming [77].

Despite the fact that a complete taxonomy of threats is something that can never be achieved due to continually emerging new technologies, an extensive taxonomy framework is still needed.

2.2.3 Vulnerabilities

Vulnerability is a property of an asset that describes an unwanted way of exploiting of this asset by a particular threat. Vulnerability as such does not cause harm, but it is a condition for it. Thus within risk analysis, vulnerability analysis is performed that includes examination of the following weaknesses: physical weaknesses, organizational weaknesses, procedural weakness, personnel related weakness, management related weakness, constructional and logical weakness of hardware and software, and information weakness [173].

The lack of appropriate taxonomies is a problem here as well. One of the first attempts in this area can be found in [215]. However, an extensive vulnerabilities framework is still needed more than ever. As with threats, an organization can improve the processes of identification of threats by use of creative thinking methods.

2.2.4 Risks and Impacts

Impacts are the consequences of a successful attack. They can be direct (e.g. disabling an asset or destroying it), or indirect (e.g. financial loss or damage to goodwill). The impacts can be assessed by using two approaches [173]:

- assessment of risks through qualitative measurement of impacts, i.e. using a descriptive scale;
- assessment of risks through quantitative measurement of impacts, e.g. through financial loss.[5]

The possibility of an unwanted impact is driven by risk. Therefore, risks and impacts are closely related. More precisely, risk is determined by the possibility that a certain threat will exploit vulnerabilities and cause damage to an asset. Thus, risks are characterized by the following two factors: the probability of an unwanted incident and its impact.

2.2.5 Safeguards and Residual Risk

Safeguards are mechanisms and procedures intended to protect assets against unwanted events. Safeguards belong to the following domains: technological,

---

[5]An average IS security breach is estimated to cost approx. EUR 20,000 [199].

organizational and legislative. ISs security and privacy usually requires a combination of safeguards, where some safeguards provide multiple functions. They may reduce vulnerability, detect incidents, limit impacts, and facilitate recovery [173].

Further, safeguards may only mitigate risks, and this mitigation is a function of the time and money invested. Thus some residual risk is often unavoidable. Besides time and money constraints, residual risk is also a consequence of organizational, environmental, personnel, technical, and cultural constraints [173].

2.2.6 The Concept of Security Management Processes

ISs security and privacy management is an umbrella process consisting of planning, organizing, executing, and supervising with corrective actions - these are the classical management functions according to Henri Fayol. ISs security and privacy management binds together an organization's objectives and strategies, the establishment of an appropriate organization structure, the derivation of security policy, its implementation and validation, its execution and compliance checking, together with adjustments, including reactions to incidents and handling of these incidents.

Configuration and change management has to take place in parallel with the above processes. *Configuration management denotes processes dealing with keeping track of system changes in order to prevent the degradation of implemented safeguards as the result of change.* Further, a systemic look at an average IS reveals a large number of elements that interact with one another in numerous ways. As a consequence, change to any asset or safeguard is likely to result in changed risk. This stresses the importance of *change management that identifies new security requirements due to changes caused by new procedures, features, software updates, hardware revisions, new users or network connections.*

Given the fact that there is no such thing as 100% security, contingency planning and disaster recovery have to be considered. Each organization needs plans about the support of business when IS processes are degraded. These plans should describe the restoration of these processes, starting with the definition of a disaster, responsibilities for activation of recovery, responsibilities for recovery activities, and description of these activities [174].

2.3 Techniques for ISs Security Management

Techniques for selecting safeguards are established as part of managing ISs security and privacy processes and they are given in Fig. 2.3. These processes are in the domain of personnel responsible for design, implementation, testing and operation of ISs. Further, they belong to the domain of personnel responsible for activities that substantially depend on ISs [174].

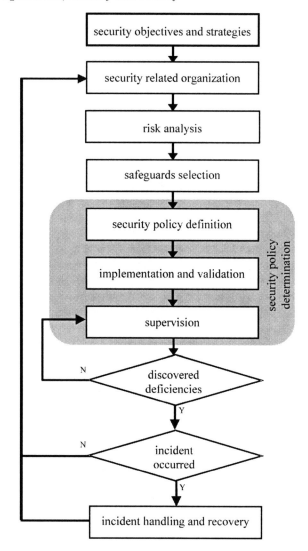

Fig. 2.3. Managing ISs security and privacy

These processes have to be harmonized to ensure appropriate levels of security (and consequently, privacy). Let us look more closely at each of these processes.

2.3.1 Security Objectives and Strategies

The initial elements to be determined are ISs security objectives and strategies. They are obtained through discussion, interviews and questionnaires, and determined by analyzing existing documents and formal frameworks. They are contained, explicitly or implicitly, in the answers to the following questions [174]:

- What is the general level of risk that is acceptable?
- How much does the organization depend on IS?
  - What are the essential decisions that depend on accurate information?
  - Which basic processes cannot be performed successfully without IS?
  - Which of them are completely dependent on IS?
- What are the critical unwanted incidents and what are their implications for the organization?
- Which is the critical data that need security?

2.3.2 Security Related Organizational Issues

An organizational infrastructure has to be built that consists of the following principal elements [174]:

- A security forum that advises on strategic planning, formulates corporate security policy, defines and monitors implementation, and promotes security awareness. This forum should consist of participants from ISs, audit, finance, utilities and infrastructure, personnel, security, and senior management.
- A corporate security officer who controls whether implementation is aligned with the plan, reports to the security forum, coordinates investigations, and manages awareness programs.
- A project or system security officer, subordinated to the security officer, who maintains security policy on a daily basis, and initiates and assists in incident investigations.
- A security administrator who performs operation level tasks (logs analysis, sets user task priorities, enables and disables various kinds of network access, etc.).

To cope effectively with personnel, roles are introduced, each of which is associated with defined authority and responsibility. Last but not least, an important aspect for the success of ISs security and privacy is the (written) commitment of the management.

2.3.3 Risk Analysis

Risk management starts with risk analysis and can be based on a variety of approaches. The most extreme case is when an organization has no risk management approach at all. But in the majority of cases, four approaches can be applied [174].

The first is the informal approach, which means a pragmatic approach without structured methods. It simply exploits the knowledge and experiences of employees. Its advantage is that it needs no additional skills and can be done in a short time. The disadvantage is that some risks are likely to be overlooked, the results are subjective, there is little justification for safeguards and change management is difficult.

The second approach is the baseline approach, which means a selection of a standardized set of safeguards for all (or parts of) IS. The advantage is obvious - there is no need for detailed risk analysis, and similar safeguards can be applied to many systems. The disadvantage is that the baseline may overshoot or undershoot real requirements and it may be hard to manage change.

The third option is detailed analysis, which involves the identification and evaluation of assets, threats and their levels of severity through assets vulnerability. Each safeguard can be justified and tailored to the level of acceptable risk. The advantage is an appropriate level of protection and controllable change management. The disadvantage is the extensive input of resources.

Therefore it is not uncommon to utilize the fourth possibility, a combined approach, in which critical systems are subject to a detailed approach, while the rest of the system is subject to e.g. baseline approach. This requires quite detailed, high-level initial analysis. The benefits of such a combined approach are the high level overview before commitment of too many efforts, enabling resources to be spent on the most appropriate aspects. The disadvantages of the initial two approaches are thus minimized.

Now how can an organization cope with detailed risk analysis? Before any technique is chosen, assets have to be identified (and it is important not to limit the identification of assets only to tangible ones). The following assets taxonomy may be helpful when identifying assets:

- information assets, which include all kinds of operational data that reside in databases, other files, and other data stored on various media (paper, micro-film, CDs, DVDs, etc.) in all forms (graphics, video, voice, e-mails);
- hardware assets, which means computers (servers, workstations, mainframes, laptops, etc.), communications equipment (terminal devices and infrastructure devices including switches, routers, cables, fibers), peripheral devices (printers, scanners, cameras, etc.), operating conditions assuring devices (air-conditioning, uninterruptable power supplies, voltage protectors);
- software and firmware assets, starting with operating systems through middle-ware to applications;
- ordinary assets including buildings, furniture, funds, manufactured goods and services;
- people, including employees, partners and customers;
- non-tangible assets, including the image of the organization (goodwill), its market share, and core business processes as such.

Once assets are identified, the risk management process requires their valuation. During this process, various views on assets have to be taken into account - assuming damage to a certain asset, one can more precisely value this asset.

Next, threats need to be identified. One taxonomy of threats, based on [175], divides threats into environmental and human factor based ones. The latter are further divided into deliberate and accidental threats:

- Environmental: extreme water, humidity, temperature, dust, vibration, electromagnetic radiation, electrostatic discharging, and earthquake.
- Human factor:
  - Deliberate: theft, physical destruction (use of arms, fire, water), indirect physical attack (air conditioning failure, electromagnetic radiation), covert attack (masquerading, eavesdropping), use and operation errors (unauthorized or illegal use, improper use, maintenance error).
  - Accidental: These threats include the same categories as above, except thefts and covert attacks.

Threats can sometimes be more easily identified by assuming potential harm. They can cause direct financial loss, they can also violate legislation, lower performance, harm an organization's goodwill, endanger personnel safety and the environment, etc.

Vulnerability has to be assessed next. A taxonomy derived from the one in [175] is given below - note again that vulnerability is constituted in relation to a threat. It is thus sometimes stated indirectly through description of the related threat:

- Hardware vulnerability: sensitivity to environmental conditions, to supply conditions, improper maintenance, and lack of or improper disposal procedures.
- Software vulnerability: bad specifications for developers, insufficient or improper testing procedures, complicated use of products, lack of or improper authentication, authorization and access control mechanisms, uncontrolled installations, lack of documentation, inadequate back-up, and lack of or improper disposal procedures.
- Communications vulnerability: unprotected media, improper management of cables and network, lack of security services.
- Infrastructure vulnerability: inadequate control or protection or stability of any kinds of supplies.
- Document vulnerability: unprotected storage, uncontrolled duplication, careless disposal.
- Personnel vulnerability: inadequate or lack of recruitment procedures, lack of personnel or training, unsupervised personnel, lack of security awareness.
- Environmental vulnerabilities: inadequate or lack of physical protection, inadequate or lack of electromagnetic protection, improper location of buildings and rooms (in terms of physical access or exposure to vibrations, dust, and humidity).

- General vulnerability: lack of policies, existence of single points of failure, poor service or maintenance support.

With regards to taxonomies of vulnerabilities and their assessment, there are some approaches that may be helpful for risk analysis:

- for general software systems [210, 96, 97],
- for operating systems [17],
- for Web based part of ISs [9],
- for intrusion detection systems [30].

To further improve these taxonomies, a number of other vulnerability databases should be used:

- Common vulnerabilities and exposures database from MITRE [240],
- CERT advisories [55],
- SANS institute archives [302],
- X-Force archives [183],
- Bugtraq archives [316].

After vulnerability assessment, risks have to be prioritized with relation to expected loss. For this purpose, various qualitative and quantitative approaches can be applied. The important distinction between them is that exact values are not used with qualitative approaches, but descriptions of ranges or levels. The main reason for using qualitative approaches is that finding exact values requires significant investment in terms of manpower and time. Moreover, in certain cases it may be practically impossible to derive exact figures.

A typical quantitative approach goes as follows [288] (see Fig. 2.4):

1. Use a complete record of the organization's assets and resources.
2. Identify threats by taking motivation of a potential attacker and human factor into account.
3. For each threat in step 2 define the probability $E(x)$ of an event occurring within a certain period (usually one year).
4. Determine damage costs $D(x)$ related to each threat.
5. Evaluate risks for the certain period by calculating expected damage $D(x) * E(x)$ in this period (this product represents expected annual loss).
6. Set priorities, where investments for prevention of threats should not exceed damage costs.

Point six above requires further elaboration. The expected annual loss has to be mitigated somehow and various options are at our disposal. For each of these options a modified expected annual loss has to be calculated, where probability is affected by mitigation factor $M(x)$, caused by applied safeguard [28]. Thus expected annual loss for mitigation option with factor $M(x)$ is $D(x) * E(x) * M(x)$.

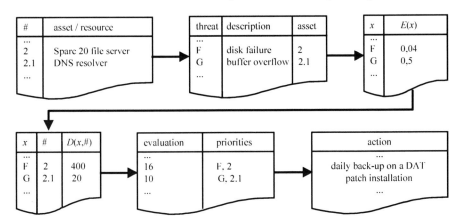

Fig. 2.4. Quantitative approach to risk analysis

For example, having D = US\$ 1,000 and E = 0.5 per annum, the first mitigation option with $M_1(x)$ = 0.5 results in expected annual loss of US\$ 250 (\$1,000 * 0.5 * 0.5). With mitigation option $M_2(x)$ = 0.1 the expected annual loss is US\$ 50 (\$1,000 * 0.5 * 0.1). Assume the cost of the first solution is US\$ 100, and of the second solution US\$ 300. The return on investment (ROI), which is obtained by dividing annual benefit by the investment amount, is calculated as follows. Firstly, savings minus mitigation costs are calculated, where savings are the difference between expected annual loss and modified annual loss [28]. Thus in the first case the savings are US\$ 500 - US\$ 250 = US\$ 250 and, in the second US\$ 500 - US\$ 50 = US\$ 450. Secondly, savings are evaluated relatively to required input, which results in the ROI for the first case to be US\$ 250/US\$ 100 = 2.5 and, for the second, US\$ 450/US\$ 300 = 1.5. This clearly identifies the winning safeguard.

Further techniques are of a qualitative nature, mostly based on various matrixes or tables like the following example of a table with predefined values. With this method a value level is determined for each asset. Similarly, for each threat the corresponding level is assessed and within these levels, sub-levels that denote vulnerability of a particular threat are introduced. An example is given in Fig. 2.5, where "L" stands for low, "M" for medium and "H" for high [175].

Techniques like the one above are security specific (in the narrow sense of this word). As far as pure availability and fault tolerance is considered, i.e. no malicious attacks from the outside world are taken into account, reliability engineering, which is a well established discipline, can be used [319].

It is a fact that, in any business, risk management is going on in the background all the time. Therefore, it sounds logical that some authors have suggested to view security as just another kind of risk management proposition [130]. The same authors argue convincingly that ISs security professionals should have a look at the extensive knowledge about risk management in the

Threat description	Threat level	low			medium			high		
	Vulnerability level	L	M	H	L	M	H	L	M	H
Level of asset value	none	0	1	2	1	2	3	2	3	4
	minor	1	2	3	2	3	4	3	4	5
	medium	2	3	4	3	4	5	4	5	6
	high	3	4	5	4	5	6	5	6	7

Fig. 2.5. An example of a qualitative approach to risk analysis

business domain, like quality management (security flaw in a product can be interpreted as a quality flaw) or finance risk management.

General and standardized applications of these methodologies tailored to the needs of ISs security and privacy are not available yet. Managing funds and quality of a product is one thing, but dealing with ISs security is another. In the former case threats have been known for decades. In case of ISs, threats are fairly new and continually changing due to changes of technology. Further, statistical aggregates of these threats that span over decades of experience are impossible or hard to obtain. Moreover, the role of human factor is more specific. It is very often the case that we are dealing with an irrational attacker who does not follow a gain vs. punishment, i.e. cost-benefit line. Such an attacker does whatever possible to exploit vulnerability, regardless of the cost. Worse than this, the number of potential attackers often far exceeds the number of entities involved with ordinary risk management. A fairly complicated situation!

2.3.4 Safeguards Selection, Security Policy Definition and its Realization

After the assessment of risks, we proceed with selection of the safeguards. Recommendations are given that define acceptable levels of risks and the benefits of selected safeguards with residual risks, which should all be described. Where estimates imply excessive risks, insurance arrangements have to be considered.[6]

The process is completed with a security policy that is defined in a written document and should specify in detail the following [178]:

- explicit commitment of management to security policy;
- statements on objectives of security policy and strategies;
- definitions of all relevant terms;

---

[6]Insurance for ISs will be overpriced [130]. In principle insurance companies sell insurance that is based on a data census of a few decades, but for the internet this simply cannot be done. As a rough guide, one can count on a premium from US$ 5,000 to US$ 25,000 and coverage from US$ 250,000 up to US$ 25,000,000. These data are based on offers from Cigna, ICSA, J&H March, Lloyds, Reliance National and Zürich Financial Services Group [290].

- description of formal (legislative and contractual) frameworks;
- determination of the level of investment in IS and potential unwanted business impacts;
- identification of threats, assets and their vulnerabilities (these may be partially confidential);
- allocation of identified assets to owners;
- required safeguards with validation procedures;
- awareness initiatives;
- monitoring, incident handling and recovery.

The realization plan is intended for coordinated action when implementing security policy, and it should be backed by common project management methodologies, e.g. [58]. This plan identifies the required resources (personnel and finance), scheduling of tasks and responsibilities. The top responsibility of security policy implementation is assigned to the security officer. After implementation of the plan, safeguards have to be validated.

2.3.5 Supervision and Incident Handling

Supervision of the security policy covers maintenance of safeguards and their monitoring, including advances in implementation of safeguards. A vital part of every IS supervision system is compliance checking. The compliance checks should start at the design and development stage, continue through the operational lifetime of IS, its replacement and disposal.

Incident handling should first cover reporting, exact chronological documentation and preservation of evidence for further investigation and potential prosecution. Next, recovery activities have to be defined to minimize unwanted impacts on business processes. Last but not least, an analysis is needed to produce "lessons learned" in order to prevent future attacks.

2.4 Particular Implementations Level

Activities at a particular implementations level result in fully defined security policies. These policies can be defined for various levels, e.g. a top level one and operational ones. Top level policy needs to address organizational infrastructure, assets classification, risk management strategies, validation procedures, maintenance and reviewing, incident and contingency strategies, personnel framework, and regulative framework. The document serves as a template for further derivation, all the way down to the level of operations and systems configurations [174].

Operational security policy should describe the scope and purpose of security policy, focused on authentication, confidentiality, integrity, availability, accountability and reliability. The operational policy should cover detailed authorities and responsibilities based on logical grouping of involved entities. So one should not think in terms of a particular employee or particular resource. Instead, groups of employees that have the same roles in assuring security have to be defined. An analogous approach has to be used for resources.

The main standard for particular implementations level is ISO 17799 [178]. This international standard is almost identical to British standard BS 7799-1 [43] that describes the code of practice for information security management. ISO 17799 is often referred to as a reference guidance for establishment of security policy, which actually means detailed specification in terms of safeguards selection.

2.4.1 General Hints for Selection of Safeguards

Security policy may concentrate on transferring risks (using, for example, insurance), reduction of threats, reduction of vulnerabilities or impacts, and detection of unwanted events with appropriate reactions to these events. Further, when selecting safeguards, one should think about ease of implementation, user-friendliness (i.e. ease of use), and types of performed functions (prevention, monitoring and detection, recovery, correction, security awareness). Additionally, constraints related to safeguards should be taken into account [175].

The bottom line to select safeguards is that their costs should not exceed the value of the assets to be protected. What approach can an organization take for safeguard selection? The basis is risk analysis, that is clear. The second step depends on the type of IS, physical and environmental conditions and assessment of existing safeguards [176]:

- The type of IS is identified by determining whether it is situated at local premises only or distributed. Further, is the IS an isolated one or integrated with some partner's IS? Further, is it based on main-frame based architecture or client-server based architecture?
- Physical and environmental conditions are identified by studying the location of buildings, identification of critical areas and nature of occupancy of these buildings. Further conditions include access control to find out who has access to buildings and what physical access controls exist. Finally, the protection of IS has to be investigated: Are there alarms and detection systems in place? What support utilities (UPS, air conditioning) are installed?
- Existing safeguards are assessed by studying documentation, interviews and by carrying out checks on the spot. The main point is to find parts that are under or over-secured.

The easiest way for an organization is to decide for a baseline approach. This means following a set of suggested safeguards to implement new safeguards, to upgrade or dismiss existing ones. Such an approach should work well with many organizations. In a case where IS is not homogenous, various parts of IS may require various baselines. Thus, responsible persons and teams should first define security levels for these baselines, and afterwards select particular safeguards.

In rare cases, a completely tailored approach should be taken with two possibilities - focusing on threats and concerns, or focusing on the type of IS. In the first, specific safeguards are implemented on top of general safeguards. In the second, all safeguards are specific, related to authentication, confidentiality, integrity, availability, reliability and accountability [176].

2.4.2 Organizational Safeguards

Organizational issues related to ISs security and privacy are given special attention in standards. An important representative of this kind is British Standards Institute's Specification for Information Security Management Systems, BS 7799-2 [44], which complements ISO 17799.

These safeguards include formalization of ISs security and privacy organizational infrastructure as described in the previous section. Having established this infrastructure, asset validation and valuation can take place. The responsible person, i.e. the security officer, identifies all assets, classifies them and labels them accordingly.[7] For each classification, handling procedures are defined. Assets are allocated to employees and related handling procedures become their responsibility; this should be clearly documented. Further, provision of feed-back should be documented. Every change to procedures or ISs must be formally approved before application. Finally, the principle of segregation of duties should be taken into account to minimize the risk of misuse of privileges.

2.4.3 Personnel Security

Personnel security safeguards protect against intentional or unintentional actions of employees, external partners or visitors that present risks to ISs security and privacy. They can be divided into the following categories [176]:

- Safeguards for internal members of an organization: These include their roles and responsibilities associated with these roles. Before signing an employment contract, personnel should be subject to recruitment checks. It is advised that employment contracts contain relevant clauses about security policy.
- Safeguards for external partners: These should include a contractual agreement about responsibilities for accessing IS. These agreements should include also consensus about monitoring, which is to be regularly performed.

---

[7]With information, these labels should reflect how critical information is in terms of its confidentiality, integrity and availability. A possible classification is: non-classified, for internal use only, confidential, extremely sensitive. Similarly, tangible assets can be labeled in terms of their value, for example: negligible value, minor value, medium value, high value, extremely high value.

- Safeguards for visitors: These should include supervision of visitors, recording their entry and departure, and instructing them. Visitors should wear visible identifiers.

Thefts are a classic risk, and they should be dealt with under ISs security and privacy management. Besides physical controls, various electronic detection techniques, e.g. sensors and X-rays, can be used. Electronic cameras and sensors can be deployed to physically protect the organization's environment. An inventory has to be maintained with all items being uniquely identified. Receptionists should check that no items are entering or leaving premises without authorization. Media with sensitive information should be handled with special care.

In order to effect the proper operation of safeguards, security awareness should be in place. It includes education, regular dissemination of information through e-mail, posters, seminars and the like. Last but not least, a disciplinary process should be defined so the employees are aware of the consequences of violation of organizational security policy. Other details are given in subsection 2.4.5.

2.4.4 Physical and Environmental Security

Physical security refers to protection of buildings, rooms and secure areas. This is done with fences, walls, guards, cameras, windows and doors with built-in protection mechanisms. Intrusion detection systems and alarms should be installed, as well as smart card or biometry based access control. Dangerous materials, redundant installations and back-up media should be located at a safe distance [178].

If possible, areas where natural disasters are frequently occurring should be avoided. But location should also be carefully studied on micro scale. Location of facilities should prevent unauthorized access, buildings should not indicate their purpose, and support equipment (faxes, photocopiers) should be placed properly. In order to prevent unauthorized access, secure areas have to be defined. These areas are also intended for handling sensitive materials that might endanger IS.

Physical and environmental security includes safeguards about clear-desks, locking of sensitive information, logging off the system, unauthorized photocopying prevention, clearance of sensitive information from printers and copiers, appropriate use of passwords, etc. [178].

In the most sensitive cases, electromagnetic protection might be needed for rooms and offices with delicate electronic equipment. All electronic devices produce electromagnetic radiation, which could reveal sensitive data.[8] Related to these threats is cabling, which should not be overlooked in order to avoid

---

[8]This is especially true for classical computer monitors. A technique is known where an attacker can reproduce an image of a computer's monitor from a distance. Such an attack is estimated to cost between US$ 500 and US$ 2,000 [315].

interference or physical damage. Further, wiretapping should be considered, which means that physical layout of cabling has to be planned in advance. In addition, transmission errors can seriously degrade performance and should be considered [178].

Physical security requires careful examination of sensitive offices for possible installation of eavesdropping devices: floor, ceiling, furniture, computers, etc. Such equipment is now extremely small and easily placed. Because it is hard to supervise all premises carefully, one should concentrate the most sensitive operations in a few rooms, which are equipped in a way that allows minimal possibility for installation of such devices. At the same time, intensive physical checks have to be performed regularly in these rooms. Electromagnetic radiation may still cause leakage of information from such rooms, therefore proper electromagnetic shielding should be considered.

There should be an assured continuous power supply by means of an uninterruptable power supply. Also proper temperature and humidity level should be assured with air conditioning devices.

2.4.5 Access Control, Communications and Operations Security

Access to computers and networks has to be restricted in order to protect system resources, applications, and information in general. Access control is defined for groups of users according to their roles and often follows the philosophy of allocating as few rights as possible, but just as many as necessary.

Logical access is dependent on authentication, where three principles can be used. The first one is based on something that only a particular user knows - this is usually a password.[9] Password issues are so vital that they can not be over-stated. Consider the following paradox. Nowadays organizations use asymmetric cryptography with keys that are 2048 bits long, and sessions are protected with 128 bit long symmetric keys. Private keys are stored on personal computers, and encrypted there by some cryptographic algorithm. This algorithm needs a password for its encryption and decryption. But passwords are often only six or seven characters long. Even if they are random, they are far too short to resist attacks. This means that the whole system security is reduced to the weakest password in the system. Therefore, passwords should be as random as possible,[10] consisting of at least fourteen alphanumeric characters, changed regularly, never written down, or told to others. Despite this, passwords can be obtained by observation, keyboard monitoring software or hardware, by packet interception, host emulation or video surveillance [100]. To prevent such attacks, regular checks for malicious software should be per-

---

[9]Personal identification numbers (PINs) are passwords.

[10]Memorizing such passwords becomes difficult, thus the following technique can be used. Compose a sentence in which the first character of each word is a character of the password. For example, to remember a password "e2digtmbtb1kob", one can use a sentence "Every two days I go to my baker to buy one kilo of bread".

formed, hardware components and rooms should be checked, host should support authentication techniques (host emulation is also prevented by providing a user with the date and time of the last successful login). Finally, to prevent the interception that happens when using unprotected passwords, strong authentication techniques or one time passwords have to be deployed.

The second principle of authentication is based on something that a user possesses, like a memory token or a microprocessor based token (smart card). The third principle is based on deploying unique attributes that are integral parts of a user, like retina patterns, fingerprints, voice, etc. - this is where biometry comes in.

Whatever the means to access resources (by password, token, or biometry), all successful and unsuccessful attempts should be logged and these logs regularly analyzed. If necessary, logs should be archived in line with data protection and privacy legislation.

After getting access to resources, fine grading of access rights takes place. These require a proper configuration of operating systems and applications that is generally based on role-based access, which allows access according to business functions. Configurations should be reviewed periodically to remain consistent with existing roles in an organization, where more attention has to be paid to privileged roles, e.g. system administrators.

The introduction of networked and Web-centric ISs requires a security policy that clearly defines the use of network services, necessary user and system authentication, physical and logical segregation of networks, enforced routes for services, and filtering and limitation of connection time for high-risk applications [178].

When considering information propagation within an organization, it is advisable to use a formal model. An example is the Bell-LaPadula model [24] with its "no write down" (NWD) and "no read up" (NRU) principle. This principle assures that sensitive information can only propagate horizontally and upwards, so there is no leakage of confidential information. It is especially suitable for hierarchical organizations.

Logical access can also be obtained via electromagnetic radiation, so an organization should consider deployment of devices with low or zero electromagnetic radiation, e.g. opto-cables. Another possibility is to intentionally add electromagnetic (white) noise to complicate attackers' efforts. A less expected violation of access control can be caused by steganography [196].

So far, we have concentrated on issues related to internal members of an organization, but external, third party access should not be overlooked. This access is defined on a basis of identified risks and includes security guards, students, visitors, consultants, maintenance staff, cleaning and catering staff, and other outsourced partners. Third party access should be based on contracts that include general security policy and description of services with logical access control. Further, acceptable levels of services (performance criteria), liability and responsibility with respect to legal matters (e.g. intellectual property rights), the right to audit responsibilities, and reporting associated with investigation of security incidents have to be defined [178].

Special attention has to be paid to internal communications and operations. Operating procedures should be documented and changes formally approved. Certain procedures that might be overlooked easily may present significant threats [178]:

- When media management is considered partially: its transport, its exchange and disposal. For example, high security measures are conducted within an organization, but neglected when transporting back-up copies to a remote location.
- When minor operations are underestimated, like leaving clocks unsynchronized, equipment unattended and automatic time-out procedures not implemented. Further, when software is not upgraded on-time, when mobile phones are used for sensitive communication in public places, when passwords are poorly managed, when paper documentation is not addressed, etc.
- When off-premises use of equipment is not authorized by management, or this equipment is left unattended, and when there is no additional insurance for such equipment.

2.4.6 ISs Development, Maintenance, and Monitoring

Operational and development systems have to be separated, which is often not the case. Development environments are typically less protected and access to their data can be used to break into the operational system. For example, testing is often performed on extracted operational data, which can easily be exposed this way. Systems have to be developed with data input checks in mind, together with control of internal processing to prevent abnormal behavior of applications. Output data validation is also needed [178].

Due to network character of contemporary ISs, network management requires proper attention.[11] Proper management of networks needs established and documented operational procedures and responsibilities. Planning is also essential, not only in terms of capacity (proper dimensioning prevents insufficient support of business requirements), but also in such "minor" issues as network topology and cabling.

Proper configuration is important for the required functioning. Documentation of this configuration should be stored in a safe place with access allowed only to authorized persons.

Maintenance ensures availability, reliability and integrity. It should be done in line with the producer's and supplier's requirements and should be performed by authorized personnel. An often overlooked element here is media

---

[11]With its technical recommendations ISO recognized that special guidance and safeguards are needed due to the growing importance of computer networks [177].

controls, in terms of its integrity verification and secure disposal, i.e. assured data destruction.

Monitoring should be activated and the resulting logs should be checked regularly for suspicious activities, and for incident detection. Effective analysis of log data should reveal a complete picture on what is going on behind the scenes. Therefore, the first step is to consolidate all logs on one server. The next is integration of the logging process into a systems management operation that is supported by appropriate tools that suit business rules [222]. But monitoring is not only about suspicious activities. It also serves to anticipate the future course, when deployed on a general level that deals with performance issues. To prevent malicious monitoring, i.e. traffic analysis, dummy traffic can be injected on the network and forced (alternate) routing can be deployed.

As far as software is concerned, regular inspections of installed software should be carried out. Safeguards against malicious code should be in place. Inspection of incoming media, inspection of e-mails for active content (attachments), and inspection of active contents from the network (Web servers, streaming media servers, etc.) should be performed. Before applying new versions of software, old versions should be archived. Software patches have to be applied where necessary - in the case of open source code products, an attacker can analyze a patch to obtain unauthorized access to resources that are not updated. It is also necessary to consider licensing, support agreements, assurance and quality agreements [178].

Special attention needs to be paid to cryptography, because cryptography based safeguards are essential to provide many security services, i.e. authentication, confidentiality, integrity and non-repudiation. The use of cryptography should be planned ahead, otherwise it may happen that it will be hard or even impossible to use it when the new system will be made operational. Once cryptographic controls are selected, the policy about use has to be set in line with information classification (algorithms, keys management, appropriate protocols). All these should be studied in relation to legislation, i.e. data protection, privacy, accountability, digital signatures use, and archiving of digital documents. Last but not least, suitability of cryptographic solutions for particular protection should be addressed [178].

To reduce maintenance costs and improve security, organizations are considering outsourcing in various domains like firewalls administration and security policy development. But such decisions should be carefully studied. There are many drawbacks, including access to the company's IS, breaches of its confidentiality, failures to meet service levels, license problems when the outsourced provider uses software on behalf of its customer, etc. [118].

Penetration Testing

Penetration testing serves as additional means to discover weaknesses in ISs, which may come from physical, technical and social channels [143]. A formal methodology, developed for certified ISs security professionals (CISSP) [333], defines *penetration testing to denote a vigorous attempt to break into a protected network using any means necessary.*

Each penetration testing must be carefully planned and methodologically sound, which means that it should focus on three principles [22]:

- reliability, meaning that testing should not cause systems to fail accidentally, assuring that results are accurate, believable and useful for taking actions;
- repeatability, meaning that when performing the tests many times, the same results will be obtained (assuming, of course, that the systems have not been altered in the meantime);
- reportability, meaning that the outcome can be communicated with a meaningful document that serves for concrete action.

These principles must support clearly defined objectives of penetration testing and success criterion.

Penetration testing can be divided into four phases [22]. In the first phase, the type and versions of hardware and software used by the company are determined. Further, possible computer account details, available services, routing policy, etc. have to be gathered. Acquisition of information about the company and details of its IS is done by use of search engines, public databases and media reports. Details of IS include domain name system records, e-mail servers communication headers, and Web servers identification records. For these purposes, special tools can be used that are now already available as system tools (examples include ping, traceroute, nslookup, nmap, netcat). This information is then used to construct an attack plan for the second phase, when hacking tools are applied. If access to the system succeeds, it is usual to try to escalate it to obtain system administrator privileges (this is done with so-called root-kits). The third phase includes establishment of proof of a successful access by setting a flag data in the system, by obtaining data or by altering existing data. The exact execution of this phase has to be defined by the contract. The last phase includes clear report about the discovered vulnerabilities, how they were exploited, and recommendations on improving the system security.

Everything about penetration testing has to be contractually agreed upon in advance: definition of systems that will be subject to testing, the description of the methodology, eventual access with escalation principles, and reporting.

Final note - successful break-in shows a vulnerability in IS that should be patched. Despite this, other uncovered vulnerabilities may still exist [233].

Social Engineering

No matter how clever and strong mechanisms are implemented, their protection can be trivially breached if users do not behave appropriately. Social engineering can be used to identify human related threats. *Social engineering is a method where an attacker exploits a relationship with an affiliate of an organization, and uses this affiliate to get unauthorized access to IS resources* [22].

Social engineering can be seen as a kind of penetration testing, but it cannot follow the above requirements for testing reliability, repeatability, and reportability. In general, it cannot be done in a repeatable manner, not to mention that it is hard to imagine how "to put flags" in this case. Above all, social engineering should be performed in a fair and moral way, otherwise it may present a weapon against organization itself. But if applied, it goes as follows [22]:

- identification of targets by gathering information like name, job position, contacting point, sex, age and interests;
- getting in touch with targets, usually by knowing them through people that know the targets (so-called strategic selling), and by gaining an understanding of targets to gain influence over them (so-called neuro-linguistic programming);
- implementing the desired actions by deploying the gained influence over targets.

Social engineering is easily accomplished, because there is usually little effort to help people to recognize it and behave accordingly [314].

2.4.7 Incident Handling

Incidents in ISs will happen, and one should prepare for bad times in order to react accordingly. Firstly, a clear reporting scheme should be in place within an organization. This means designation of a person to whom all reports are sent. It also means existence of established feed-back channels to the initial reporters.

Secondly, for serious incidents, a management scheme should exist that should take into account limiting damage. Further, the function of incident response is to discover how the incident occurred and what damage has been caused. At the same time, steps have to be taken properly to ensure sufficient admissible evidence to make prosecution feasible [84]. Therefore careful planning is required in advance and it should be formalized with security policy.

2.4.8 Business Continuity Planning

To protect organizations for worst cases that may follow certain incidents, critical business processes have to be identified and strategies for their continuity set. Critical business functions need to be prioritized, depending on their impact. Next, impacts on these processes caused by major failures of IS have to be defined.

This forms the basis for justification of related investments into equipment, procedures and training, and to enable recovery within the necessary time frame. Business continuity planning should not overlook external consequences like interruptions of partners' processes, loss of credibility and loss of image. Last but not least, a business continuity plan should be tested, and this holds true also for the first time of its acceptance [178].

2.4.9 Compliance and Auditing

Security policy has to be subject to regular compliance checking. Firstly, if the policy is not aligned with relevant laws and regulations, it may be even null and void - this kind of compliance should be checked on a case by case basis with the regulatory requirements of particular country. Secondly, compliance with security policy as such should exist within an organization.

As information security management in e-business systems is becoming a common practice, standards for auditing are a necessity. These standards assist management to consult proactively on ISs security. There are two mainstream auditing methodologies for ISs. The first is based on the already known ISO 17799 standard, and the second is defined by Information Systems Audit and Control Foundation (ISACF).

If an organization decides for ISO 17799 (BS 7799) certification, it can expect two visits [232]. The first visit from an accredited organization is focused on the organization's documents:

- review of documents about the organization's information security management system;
- review of structure in relation to market objectives, security policy and its applicability.

Approximately one month after the first visit, the second visit takes place. During this visit, actions taken as a response to the first visit are checked. Further, auditing is performed to find out which controls are in place and how they are used. After this visit a summary report is written by an accredited organization and examined independently. If all goes well, the organization is certified. It is not uncommon that accreditation does not go as planned, because people with a security background focus mostly on technical issues, and ignore business processes. On the other hand, auditors focus on business and do not get down to technical details [74].

ISACF auditing methodology is called Control Objectives for Information and Related Technology (COBIT) [71]. COBIT is oriented towards understanding and managing business risks that are associated with implementation of new technologies. Put another way, it bridges gaps between business risks, control needs and technical issues, by providing good practices to structure and manage activities. These activities are related to business objectives and they are structured into four domains: planning with organization, acquisition with implementation, delivery with support, and monitoring. Each of these domains consists of processes that have to be performed and there are thirty four such processes, from a definition of a strategic plan to independent monitoring. Using these processes, two additional views are covered: information criteria (quality, fiduciary, security) and resources (people, applications, technology, facilities, data).

An important organization in the field of compliance is the International Information System Security Certification Consortium (ISC2) [129]. It is not directly involved in auditing, but deals with compliance and accreditation of knowledge of security professionals. Approval by this consortium is given on the basis of a successfully passed test that takes six hours to answer two hundred and fifty multiple-choice questions. Those who answer correctly at least 70% of these questions are licensed for three years as a Certified Information Systems Security Professional (CISSP). CISSP covers the following areas: security management practices, access control systems, telecommunications and network security, cryptography, security architecture and models, operations security, applications and systems development, business continuity planning and disaster recovery, law concerning investigations and ethics, and physical security [211]. The CISSP certificate is recognized by organizations such as the Computer Security Institute, the Information Systems Security Association, and the Canadian Information Processing Society [129].

2.4.10 Security Awareness

The basis for successful management of ISs security and privacy in every organization is the informed, educated, and loyal employee. This is the most important factor for minimizing human error, misuse, fraud and theft. Improving security awareness requires proper training and education, where employees become familiar with security policy. Employees should be allocated responsibilities and they should know the consequences of not adhering to security policy.

Appropriate security awareness takes into account factors that influence security behavior, and can be divided into two groups [217]. The first group covers factors related to users' understanding of expected behavior. This understanding is determined by what employees are told, by behavior demonstrated by co-workers (especially senior management), by their security common sense, and by decision making skills. The second group covers factors related to users' willingness to comply with accepted norms. Their willingness in this case is determined by their personal standards and values, by psychological contract with their employer, and by difficulties associated with compliance.

2.5 Standardized Safeguard Templates

Standardized templates mainly cover organization related issues. Some of them are of a general nature. On the other hand, some of them are aimed at special fields like the banking or healthcare sectors.

2.5.1 Organizational Safeguard Templates

Related standards that can be seen as organizational safeguards templates are summarized below:

- ISO 17799 - IT Code of Practice for Information Security Management [178],
- DIN IT Baseline Protection Manual [46],
- NIST, Computer Security Handbook [249], which also served as the basis for Canadian Handbook on IT Security [138],
- ETSI Baseline Security Standard [112],
- ISO Information Security Guidelines for Banking and Related Services [170].

The most widely accepted is the first one mentioned above. It is of a generic nature, very much concentrated on managerial issues related to initiation, implementation and maintenance of ISs security. This standard is a collection of best practices, and can be used as a quality reference for deriving organizational security policy.

However, it is concentrated on safeguards from the managerial point of view. Luckily, there is another quality standard that complements it by concentrating also on technology and technical details. This is the DIN IT Baseline Protection Manual, with over two thousand pages. It provides detailed and concrete steps for configuration and administration of a wide variety of platforms, starting with particular operating systems, through networking infrastructure, and ending with most common applications. These two standards should cover ISs security policy needs for the great majority of organizations.

2.5.2 Technology Compliance Safeguards

When buying commercial off the shelf (COTS) products, it is necessary to pay attention to independent evaluation of their security properties. A few years ago, the main approach in Europe in this field was through the Information Technology Security Evaluation Criteria (ITSEC), while in the US this was Trusted Computer System Evaluation Criteria (TCSEC). Joint harmonization efforts are now underway within ISO, called Common Criteria for Information Technology Security Evaluation (CC) [172].

CC defines requirements that products have to fulfill from the security point of view. They present a basis for comparing different security evaluations. Consumers can determine if a certain product is secure enough for the intended use, developers can determine the desired security properties and declare them in a standardized way, and evaluators can verify them.

CC consists of four parts: the first part presents a general model for evaluation, the second provides a catalog of security functional requirements, the third contains assurance requirements, and the fourth contains examples of protection profiles. There is a part in preparation that will contain functional and assurance security requirements for cryptographic support in distributed systems and networks.

Functional requirements consist of functional classes, where each of them contains various families. Similarly, assurance requirements consist of assurance classes, where each contains various families. An important notion, introduced by CC, is that of evaluation assurance levels (EALs). These predefined assurance packages present the baseline set of assurance requirements for evaluation [172]:

- EAL 1 refers to functionally tested products at the lowest assurance level for which evaluation is meaningful and economically justified. It is intended to detect obvious errors and is applicable in circumstances where risks to security are not serious.
- EAL 2 refers to structurally tested products and can still be used without imposing additional tasks on the developer. If the developer applies reasonable standards, this level may be feasible without developer's involvement, other than support for security functional testing. EAL 2 is applicable to a low or moderate level of security without the need for a complete development record.
- EAL 3 refers to methodically tested and checked products. This level can be assured by using security engineering at the design stage (there is no need for substantial alteration of existing sound development practices). Therefore, EAL 3 provides a moderate level of assured security.
- EAL 4 refers to methodically designed, tested, and reviewed products. It provides maximum assurance based on good commercial development practices. These practices still do not require substantial specialist knowledge and skills. EAL 4 is likely to be economically feasible for implementation within an existing product line. It provides moderate to high level security for conventional products, with minimal additional engineering costs.
- EAL 5 refers to semi-formally designed and tested products. It requires security engineering based on rigorous commercial development practices supported by moderate security engineering techniques. Although additional costs should not be excessive, EAL 5 provides a high level of security.
- EAL 6 refers to semi-formally verified design and testing of products. It provides high assurance by using a rigorous development environment and techniques. EAL 6 products are for protecting high value assets against significant risks.

- EAL 7 refers to formally verified design and testing of products and constitutes the upper bound for practically useful products. It is aimed at security products for application in extremely high-risk situations or where the high value of the assets justifies these costs.

The important advantage of Common Criteria is that it is focused not only on IT security as such, but also on production processes [314]. However, CC is a very extensive standard. And it seems that extensive standards with hundreds of pages are highly probable to fail. History records a lot of such examples: OSI family of protocols [169], Secure Electronic Transactions (SET) standard with its predecessor Secure Electronic Payment Protocol [230], etc. And CC appears to approach the line, too [151, 87].

*   *   *

Final cautious remarks. Security policy should not be overly top-down driven, because lack of visibility at the bottom is likely to result in an unimplementable or inapplicable policy [357]. Further, paperwork related to formalization of security policy should not be over-emphasized. This burden prevents experts from using their skills and creativity in deploying security solutions. Further, overly complex schemes for security policies should be avoided. Although they might look impressive, people cope with them only with difficulty. Last, but not least, complex security policies entail higher "transaction costs".

Summing up, the *cumini sector*[12] approach will result in an effect that will be the opposite to that planned. Thus, a good portion of common-sense and feeling for human resources has to be practiced.

---

[12]The hairsplitter.

3

Security Technology: Concepts and Models

Arma tuentur pacem.[1]

This chapter will discuss technologies that belong to the basic arsenal of tools for provision of ISs security and privacy. Although the chapter is about technology, the field will be presented conceptually with graphical models. Thus no particular experience with bits and bytes, or lemmas and theorems, is required. Mathematical and other formal details will be covered in the appendix for those readers that are interested in a deeper understanding of this area.

The meaning of core graphical notation that will be used throughout this book is given in Fig. 3.1.

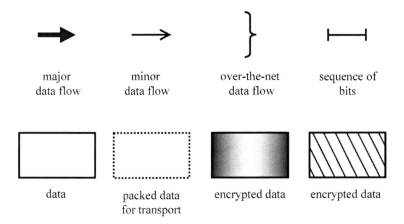

| major
data flow | minor
data flow | over-the-net
data flow | sequence of
bits |

| data | packed data
for transport | encrypted data | encrypted data |

Fig. 3.1. The meaning of graphical notation

---

[1] Arms maintain peace.

In case of encryption, two different notations will be needed for this operation. The reason is that schemes will sometimes present application of two consecutive encryption processes. In this case, for clarity reasons, these different notations will be used. The meaning of the rest of symbols will be explained when they will be used for the first time.

Despite the more reader friendly approach, the reader should be able to grasp the essence and principles of functioning of the relevant technologies. In addition, a historical perspective will be added to better understand contemporary management of ISs security and privacy, and to enable anticipation of future developments.

3.1 Security Mechanisms

Security mechanism denotes a process (or a device incorporating such a process) that can be used in a system to implement a security service that is provided by or within the system [146]. Security mechanisms include pseudorandom generators, one-way hash functions, cryptographic algorithms, logical, and physical mechanisms. At the heart of many security mechanisms is *cryptography, which is a scientific discipline that deals with transformations of readable texts (plaintexts) into unreadable forms (ciphertexts), and vice versa, to protect the contents of texts.* Transformation from plaintext to ciphertext is called encryption, and transformation in the opposite direction is decryption.

3.1.1 Pseudorandom Number Generators

Random values play an important role in the implementation of ISs security and privacy, primarily with cryptographic algorithms and cryptographic protocols. For example, symmetric cryptographic algorithms depend on session keys that have to be genuinely random values as much as possible. Further, cryptographic protocols are prone to threats like replays and these may be prevented by inclusion of random numbers.

Random bit sequences, i.e. random numbers, *can be defined as sequences, where each of these sequences is equally likely.* To obtain truly random bit sequences, processes like coin-tossing or measurement of (intervals between) hits on a Geiger counter during radioactive decay can be used. But these are impractical for computing environments, thus computers themselves are used to produce appropriate sequences of bits. These sequences are referred to as pseudorandom sequences, because they are produced with pseudorandom generators, where *pseudorandom generator means an efficient algorithm that, being driven by a seed on its input, produces a sufficiently long sequence of bits as output, which is apparently random.* The scheme of such a generator is presented in Fig. 3.2.

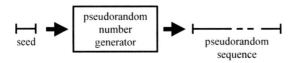

Fig. 3.2. Model of a pseudorandom number generator

Practical implementations of pseudorandom generators are done on the basis of cryptographic primitives like symmetric algorithms [197], strong one-way hash functions [209], or by use of congruencies [113]. The seminal work in this field has been done by Blum, Micalli and Yao [32].

3.1.2 One-way Hash Functions

One-way hash functions are cryptographic primitives that take an arbitrary input file (plaintext) and efficiently produce a fixed length output (ciphertext), but finding the input on the basis of a known output is not computationally feasible. A model of a one-way hash function is given in Fig. 3.3.

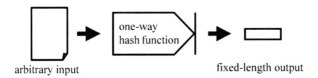

arbitrary input   fixed-length output

Fig. 3.3. Model of a one-way hash function

The output of a one-way hash function is called the fingerprint of the plaintext, because it unambiguously represents a particular plaintext, and because it is a shrunk value (a hash) of its input. Therefore in the rest of the book we will use terms hash functions and one-way hash functions interchangeably, referring always to one-way hash functions.

Important representatives of hash functions include the SHA family [252] and RIPEMD (RIPEMD-160) [180]. Historically, the MD family of one-way hash functions has special status, with the most popular representative being MD5 [293].

One-way hash functions play a fundamental role in digital signatures, so let us concentrate on this issue for a while. A principle of digital signatures forgery will be presented that is inherently tied to properties of these functions. It will provide some insight into cryptanalysis, which sometimes finds surprising ways to reduce the strength of cryptographic mechanisms. The principle will only be outlined in this subsection, while more detailed discussion is given in the appendix.

Assume a large population of people. It is reasonable then to assume that the probability for any person having birthday on a particular day is equal for all days. Thus birthdays are equally distributed among the members of this population. Now imagine the following two variants:

1. A randomly chosen person walks into the room and we record her birthday. How many additional randomly chosen persons have to enter the room to have a probability of at least 50% that there is a match with the birthday of the first person?
2. Randomly chosen persons walk into the room and we record the birthday of each of them. How many randomly chosen persons have to enter the room to have a probability of at least 50% that any two of them have the birthday on the same day?

In this particular case of 365 birthdays, the first variant yields 253 persons, while the second variant yields only 23 persons. This result is surprising. In the first case, to achieve probability of more than 50%, the required number of persons is close to the total number of possible birthdays and is of the same order of magnitude. In the second case, the required number is on the opposite side of the expected interval, one order of magnitude smaller.

What does this experiment mean for falsification of digital signatures? One way hash functions are used to produce digital signatures. These functions map a set with a large number of elements into a set with a relatively small number of elements. This means that certain elements from the first set will map to the same element in the second set, and such cases are called collisions. In the case of digital signatures, two different texts will produce the same digital signature - with the above example, persons correspond to texts, and birthdays correspond to hashed values.

The conclusion is that having a fixed text, it is much harder to find a falsified text that produces the same hashed value - this corresponds to the first variant above. However, if the right text and the forged one are allowed to be represented with numerous variations, this reflects the nature of the second variant and significantly improves chances for forgery. In this case, one systematically generates variants of a harmless text together with variants of harmful text, e.g. [331]:

- Dear [Prof./Dr./Prof. Dr.] Johnson, this is to express my [honest/sincere] opinion about the [teaching qualifications/academic qualifications] of [Prof./Dr./Prof. Dr.] May. His [excellent/outstanding] achievements in his field with [numerous/many] references...
- Dear [Prof./Dr./Prof. Dr.] Johnson, this is to express my [honest/sincere] opinion about the [teaching qualifications/academic qualifications] of [Prof./Dr./Prof. Dr.] May. His [poor/weak] achievements in his field with [irrelevant/minor] references...

It can be seen that the number of available messages for both cases, harmless and harmful, can easily be taken to extremes. This enables the application of the principle from the second variant of the birthdays experiment. When a match is found for both variants, the harmless text is submitted for signing. After being signed, the signature is stripped-off, and appended to the harmful text. And indeed, this is how it is done with digital signatures.

In brief, what are the implications for management of ISs security and privacy? Firstly, one should be cautious about the strength of cryptographic mechanisms. In 2003, SHA-1 was treated as probably the best cryptographic hash algorithm in the world [258], and a year later it was predicted that SHA-1 is safe for the foreseeable future [323]. However, in 2004 this hash function has been successfully attacked [310]. Secondly, breaking one-way hash functions is normal evolution in this field. The same situation happened to the very popular hash function MD5 roughly ten years ago [293]. The first dangerous signs for MD5 appeared only one year after its standardization [35], while the efforts successfully ended four years later [94].

But there is no reason for panic. Users will have to get used to such situations. If computers are getting exponentially faster according to Moore's law,[2] so are the cryptographic primitives "aging" with the same speed. In this case, luckily, we already have stronger variants like SHA-256 at our disposal. Besides, there are other measures that can complement one-way hash functions, and may be taken into account in certain cases [339]:

- Documents can be highly structured with only certain fields (parts) allowed to contain varying values. Further, the set of applicable values for changeable fields should be only as large as necessary.
- For each transaction, two documents with different syntax, but the same semantics, can be signed. This can be achieved by rearrangement of words in a document, or even easier by insertion of additional blanks.
- Documents can be segmented into two or more parts, which both have to be signed.

All the above described measures further reduce the possibility of successful electronic document forgery.

3.1.3 Symmetric Algorithms

A model of a symmetric cipher is presented in Fig. 3.4. It can serve for deriving a definition of *symmetric algorithm, which is an algorithm that uses the same key for encryption of plaintext as for decryption of ciphertext.* The main advantage of these algorithms is that they can be implemented efficiently in computing environments. Their main disadvantage is complex key manage-

---

[2]The well-known Moore's law states that available processing power and storage capacities double every eighteen months, which means exponential growth of available resources. This experience based observation has held true since the sixties, when it was stated by the co-founder of Intel, Gordon Moore.

ment. The number of secret keys needed to enable each pair of participants to communicate securely is proportional to n^2, when there are n participants.[3]

Two major players in the world of symmetric ciphers are Triple DES (3DES) [250] and its successor Advanced Encryption Standard (AES) [251]. Triple DES is a variant of Data Encryption Standard (DES) [246] that used to belong to the golden arsenal of cryptographic tools for protecting computers and computer communications. Ordinary DES is based on the IBM's cipher, called Lucifer [117] and when the National Bureau of Standards launched its call for a national cipher standard in 1973, IBM jumped into the game with an improved version of Lucipher. IBM won the call and this gave the birth to one of the most successful standardized ciphers worldwide - DES algorithm.

DES stayed on the scene as a major symmetric cryptographic algorithm for almost thirty years. It finally became clear, in 1999, that the power of available computing resources made it vulnerable. In this case, brute-force attack is assumed, which means systematic generation of all possible keys and their application to a ciphertext in order to recover the corresponding plaintext.

NIST, therefore, issued a new standard for a DES based derivative, the above mentioned 3DES. At the same time NIST started to look for successor of DES. The successor came in the form of an Advanced Encryption Standard that was officially confirmed by NIST in 2001. This algorithm was developed by two Belgian cryptographers Daemen and Rijmen and has many advantages over 3DES. The most notable is that it can be more efficiently implemented in software, is thus faster and can operate on larger blocks than 64 bits, i.e. 128, 192 and 256 bits. This latter property also has cryptographic significance. Additionally, keys may have various lengths, the shortest being 128 bits (standardized version).

However, it is important to note that the base of applications with ordinary DES is very large. Taking into account that 3DES systems can be used directly within DES based environments, this significantly reduces the costs. Therefore 3DES is anticipated to prolong the life-time of DES for quite some years [323] (even some recent implementations that are started from scratch are 3DES based [57]).

The above facts provide the guidelines for the management of ISs security and privacy. An organization may stick with 3DES, especially if it already has a large base of DES implementations. But if an organization is starting a project from scratch, a better approach is to use AES.

Symmetric ciphers depend heavily on principles that have been known for a long time. These basic principles include permutations, substitutions and

---

[3]More precisely, the number of required keys for secure communication of each pair in an environment with n participants is $n*(n-1)/2$. Each participant shares a key with $n-1$ other participants. As there are n participants, the total number is $n*(n-1)$, but this means that each key was counted twice. Thus the final result is obtained after division by 2.

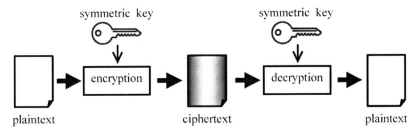

Fig. 3.4. Model of a symmetric encryption algorithm

transpositions. A typical example of a cipher that is based on these principles is 3DES. Because of the historical importance of DES, its relative simplicity, its wide use and suitability for contemporary applications, the detailed structure and functioning of 3DES will be given in the appendix.

Substitutions

With substitutions, the characters of plaintext are replaced by other characters according to some rule, also called the key. There are two families of substitutions: mono-alphabetic and poly-alphabetic. An example of mono-alphabetic substitution is given in Fig. 3.5. In this case, plaintext "this is a cipher" is transformed into "wklv lv d fltkhu".

a	b	c	d	e	f	g	h	i	j	k	.	.	.	u	v	w	x	y	z	plaintext
d	e	f	g	h	i	j	k	l	m	n	.	.	.	x	y	z	a	b	c	ciphertext

a	b	c	d	e	f	g	h	i	j	k	.	.	.	u	v	w	x	y	z	plaintext
d	e	f	g	h	i	j	k	l	m	n	.	.	.	x	y	z	a	b	c	ciphertext 1
f	g	h	i	j	k	l	m	n	o	p	.	.	.	z	a	b	c	d	e	ciphertext 2

Fig. 3.5. An example of mono-alphabetic substitution (top) and poly-alphabetic substitution (bottom)

With mono-alphabetic substitution one uses an alphabet character sequence and another sequence with permuted characters. Each character of plaintext is replaced by the corresponding character from the permuted sequence to produce ciphertext (to obtain the plaintext, one uses the reverse procedure). The problem with this procedure is that it preserves the statistical properties of the plaintext. Thus an attacker has only to calculate the frequency of characters in the cipher text and replace them with appropriate characters that have the same frequency in the language. This reveals the plaintext.

To complicate such an attack, poly-alphabetic substitutions can be used. They work as follows: A set of different substitution sequences is defined and each substitution sequence is applied to the plaintext according to a certain rule. For example, one defines two substitution sequences and uses the first one for the first letter, the third letter, and so on, while the second sequence is used for the second letter, the fourth letter, and so on. So, for example, plaintext "this is a cipher" is transformed into "wmlx lx d hlvkju", using the second cipher from Fig. 3.5.

These kind of ciphers have received a lot of attention, especially a variant called Vigenere cipher, but they are all vulnerable to statistics based attacks [323].

Transpositions

With transpositions one permutes the group of plaintext letters, e.g. by writing plaintext in a rectangle and permuting the columns. An example of transposition is given in Fig. 3.6, where the plaintext "thisisasimpltext" is transformed into "htsisisamilptexe-t–". Padding with "-" is used to form blocks of dimensions $5 * 4$.

plaintext			
t	h	i	s
i	s	a	s
i	m	p	l
e	t	e	x
t	-	-	-

ciphertext			
h	t	s	i
s	i	s	a
m	i	l	p
t	e	x	e
-	t	-	-

(key: $1, 2, 3, 4 \rightarrow 2, 1, 4, 3$)

Fig. 3.6. An example of transposition

Pure transposition is again easily recognized, because of the same letter frequencies as in the original text. If an attacker assumes that transposition has taken place, ciphertext can be arranged in columns and permuted. Using two or more-stage transpositions makes this process harder, and the cipher becomes stronger. But despite these efforts the resulting cipher still preserves statistical properties of the plaintext.

Such ciphers as described above are called block ciphers, because they operate on blocks of data. On the other hand, stream ciphers operate on one data character at a time.

Product Ciphers

Symmetric key crypto-systems can be also obtained by the combinations of substitutions and transpositions, where substitutions are used interchangeably with transpositions. This hides the statistical properties of the plaintext and results in a much harder cipher. Such combinations are called product ciphers and an example is given in Fig. 3.7. Decoder, denoted by D in Fig. 3.7, takes three bits on input and maps it to output according to the table in Fig. 3.8 through an encoder (denoted by E).

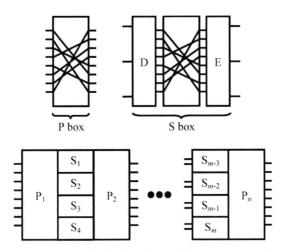

Fig. 3.7. Permutation box P, substitution box S (above), and product cipher (below)

plaintext	ciphertext
000	101
001	111
010	100
011	001
100	110
101	010
110	011
111	000

Fig. 3.8. Mapping table example for substitution box

3.1.4 Asymmetric Algorithms

In the late seventies, the principles for asymmetric cryptography, also called public key cryptography, were set by Diffie and Hellman. They proposed the novel idea of using computational complexity theory for a brand new approach in cryptography [90]. Soon, the first (and still the most famous) fully functional public key algorithm was developed by Rivest, Shamir and Adleman, called

RSA [292] (because of its importance, this algorithm is addressed in detail in the appendix). Other representatives of asymmetric cryptography are Diffie-Hellman (DH) [90], ElGamal [102], Digital Signature Standard (DSS) [248], and elliptic curve based cryptography (ECC) [189].

Based on Fig. 3.9, the following definition can be obtained: *Asymmetric cryptography is a process with two complementary keys that are used for cryptographic transformations, where one of these keys is publicly announced and the other one is kept secret.*

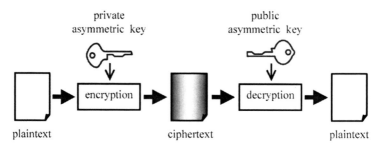

Fig. 3.9. Model of asymmetric algorithm

Public key cryptography has many advantages over ordinary, symmetric key cryptography. One can communicate securely by keeping one key, i.e. the private key confidential, while the second key, the public key, can be communicated to anyone. These keys are different, but complementary. Knowing one key gives no hint to an attacker about the other key, because deriving the other key from the known one is computationally hard.

When an owner of the private key encrypts a message, anyone having the public key can perform decryption and be assured that the message came from the owner of the private component. This effectively embodies the signature principle, thus the procedure is called digital signature. On the other hand, if someone uses the public key to encrypt the message, only the owner of the corresponding private component can perform the decryption, which means that confidentiality is assured.

Another benefit of using asymmetric cryptography is reduction of key management complexity. Suppose there are n users in the system and each user wants to securely communicate with every other user. To enable such communication, the number of keys needed is proportional to n, which means easier key management than with symmetric cryptography. Note that secure communication denotes confidential communication in an authenticated way. This may be achieved by using the partner's public key to encrypt the message for confidentiality and afterwards encrypt the result with the sender's own private key to provide authentication. On receipt, the partner uses the sender's public key and obtains the intermediate result. Afterwards, the private key is used to retrieve the plaintext.

However, asymmetric cryptography also has drawbacks. The first one is its computational complexity. To achieve comparable strength to symmetric cryptography, a few orders of magnitude longer processing time is needed than with conventional cryptography. This most notably holds true for algorithms like RSA, and those that are based on similar principles. This is a drawback for many devices that have low processing capabilities, like smart cards or hand-held terminals. The problem is a general one, because desktop systems are far less limited in dimensions than mobile devices. Therefore the latter type of computing devices will be always inferior to others. Luckily, not so long ago, elliptic curve based cryptography was developed [189]. Corresponding algorithms offer the same functionality, but they use significantly shorter keys for comparable strength. Therefore, the processing burden is reduced.

The second drawback of asymmetric cryptography is the inherent need for assuring the binding between a public key and corresponding entity. This requires the introduction of a so-called *certificate that is a digital document, issued and signed by the certification authority (CA), aimed at providing assurance that a certain public key indeed belongs to the claimed entity.* Thus everyone who knows the public key of the particular CA, can verify digital signatures on its certificates, and be assured about valid relationships between entities and their public keys.

CA related issues looked simple at the time of invention of asymmetric cryptography. A good decade later it started to become clear that digital certificates are the beginning of a whole new and complicated story, called public key infrastructure (PKI), which will be discussed in subsection 3.4.1.

It is good to have some basic idea about the meaning of cryptographic strength. A comparison of strength of few cryptographic algorithms is given in Fig. 3.10 [128]. It can be seen that it is expressed as the estimated number of MIPS-years to break a cipher (MIPS stands for millions instructions per second). The above estimates are already five years old, but the figure is still very descriptive. The relative strength of one method to another remains the same, except if a short-cut kind of attack was to be found. However, the strength of all methods in terms of required time efforts should be reduced by a common factor. This is needed to reflect the current situation due to advances in technology, and the factor is determined, as expected, by Moore's law.

But one should be warned - such comparisons are based on certain estimates that may be false. For example, RSA is based on the assumption that factoring certain kinds of numbers is computationally hard. In 1977 it was estimated that factoring a 125-digit number would take 40 quadrillion years, but less than twenty years later, in 1994, a 129-digit number was factored [306]. This is another example that estimates about strength of cryptographic algorithms should be taken with caution. The reason for problems with such estimates is the fact that, for many principles on which cryptographic mechanisms are based, there exists no formal proof about their bottom line computational complexities. This refers to idealized mechanisms, thus once (and if)

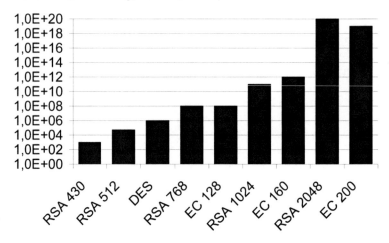

Fig. 3.10. Strength of cryptographic algorithms according to key lengths, where vertical axis presents MIPS-years for a crypto-algorithm to break (this graph first appeared in the June 2000 issue of ISO Bulletin - now entitled ISO Focus (www.iso.org/isofocus) - The Magazine of the International Organization for Standardization, and is reproduced here with the permission of ISO Central Secretariat (www.iso.org))

such proofs are found, it has to be further assured that concrete implementations preserve these idealized properties as well.

As a practical consequence, an organization should plan transition to longer keys or new algorithms well in advance by following the latest news about the "aging" of cryptographic mechanisms, be it mechanisms as such, or their key-lengths.

3.1.5 Steganography and Watermarking

The word steganography is of Greek origin and means covered writing. *Steganography is a method by which a message contains additional hidden information.* This technique is radically different from cryptography. With cryptography, the existence of a message is evident, although the content is not accessible. The approach with steganography is the opposite one - the existence of a message is kept secret. This is achieved by using a harmless message, called cover message (or cover object), and embedding the secret message into this cover object, usually by using some key, called stego-key. A particular cover object is randomly chosen from a set of equally likely cover objects, thus an attacker is not able to decide which cover object contains hidden information [196].

Encrypted information can attract attention and is thus more likely to be a subject of analysis. So it is not uncommon to see claims that steganographic techniques give further level of protection to classical cryptography by

Fig. 3.11. Hiding information within graphics file - the original graphics at the top, the graphics with embedded subsection 1.1 of this book at the bottom (photo courtesy of T. T. Pečak)

additionally applying steganography [88]. But cryptography is sensitive to the smallest changes of transformed data at the bit level, which cause the recovery process to fail. With steganography, the processing of a stego-object may lead to changes of embedded information, and if this information is encrypted, it is lost.

One of the simplest forms of steganography uses color values of pixels in graphic files. If one uses the least significant bit of each pixel in such file, where the pixel has a color depth of sixteen bits or more, the change of this bit will be invisible to a human eye. An example of a graphic file that contains hidden information is given in Fig. 3.11. This example shows that it is possible to secretly convey the whole section 1.1 of this book within a picture (the original picture with embedded information has been scaled to fit on the page).

Problems with such techniques as presented in Fig. 3.11 emerge if graphics are processed. In this case, the hidden information becomes distorted. If this hidden information is encrypted, it will become useless. More resistant techniques are watermarking techniques [196], which can be seen as steganographic techniques with additional property of being robust against possible attacks. This is especially important for protection of intellectual property rights with digital content, to which various lossy compression techniques may be applied.

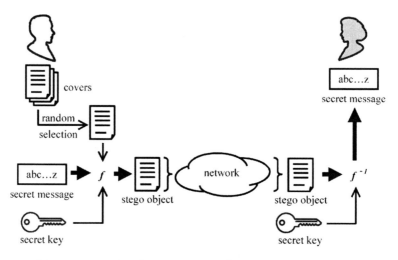

Fig. 3.12. Model of steganography (f denotes stego function)

A model of steganography is presented in Fig. 3.12.[4] The topic of steganography and digital watermarking exceeds the scope of this book, so for detailed coverage of these topics the reader is advised to consult e.g. [196]. But for the management of ISs security and privacy it is important to keep in mind that there may exist some exchange of secret information behind the scenes, and prevention of such activities has to be considered.

3.2 Cryptographic Protocols

Before proceeding further with security and privacy methods and tools, one has to have a basic understanding of computer networks, i.e. computer communications. This topic will be covered briefly in the next subsection.

---

[4]Reproduced by permission from Katzenbeiser S., Petitcolas F.A., *Information Hiding - Techniques for Steganography and Digital Watermarking*, Norwood, MA, Artech House, Inc., 2000. ©2000 by Artech House, Inc.

3.2.1 A Brief Overview of Computer Communications

Computer communications deal with the complex process of exchange of information between computers. To cope with it, the whole communication task is divided into sub-tasks, and these sub-tasks are assigned to so-called layers. Layers are just abstractions for hardware or software that performs certain functions. From the standardization point of view it is not important how a particular layer performs a certain sub-function. What matters is the way of communication with the peer layer, i.e. the communicating layer on the other side of network, and with layers above and below it.

The most widely accepted model of computer communications is the TCP/IP reference model [278]. This model is the core of the winning Internet technology and is presented in Fig. 3.13.[5]

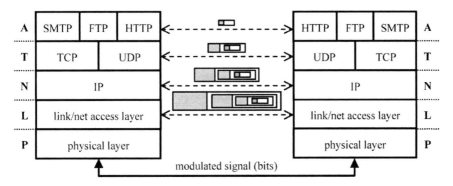

Fig. 3.13. The TCP/IP reference model ("A" stands for application layer, "T" for transport layer, "N" for network layer, "L" for link layer, and "P" for physical layer)

Layer entities communicate with peer entity layers by exchange of data streams that are referred to as segments, packets, and frames (depending on the layer). These streams consist of headers followed by payloads, and they are optionally ended with trailers. When an application wants to communicate with another application, it forms a stream of data, prepends it with a header and hands it over to the transport layer, as shown in Fig. 3.13. The transport layer treats the received payload and header as a new payload, so it prepends its own header that is needed for proper processing and hands over the result to the network layer. This game goes on to the level of the physical layer, where data are transmitted to the other party (or some intermediary systems before reaching the final recipient). The intended recipient picks the data from the medium and the link layer parses the header to know how to process the

---

[5]When written with the capital letter, Internet refers to the plain TCP/IP global area network. When written with small letter, internet refers to a global network as a conglomerate of all protocols in use (of course, the majority of them nowadays are TCP/IP based).

data. It then passes only the payload upwards to the network layer. This layer parses the network layer header and accordingly processes the payload before handing it over to the transport layer and so on. Thus physical flow of data goes from the application layer to the physical layer, where the data are sent over the network. At the other end, the flow of data starts at the physical layer end ends at the application layer. However, the logical data flow takes place between similar entities (see dashed lines in Fig. 3.13).

The task of the physical layer is to transmit bits across a particular medium, taking into account its properties. It therefore deals with physical interfaces, signal levels and frequencies, their modulation and the like. The link layer takes care of communication with the next communicating entity on the network. It is responsible for low level addressing issues, proper structuring of data (depending on characteristics of the medium), error correction, etc. The network layer is not concerned with the transmission medium, but deals basically with routing of data from the source address to the destination address. The network layer in the TCP/IP model does not ensure delivery, so the transport layer has to take this responsibility. The Transmission Control Protocol (TCP) [279] does this by ensuring that all data streams are transmitted without errors and in correct sequence. The TCP protocol is said to be connection oriented, because it provides reliable delivery, where sending and receiving layers are in permanent interaction during exchange of data. There is another transport protocol, called User Datagram Protocol (UDP) [277], which does not provide reliable delivery and is connectionless by its nature (connectionless service means that an entity does not maintain a session with its peer, thus delivery is not reliable). What then is the function of UDP?

As well as TCP, UDP manages sending and delivery of data streams by appropriately structuring them as required by network layer. Further, like TCP, it acts on behalf of an application and thus knows which data are intended for which application. This is achieved through so-called ports, where each application is assigned a port number, while the host, where the application resides, is identified through an IP number. So, in essence, the connectionless nature of UDP is the main difference from TCP. This enables simpler and more effective implementations, because the protocol requires less overhead, which is suitable for certain applications. But no matter which transport layer protocol is chosen, it handles data on behalf of the application layer by taking care of all communication details and making them invisible to applications.

The last layer is the application layer that consists of various protocols, which can be seen as self contained applications. In our case, these are Simple Mail Transfer Protocol (SMTP) for e-mail [280], File Transfer Protocol (FTP) for files transfer [281], and Hypertext Transfer Protocol (HTTP) for transport of Web documents [119]. Application layer protocols may further provide services not only to human users, but also other stand-alone applications.

3.2.2 Security Services

Security service denotes a service aimed at protecting resources. Security services are implemented by deploying cryptographic mechanisms (pseudorandom generators, one-way hash functions, symmetric and asymmetric algorithms). The rest of protection is done by deploying logical and physical mechanisms.

Most often, security services are implemented in a form of *cryptographic protocols, which are protocols enhanced with cryptographic mechanisms, where protocol means a procedure for setting-up, maintaining and releasing a connection.*

The following security services are the ones most often defined in the literature (see e.g. [168]):

- *Authentication that ensures that the communicating peer entity is the one claimed, or that the data are coming from the claimed source.*
- *Confidentiality that protects the data from unauthorized disclosure.*
- *Integrity that enables detection of any modification, insertion or deletion of data.*
- *Non-repudiation that provides the recipient with the proof of origin and the sender with a proof of delivery, where false denying of the message content is prevented.*
- *Access control that prevents unauthorized use of resources.*
- *Auditing (logging) that enables administrative recording of events for detection of suspicious activities, analysis of successful breaches and evidence for resolving legal disputes.*

To better understand the logical functioning of the above security services, the following subsections present and discuss model implementations.

3.2.3 Models of Security Services

A model of an authentication service is given in Fig. 3.14. It is implemented by use of a symmetric algorithm. With a shared symmetric key, entity A produces a ciphertext that is appended to the plaintext, and both parts are sent over the network. On receipt, entity B recovers the ciphertext and compares it with the received plaintext. If values match, entity B can be assured that entity A is the originating entity of the message. In this case, ciphertext plays the role of authenticating data, and is thus referred to as the message authentication code (MAC).

A model of authentication service with asymmetric crypto-algorithm is given in Fig. 3.15 (attention should be paid to the color of the asymmetric keys - white keys always belong to entity A, gray to entity B). Sender encrypts a message with his private key and sends plaintext with corresponding ciphertext over the network. A receiver uses sender's public key and decrypts

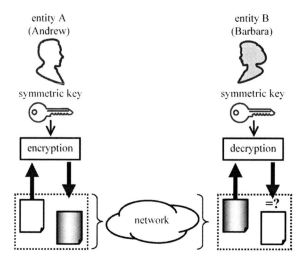

Fig. 3.14. Model of authentication with symmetric crypto-algorithm (dashed line denotes the complete message that is sent over the network)

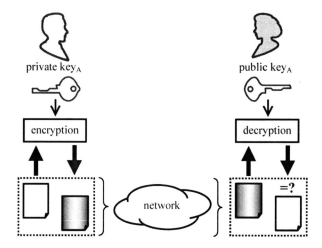

Fig. 3.15. Model of authentication with asymmetric encryption

the received ciphertext. The decrypted message is compared with the received plaintext and if values match, the message is authenticated.

A similar approach is used in case of confidentiality (see Fig. 3.16). The only difference is that the plaintext is not accompanying the encrypted text to assure confidentiality. Using confidentiality by sending only ciphertext over the network may be suitable for texts, where integrity problems would result in an unreadable file at the recipient end. In this case, the recipient would recognize that something unwanted has happened to the message along the way. But generally, using only confidentiality does not assure integrity.

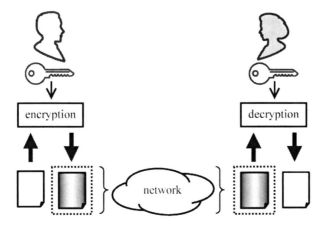

Fig. 3.16. Model of confidentiality with symmetric encryption

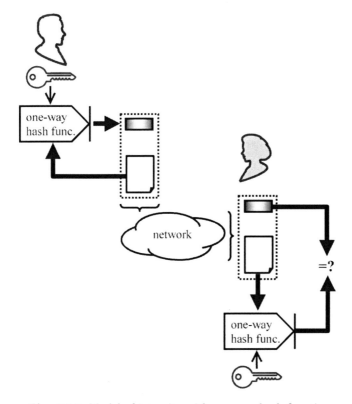

Fig. 3.17. Model of integrity with one-way hash function

The most common approach to ensure integrity is to use a one-way hash function to calculate the fingerprint of a file. Due to the fact that calculation of such fingerprints involves secret keys that are submitted to hash function together with the plaintext, the results present means for message authentication. That is why they are also called message authentication codes. In this case, sending entity A hashes the plaintext and the secret key that is shared with peer entity B. The result is appended to the plaintext, and both parts are sent over the network (see the dashed line in Fig. 3.17). On receipt, recipient B uses the secret key and received plaintext to calculate the MAC value. This value is then compared with the received MAC value and if there is a match, the receiver can be assured of message integrity and authenticity.

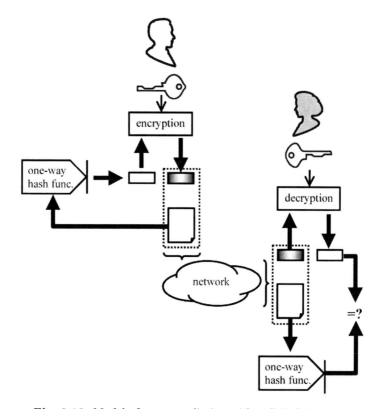

Fig. 3.18. Model of non-repudiation with a digital signature

A similar approach is used to produce a digital signature, which ensures non-repudiation. Entity A produces first a hashed value of the plaintext and encrypts it with the private key. This encrypted hash presents the digital signature and is appended to the plaintext to be sent together with the plaintext over the network. Upon receipt, the receiver uses A's public key to decrypt the hash, which is compared with the newly produced hash value of the plaintext. If these values match, integrity and authentication (thus non-repudiation) are

assured (see Fig. 3.18). The deployment of asymmetric cryptography constitutes the main difference from the integrity approach in Fig. 3.17, where two
entities share the same key, thus one entity can always claim not to be the
author of the message.

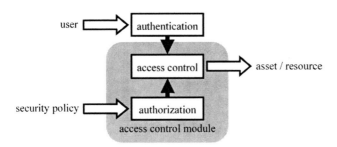

Fig. 3.19. Model of access control

The last model presents access control service and is given in Fig. 3.19.
This service is implemented with appropriate logical controls (usually within
operating systems), being dependent at the same time on authentication. The
authorization is performed on the basis of matrices or lists, where an entity
is associated with allocated resources, or vice-versa - a resource is associated
with entities that are allowed to access it.

Traditional access control models can be classified as follows [225, 271]:

- The first group comprises discretionary access control models. These models are based on four sets: objects (resources that need to be protected),
subjects (entities interacting with objects), access rights (defining the kind
of interactions between objects and subjects) and predicates (expressing
constraints). Access rules are most often stored in a matrix.

- The second group comprises mandatory access control systems. The basic
philosophy with these systems is concentration on the flow of information. Objects and subjects are classified and labeled accordingly. Based on
classification, various information flows can be enforced. The most famous
one is Bell-LaPadula [25]. With its "no read-up" and "no write-down" approach it enables dissemination of information only among the subjects of
the allowed class and superior subjects. Thus less sensitive information can
enter a domain with higher sensitivity, but information from the domain
with higher sensitivity cannot propagate downwards (see Fig. 3.20).[6] This
model is not very suitable for implementation within computer systems.
However, it is easier implemented organizationally, especially in highly
hierarchically structured environments.

---

[6]Formally, the model is written as follows [11]:

$\forall s \in subjects, o \in objects : allow(s, o, read) \Leftrightarrow label(s)\, dominates\, label(o)$ (NRU),

$\forall s \in subjects, o \in objects : allow(s, o, write) \Leftrightarrow label(o)\, dominates\, label(s)$ (NWD).

- The third group comprises role-based access control models. They consist of two relations. With the first, roles are associated with permissions, while the second relation binds subjects to roles. The philosophy behind these models is to tie access rights to business functions and processes. The position within an organization, i.e. a person's business roles, imply permissions.

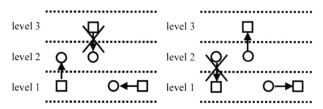

Fig. 3.20. The Bell-LaPadula model - NRU left, NWD right (squares represent objects, circles subjects)

Besides these classical models, some other models have been introduced, like Clark - Wilson model [67] and Chinese Wall Policy [41], none of which gained much importance. As far as traditional models are concerned, many authors argue (see e.g. [225]) that they cannot be used in a networked environment with various operating systems, where sets of objects, subjects, roles, etc. are permanently changing.

3.2.4 The Relationships Between Security Services

An important question with regards to security services is whether the set of services as defined in subsection 3.2.2 can be somehow reduced. Put another way, does there exist a basic set of services, which would enable derivation of all other security services? Looking at the definition of security services from a computing environment perspective, it is clear that cryptography is at the heart of the first four services: authentication, confidentiality, integrity and non-repudiation. The last two services, access control and auditing, are implemented with logical or physical mechanisms, and not directly with cryptographic mechanisms. Further, they are also independent of one another - access control may exist without logging, and logging, in principle, may exist without access control services.

Now considering cryptography related security services (authentication, confidentiality, integrity and non-repudiation), what are the relationships between these services? Which of them are orthogonal or which of them can be derived from the others? Considering the historical importance and success of BAN logic [48] (discussed in detail in the appendix), the importance of authentication cannot be denied. However, as long as integrity is not assured, there can be no authentication. The reason is that authentication is achieved by exchange of encrypted messages, and if any of those bits is changed, the result is useless. The similar holds true for confidentiality with regards to integrity. If one bit in ciphertext is flipped, integrity is broken, and although information is not disclosed, it becomes useless. It can be concluded that successful authentication and successful confidentiality imply assured integrity.

But starting with integrity, things are even more complex. The integrity that we are interested in is provided by the use of cryptographic mechanisms. A message is cryptographically processed, the result is appended to the message and both parts are sent over the network. Most frequently, this appendix is computed with a one-way hash function and an additional secret key, which results in a MAC as already discussed. Thus, to enable integrity, one has to use encryption, which requires authenticated and confidential exchange of keys (CRC codes are not the right answer, because everyone can easily change the message and re-calculate the code). So if we are strict, there is no integrity without confidentiality and authentication.

This reasoning suggests that confidentiality, integrity and authentication constitute the basic cryptographic security services. They exist either together, or not at all. In order to cope with this situation, we use an "intellectual knife" and first separate integrity. When integrity is in our focus, authentication and confidentiality have to take place beforehand. This is the main difference from the situation when authentication or confidentiality is in our focus. In this second case, authentication and confidentiality take place simultaneously with integrity. Secondly, although it appears to be a fact that these three basic services are tied one to another and cannot exist separately, we can further decouple conceptually authentication from integrity, and confidentiality from integrity. When we concentrate on authentication, we are aware of the fact that it is taking place simultaneously with integrity. The reasoning with confidentiality is the same. And when we concentrate on integrity, confidentiality and authentication that are needed for this very integrity are neglected - they have taken place at some time previously and are now taken for granted. Now if this is the case, the only conceptually compound service is non-repudiation, which consists of authentication and integrity.

It might seem that the above issues are rather philosophical, which is not the case. The above questions are important, because their understanding reduces the chances of design and implementation blunders and consequently vulnerabilities of ISs. The basic three services have to be addressed as separate issues. For example, if we use the same symmetric algorithm for confidentiality and integrity, we should logically separate these services by using one symmetric key solely for integrity, and another solely for confidentiality. This prevents confusion about the intention of use of cryptography, and such explicit use disables flaws in implementations [1].

3.3 Key Management

Key management denotes *procedures that cover generation, certification (registration), distribution, installation, activation/de-activation, storage, archiving, revocation (de-registration), recovery and destruction of keys.* In short, key management covers processes of a complete life cycle of keys.

Although key management has its roots in technology, the majority of the above processes cannot be solved without addressing organizational and legal issues. Experience shows that key management is anything but a trivial task. However, it is of immense importance, because security services depend directly on it.

3.3.1 Key Generation

With regard to generation, asymmetric keys are determined by algorithms used for this kind of cryptography. Symmetric keys, however, have to be pseudorandom and they are generated with quality pseudorandom generators.

3.3.2 Key Distribution

For key distribution, the most straightforward approach is to use physical means, including ordinary mail and couriers. This kind of distribution is also referred to as out of band key exchange. But for an online key distribution, a few basic principles can be identified. They are shown in Fig. 3.21, Fig. 3.22, and Fig. 3.23. The first one is hierarchical symmetric key distribution. The top level key is called the master key, which is exchanged rarely. It serves for encryption of session keys that have to be frequently exchanged and have short life-times.

The second principle is public key based distribution (see Fig. 3.22). Instead of using a symmetric master key, a public key of the intended recipient can be used to encrypt a session key, which can be only decrypted by the holder of the corresponding private key. The procedure can be applied in both directions to assure authentication of both parties.

This principle is often applied in such a way that the encrypted session key (the one that serves for processing corresponding ciphertext into plaintext) is sent over the network together with the ciphertext. The session key is encrypted with recipients public key. Such a combination is referred to as a digital envelope. For this model to be operational, authenticated public key exchange has to take place beforehand. This is accomplished with digital certificates, issued by CAs (see Fig. 3.23).

Another basic principle exists that is used for session key exchange and is shown in Fig. 3.24. It is a public key algorithm called Diffie-Hellman (DH) [90], which has a special functionality. In fact, DH was the first public key algorithm, its main point not being encryption of plaintexts and decryption of ciphertexts, but session key exchange. With DH, entities first generate a

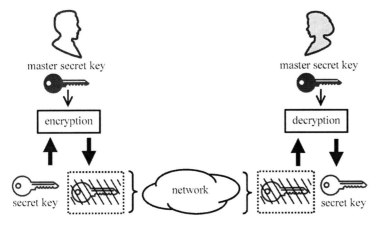

Fig. 3.21. Model of a session key exchange using master secret key and symmetric cryptography

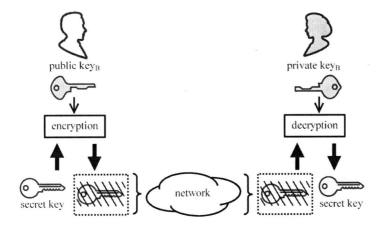

Fig. 3.22. Model of a session key exchange using asymmetric cryptography

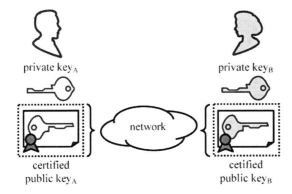

Fig. 3.23. Model of authenticated public key exchange by use of digital certificates

public component, while a private value is generated separately by each party. Using special computations, each private value is "merged" with the public component and sent over the network. It is not possible to derive secret values from the exchanged merged value. On receipt, parties use private value to compute a session key by applying it to the received merged value.

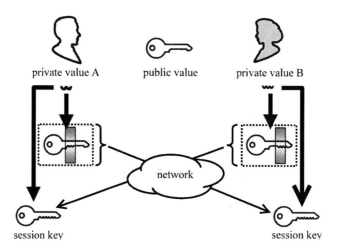

Fig. 3.24. Model of Diffie-Hellman key exchange

3.3.3 Complementary Key Management Activities

Installation and activation of keys is a matter of local system or application dependent administration. More general issues are storage, archiving, recovery and destruction. Long-term symmetric keys and private asymmetric keys in particular have to be stored in tamper-resistant devices. In practice, instead of using tamper-resistant devices, these keys are often encrypted by a symmetric algorithm and stored on a local hard disk. In this case a password is used to produce the encryption key, which results in the known problem of reducing the security of the whole system to the quality of this password. But even with tamper-resistant devices, things are not that straightforward, therefore a more detailed discussion of this issue is given in subsection 3.4.10.

An increasingly important issue for organizations is key recovery. Clearly, with data constituting a key asset of an organization, they have to be available when needed. When a user is not present to provide the key, or the key is lost, or when an organization wants to monitor encrypted traffic, means have to exist to resolve such a situation. This is achieved with key recovery techniques. For a choice of appropriate techniques the reader is referred to [86], which gives a comprehensive overview of key recovery techniques.

Due to the importance of key management, this area is often a subject of standardization. One of the first standards in this field was ANSI X9.17 [10], which was aimed at financial institutions and was based on symmetric algorithms. The standard defines the protocols for transfer of encryption keys, where the highest level belongs to the master key, which is manually distributed. The next level consists of key-encrypting keys that are distributed over the wires and serve for further distribution of the lowest level keys, called data keys. Data keys are distributed online as well. They are used for bulk data encryption, and they should be changed with each session, but not less frequently than on a daily basis.

Generally, this ANSI standard is gradually being supplemented by public cryptography based exchanges of keys. Thus new standards for key management are, in principle, based on public key cryptography and will be dealt with in the rest of the book. A further important consequence of this trend is that registration with de-registration and certification with revocation processes are becoming strongly tied to public key infrastructure.

3.4 Security Infrastructure

Organizations set up security infrastructures by deploying particular services and organizational counter-measures that minimize the vulnerabilities of their resources. Many of these counter-measures are nowadays standardized. It all starts with the public key infrastructure, which plays a special role within every security infrastructure, but this itself is far from being simple.

3.4.1 Public Key Infrastructure

A public key infrastructure (PKI) is a set of technologies and procedures that enables deployment of public-key cryptography based security services. Public key cryptography requires public key infrastructure for a simple reason - to assure that a particular public key belongs to a claimed entity. This is done by certification authority (CA), which issues a certificate that assures this binding. Such a certificate can be verified by anyone knowing CA's public key, because the certificate is digitally signed.

However, every cryptographic material has a limited life time because of growing processing power, and it may happen that the old key becomes insufficiently long sooner than expected. Also, a private key may be compromised. Finally, a user may be using a certificate and its related private key in a way that is not appropriate. In all these cases it is necessary to revoke public key certificates in order to prevent further acceptance of cryptographic materials produced with these private and public keys. For this purpose, each CA maintains a certificate revocation list (CRL) that should be checked every time before a certificate is accepted.

To provide authentication in computer systems and communication networks, asymmetric algorithms are used because of low key-management complexity. But due to their computational complexity, symmetric algorithms are used for protecting sessions once entities have been authenticated, which enables more efficient cryptographic processing of data. Summing up, to perform authentication, public key cryptography is used, but to provide bulk data confidentiality once entities are authenticated, symmetric key cryptography is used. This is a fundamental approach that provides the right trade-off between key management complexity and processing requirements for cryptography.

The ultimate certificate and certificate revocation list specification is X.509 standard [185], which is the basis for IETF PKI profiles [159]. According to X.509, the main certificate fields are serial number, issuer (i.e. trusted third party), subject (i.e. an owner of a public key), public key itself, validity and signature of a certificate. There are also fields that are required for processing instructions (algorithm identifiers), and extensions that are needed to support issues that are not yet fully resolved: automated CRL retrieval, their storage point and distribution, security policies issues, etc.

Before a certain public key is used, the user should check the validity of a certificate against the corresponding CRL. Because of the importance of this procedure, the procedure must be crystal clear to each user of contemporary ISs services. Its general form is given in Fig. 3.25. In step 1, the validity of the public key of the final signer (white color) has to be checked by verifying the digital signature on the corresponding certificate that was signed by this user's CA (gray color). Next, the CRL of this CA has to be checked to see if it contains the user's certificate (step 2). If both tests pass, the signature produced with the user's private key is valid. If the user CA's public key is not trusted, it has to be checked using certificate issued by top-level CA (black color). In step 3, the signature on the certificate of user's CA has to be checked with the top-level CA's public key. In step 4, the top-level CA's CRL has to be checked if it contains user CA's certificate. If all is correct, the user CA's public key and, consequently, the user's public key are successfully verified.

The above checks are often performed manually because of open issues about technical details for automated certificate status verification. Further checks include CA's security policy, which generally describes its terms of business and operations. Issues that are of particular importance to certificates are stated in a certification practice statement (CPS). They include details about issue and revocation of certificates, how often CRLs are published, how they are distributed, and the like.

Distribution of public keys is done through a globally distributed directory. The most frequently proposed system for this purpose used to be X.500 directory [184], but the Web is actually taking its place. The main protocol for accessing certificates and CRLs is the lightweight directory access protocol (LDAP) [184]. Additionally, to access certificates and CRLs, FTP and HTTP can be used [160] (all these protocols are referred to as operational PKI protocols). But these are not the only protocols within PKI - the full deployment

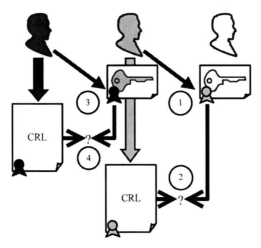

Fig. 3.25. General procedure for verification and validation of a public key

of PKI requires management protocols for interaction between entities and PKI [3], and message formats, like the one for certificate request [194].

Registration Authority (RA) is an interface between a user and a CA that identifies a user and submits certificate request to a CA. Because registration of a user is a different procedure from certification, RA not only off-loads the administrative burden from a CA, but through this split of functionality reduces the possibility of system security subversion. The process of issuing a certificate starts at the RA, which checks and validates the identity of an entity requesting a digital certificate. After successful validation, the request is handed over to the CA, which issues a certificate.

Besides CA and RA, PKI requires a synchronized time base system and the official protocol for this purpose is the Network Time Protocol (NTP) [238]. Timestamping is a must for proper operation of cryptographic protocols and means inclusion of time values in data objects and packets (in cases where there is no timestamping service, random values are used for data packets). Further, the purpose of PKI is administration of public key credentials (certificates and CRLs), which inherently depend on time values. Last but not least, in case of breaches and formal disputes, proper sequencing of events has to be proved and reconstructed, which again requires a synchronized time base.

But timestamping has additional meaning in the context of PKI. Timestamping is also referred to the following functionality. Assume a digitally signed document that is about to become endangered because of advances in cryptanalysis or due to increased processing power. At the time when the particular document is still valid, timestamping is performed. The original signature and the corresponding document are treated as a unit that is to be signed anew. The timestamp is added and a hash is produced, which is signed.

This new signature, together with the timestamp, is appended to the above mentioned unit and the validity of the old document is preserved.

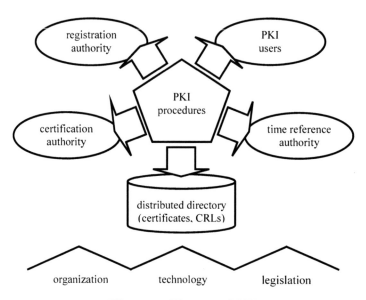

Fig. 3.26. Elements of PKI

Putting the above mentioned elements together with appropriate procedures results in the model of PKI depicted in Fig. 3.26.

When an organization decides for setting up a PKI, there are many implementation concerns that have to be addressed [2]:

- procedures covering key management;
- supporting protocols covering operational and PKI management protocols together with timestamping;
- staff issues covering education and training;
- hardware and software related issues covering flexibility, scalability, ease of use, costs, and standardization;
- consultation for covering specific issues.

An important element of PKI is CA and its malicious actions should be prevented as much as possible. The basic threat is abuse of a private key. In order to ensure that a private key is known only to a user, a common practice is that the latter generates a key pair. However, there are also many other threats that need to be minimized [297]:

- loss of private key confidentiality, including compromise of local key storage, interception during transmission from key storage unit to the processing unit, and compromise of the key generation process;

- modification of data, which includes modification of certificate contents and modification of attributes before being packaged in a certificate;
- masquerade, which should consider parties, users and CAs (with masquerade an entity is pretending to be some other entity);
- false repudiation, which includes a user denying requesting a certificate or requesting a certificate revocation;
- misuse of privilege, which includes CA issuing incorrect certificates or revocation lists.

Procedures for initial key exchange have to be defined before certificates can be issued. Initially, a user physically contacts RA, is identified on the basis of a valid document, and signs a request. The rest of the procedure may vary and is defined locally. In Web environment, a common procedure goes as follows. CA maintains a Web server that supports SSL protocol [126] and has installed this CA's certificate. A user, who has enrolled at RA, is sent two secret strings through two channels, e.g. e-mail and ordinary mail. After receiving these strings, the user connects browser to the server, which automatically establishes a secure connection through activation of SSL. CA's certificate, installed in a server, assures the user of being connected to CA's server. Subsequent confidential exchange of data, together with their integrity, is assured through SSL. After checking CA's certificate, a user enters personal data and secret sequence strings, which authenticate the user to the server. The server then triggers the browser to produce a key pair and a public key is transmitted over the network for signing. When the certificate is produced, the user is instructed to download it into the browser.

The basic question for an organization is whether to establish PKI within the organization or whether to outsource these operations. CA operations are very sensitive and require significant knowledge, manpower and financial investment. Before deciding for outsourcing, the following questions have to be answered: What are the risks associated with outsourcing? Will certificates be issued only to the employees, or also to suppliers and customers? What is the expected total number of certificates to be issued?

Further, the total cost of ownership has to be calculated, which requires properly defined costs that can be grouped into six categories [2]:

- PKI systems: user and server certificate fees, certificate hardware and software platforms, CA and directory software.
- Client software: client software acquisition and distribution.
- Maintenance: hardware, software, disaster recovery systems.
- Services: PKI design and planning, installation and configuration, integration and testing, training, root key notarization, cryptography health checks, audit and certification, disaster recovery, secured facilities and procedures for logical and physical protection, transaction insurance, financial and legal liability assistance.

- Staff: engineering costs, integration and testing, project roll-out, project management, IS administration, certificate repository and maintenance, PKI procedures, help desk, training, security monitoring and audit.

According to the Aberdeen group, three-year costs of ownership ranged from approx. US$ 3 to US$ 22 per seat for 500,000 users and from US$ 50 to approx. US$ 200 per seat for 5,000 users [2]. More recent studies predict that the establishment of PKI takes up to one year and a half, from initial planning to external accreditation. Of this, three months are needed for testing, three months for piloting, and six to twelve months to cover the entire organization [132]. In terms of software costs, the cost in 2000 for Entrust technology was US$ 25,000 per 10,000 users [365, 214].

Currently no global PKI exists. What exists are administratively and functionally closed implementations within the business sector (typical examples include Verisign or Thawte) and government environment (examples of the latter include US e-Authentication Gateway [351] and UK Government Gateway [345]). It is a fact that PKI is not the overall success that was expected some ten years ago. Why so?

There are various problems that prevent successful adoption of PKI. One is that certificates are commonly issued on a per application basis, where applications dictate specific interfaces, tied to particular vendors [186]. So separate certificate hierarchies exist for certain applications.

Another problem is complexity of a certificate structure that is intended to serve as a universal credential for security services. Thus it includes not only binding between a public key and a subject, but also various extension fields with e.g. roles of a subject. Roles change more frequently than other elements of a certificate, thus issuing new certificate for each change of a role results in impractical and expensive operations.

Further problems are related to revocation of certificates. One basic question is how frequently CRLs should be issued. This affects the interval between the time when a private key becomes compromised and when its certificate is revoked. As long as the certificate is not revoked, other users cannot be aware of the important fact that this private key has been compromised.

Further, CRLs will grow larger and larger, requiring more and more resources. Assuming that they are located on some server, requesting thousands of copies simultaneously from this server is a good precondition for denial of service. It is true that CRLs can be partitioned through a CRL Distribution Point feature, and thus cannot grow excessively [57]. But this only partially solves the problems. One proposed solution to cover the above gap is to issue so-called delta CRLs, which include certificates revoked since the last CRL, and can thus be significantly smaller and issued when needed. Some authors suggest avoiding revocation mechanism by issuing certificates with a short validity period [296]. But this brings new drawbacks - issuing certificates is costly and complex.

Further, support for automatic revocation of certificates is also an open issue with PKI. The core of the problem is lack of formalization of relevant policies [348]. Moreover, certification paths are expected to grow in a globally connected infrastructure, and discovering the placement of corresponding CRLs will not be a trivial task. To do away with all these problems, IETF does not require CRLs to be issued. Instead, it has defined protocol, called Online Certificate Status Protocol (OCSP) that enables real-time checking of certificate validity [244]. Taking all these issues into account it is not surprising that some authors are considering avoidance of PKI altogether by introducing non-PKI based methods for public key distribution [272].

After more than a decade from its introduction, PKI is giving some signals that it may be headed into a dead-end street. Some researchers think it is just "resting" and waiting for its time to come [145], while others think nothing will change without correct standardization efforts [267]. True, some PKI issues have remained unresolved for almost a decade (for some additional details see e.g. [335, 336, 338]). But it is probably wrong to claim that PKI is a failure, because it really is an infrastructure, and infrastructures have long introduction and payback periods. So it is likely that PKI will yet gain momentum, especially taking into account the fact that many important players have decided in favor of this technology. Of course, it may take some years, or even a decade, to resolve the above issues, but such a long lead-in time would not be an exception in the field of high technology. Smart cards are similar example in the field of security being developed in the seventies, but taking more than three decades before the technology really took hold.

Therefore organizations have to be prepared to use PKI, but at the same time they should take into account all the unresolved issues to apply necessary compensations.

3.4.2 Authentication and Authorization Infrastructure

It has not been uncommon practice to use PKI certificates for authorization, which violates the principle of separation of security services from administration. Actually, what the certificate provides is authentication, while authorization is a matter of policy. More precisely, *authorization means allocating rights to entities to access and use resources in line with a policy*. For this separation of authentication and authorization so-called attribute certificates and establishment of an authorization infrastructure have been proposed [185, 116]. Separation is also needed because of many scenarios where authorization counts more then authentication. For example, a merchant is usually more interested in a customer's authorization than authentication.

Attribute certificates are similar to ordinary digital certificates, but without public keys. This approach not only separates authentication and authorization, but also makes PKI operations cheaper. Additional justification for this infrastructure is based on observations that traditional approaches to authorization and access control, i.e. discretionary, mandatory and role based access controls, are not appropriate for contemporary networked systems [225].

It should come as no surprise that authentication and authorization infrastructure (AAI) initiatives use PKI for the authentication part [163]. AAI and PKI are similar, and main difference is resulting from attribute certificates. Although public and attribute certificates are logically bound, PKI and AAI have to coexist as separate infrastructures. The reason is not only the principle of separation, but also the intended way of deployment. One wish behind AAI efforts is to enable use of resources in a global networked environment with a single sign-on procedure. A user would sign-on only once within a particular security domain. When crossing the borders with requests, the AAI would automatically provide authentication and authorization.

Some research implementations of AAI exist [56], but internet-wide and general deployment of AAI is taking place only now [120]. However, more moderate and local environment oriented implementations of AAI have existed successfully for quite some years. One particular case is system Kerberos [256].

Fig. 3.27. Kerberos pre-operation state (symmetric keys that are shared beforehand)

Kerberos was designed in the eighties under the project Athena at M.I.T. and became a success story a few years later, when version 4 became an industry-wide standard. The current version is version 5 which, unlike version 4, is not tied to DES. But generally it is more complex, so version 4 will be explained. In addition, we will base our explanation on a simplified version, given in [331]. This simplification is only to enable a clearer explanation. Otherwise, such simplifications are not allowed, because a minimal change in a cryptographic protocol may result in flaws, as will be discussed in the appendix.

Kerberos consists of three servers: authentication server (A), ticket granting server (T) and server that performs the actual job - job server (J). The first server authenticates a user. The second provides means for direct access to the job server that performs tasks that authenticated entities are authorized to use. All this is achieved without sending a password over the network, while each user shares a secret with A. Further, a notion of tickets is introduced, where tickets denote the encrypted identity strings and the session keys that this user will be using in communication with T and J respectively. This pair (ticket) is encrypted with the shared secret key between the respective enti-

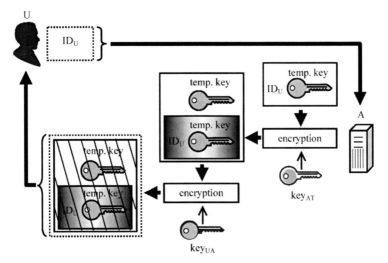

Fig. 3.28. Kerberos operations - the first cycle (the cycle starts at the user and goes clockwise)

ties. The secret keys that are shared in advance are shown in Fig. 3.27. They include shared secrets between U and A, A and T, and T and J.

Now the protocol can be described. It consists of three cycles. First a user authenticates with A by sending only his name over the network. Server A responds by sending back a temporary session key and encrypted ticket. Both are encrypted by the shared secret key between U and A (see Fig. 3.28).

After decryption, the user obtains an encrypted ticket, which is forwarded to the T together with the identity of J and encrypted timestamp (see Fig. 3.29). This timestamp is encrypted with the extracted temporary key. On receipt of this message, T constructs two encrypted pairs. The first pair consists of the identity of J and the session key for communication of a user with J - this is encrypted with the session key obtained in the first step from the A. The second pair consists of the identity of U and the same session key as contained in the first pair - this pair is encrypted with the key that is shared between T and J. Both pairs (tickets) are sent to the user (see Fig. 3.29).

Now the third cycle starts (see Fig. 3.30). User U extracts the session key that will be needed for communication with J, encrypts a timestamp with this key, and sends it with the second pair (ticket) from the previous step to J. Server J responds with an incremented encrypted timestamp by using the obtained secret session key.

Where is the password in this game? The password is entered by the user after the second message is received to construct the session key that is needed to decrypt the content sent by A. Immediately after decryption, the key and the password are destroyed by the system. Further, when the user wants to use

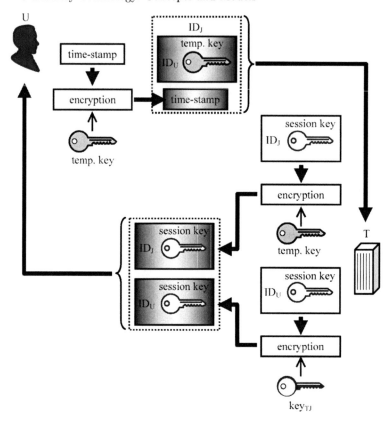

Fig. 3.29. Kerberos operations - the second cycle

some other server J, he just contacts the server T by sending it the message from the first cycle.

As a result, using Kerberos is a comfortable way of deploying distributed resources in an authenticated and authorized manner, in which the basic secret (password) never crosses the network.

3.4.3 Network Layer Security - IPSec

IPSec is a family of standards [202] that specify security enhancements for both IP protocol versions, version 4 and version 6.[7] IPSec enables secure communication across local area networks as well as across the global internet. It provides data origin authentication, connectionless integrity, confidentiality, access control, limited confidentiality of traffic flow and replay prevention. Security features are implemented by introducing extension header that is the

---

[7]Version 6 is currently replacing version 4 primarily because of support of larger address space and support for contemporary network services.

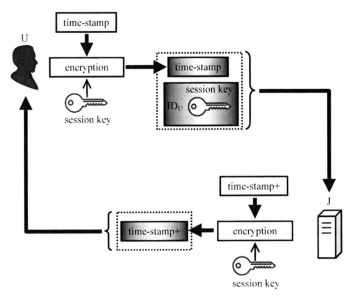

Fig. 3.30. Kerberos operations - the third cycle

basis for security related processing details. One major advantage of IPSec is a possibility of establishing virtual private networks (VPNs). These are logically closed networks laid over physical networks that are shared by many organizations.

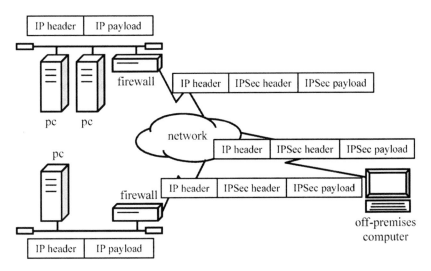

Fig. 3.31. IPSec use scenario, where IPSec is deployed between firewalls and off-premises computer, but not on local networks behind firewalls

A scenario of IPSec use is shown in Fig. 3.31, where IPSec is implemented in both firewalls [323]. Thus security related processing overhead is not incurred for local interactions, while traffic that is leaving an organization is protected accordingly. IPSec can also be applied individually. This is the case with employees that use e.g. their laptop computer to work off-premises, which is also shown in Fig. 3.31.

Because IPSec operates at the network layer, its operations are transparent to end users and applications. Applications can be changed without being affected by the security features of the underlying networking infrastructure, while there is no need to train users to use security services or perform key management.

IPSec offers two kinds of service: Authentication Header (AH) and Encapsulating Security Payload (ESP). Both can operate in two modes - transport mode and tunnel mode. Transport mode provides protection primarily to upper layer protocols and is used for end-to-end communications. AH in transport mode authenticates IP payload, while IP header is only partially authenticated. ESP in this mode provides confidentiality of IP payload and optionally authenticates it, excluding the IP header.

In tunnel mode the complete packet can be protected by authentication or confidentiality. The entire packet is wrapped by a new packet and is treated as a payload of this new packet. This approach is called tunneling because the original packet travels hidden, like being send through a tunnel between two points on the network. To be exact, this description best reflects ESP, and not so much AH - in the case of ESP, the entire packet is indeed completely hidden. In the case of AH, this should be called authentication tunnel, because the content remains visible. Authentication of the whole original packet is assured.

The transformation starts by adding AH/ESP header fields. In the case of ESP it ends by adding trailer fields to the original IP packet, while AH uses no trailers. The resulting structure presents the payload of a new IP packet, defined by a new header. This packet is routed over the network and routers along the path are not able to attack it. Moreover, the new packet may have an entirely different IP address, which assures traffic flow confidentiality. Tunnel mode operation is common between firewalls, or between an off-premises computer and a firewall. With regard to the two kinds of service, ESP in tunnel mode encrypts and optionally authenticates the original IP packet, while AH in tunnel mode authenticates the entire original packet and selected parts of the new IP header of the wrapping packet.

An important concept with IPSec is Security Association (SA). SA is a one-way relationship between a sender and a receiver with related security services. A complete peer relationship thus requires two SAs. Each SA is uniquely identified by the following parameters [202]:

- Security Parameters Index (SPI), which is a bit string assigned to an SA and is carried in AH and ESP headers to enable the receiver to select processing details.

- Destination Address, which is an ordinary IP address - currently, only a single receiver is allowed.
- Security Protocol Identifier, which indicates which kind of service is used for security association, AH or ESP.

The operational details of a particular SA are defined with the following parameters [202]:

- The Sequence Number Counter parameter is a 32-bit value used to generate a Sequence Number field in AH and ESP headers. This is a monotonically increasing number, assigned to each packet to prevent replays. Packets are ordered on the basis of these sequence numbers to properly reassemble IPSec data before processing it at the receiver.
- Sequence Counter Overflow is a flag that indicates whether overflow of the Sequence Number Counter should generate an alarm and stop further transmission. Only a limited number of bits can be assigned for Sequence Number Counter, thus after a certain number of packets has been sent, the counter starts repeating its values. This would result in duplication of packets (counter overflow), which has to be prevented.
- Anti-Replay Window is a parameter that is in a tight relation with Sequence Counter Numbers and prevents replays. It defines the interval of incoming packets that are still under processing, before being accepted as correct ones.
- AH data determine authentication algorithm, mode, keys, their lifetimes and necessary parameters required for AH implementation.
- ESP data determine encryption algorithm, authentication algorithm, mode, keys and their lifetimes, and related parameters required for ESP implementation.
- SA Lifetime defines a time interval (or byte count) after which SA is terminated or replaced by a new SA.
- IPSec Protocol Mode defines, besides the already mentioned tunnel and transport modes, a wild-card mode. This mode means that the packet is either transport or tunnel mode.
- Path MTU determines the maximum packet size that can be sent without fragmentation. It is obtained during operation through control messages and stored as SA parameter to enable efficient operation of IPSec.

IPSec depends operationally on a Security Policy Database with entries that enable traffic to be associated with related SAs. When a packet is sent (received), so-called selector fields are checked in the database to select (retrieve) SAs, associated with this traffic. After SAs are retrieved, packets are processed as required by SAs. The main selector fields that determine an entry in the security policy database are source and destination IP addresses, ports, data sensitivity levels, kind of transport protocols (TCP or UDP), and IPSec details (AH, ESP or both).

Authentication Header

The AH provides authentication and integrity of IP packets, which prevents data modification. This, in turn, prevents attacks with e.g. address spoofing. Authentication and integrity are achieved by use of keyed one-way hash functions that produce MACs (MAC is also referred to as integrity check value, or ICV for short).

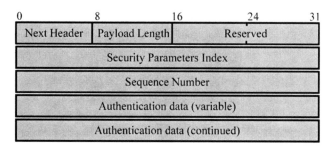

Fig. 3.32. IPSec AH format, where numbers on top denote sequence numbers of bits (the packet is divided into 32 bits long sequences to fit on the page)

In order to gain an insight into functioning of the protocol, the structure of its messages should be studied, because it reflects its functionality (see Fig. 3.32) [203].

The meaning of the fields is as follows. `Next Header` field identifies the type of the payload following Authentication Header, `Payload Length` gives the length of AH, and `Security Parameters Index` identifies an SA. `Sequence number` is a monotonically increasing value that prevents replay attacks. Besides `Reserved field` (for future use), the header contains also a variable-length `Authentication Data` field with ICV for this packet.

AH authenticates the complete packet for transport and tunnel modes as shown in Fig. 3.33 [203]. The only exceptions are fields that do not preserve fixed values on their way from source to destination (routers on the way modify certain fields in headers of packets for their own processing purposes). These fields are set to zero before calculating MAC. For MAC derivation, MD5 or SHA-1 is used, where the output is truncated to the first 96 bits because of the default length of the authentication field.

Encapsulating Security Payload

ESP provides message confidentiality, limited traffic flow confidentiality and optionally the same authentication services as AH. Authentication services are achieved as described for AH, while message confidentiality is provided by replacing the original IP packet and transporting its ciphertext. In transport mode, the original header remains unencrypted, but in tunnel mode the

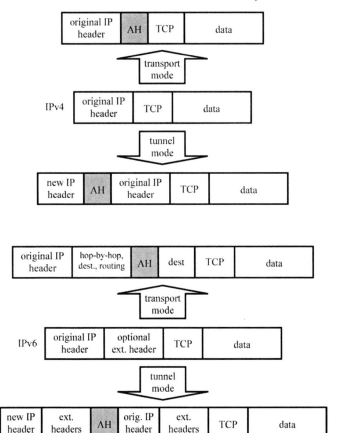

Fig. 3.33. AH transformed IP packets - IPv4 (top) and IPv6 (bottom)

original header, with header extensions for IPv6, is sent in a ciphertext. Additionally, ESP adds trailer to all packets. There are two kinds of trailer: while the first is needed because of padding, the second one is optional and is appended in case of authentication.

The reasons for mandatory extension are, firstly, application of encryption. Block ciphers require fully filled blocks of data to perform their operations. If the original data does not meet this requirement, it has to be padded. Secondly, information on the number of padded bits has to be put in this extension. Besides padding related data, this mandatory extension includes also the Next Header field that identifies the type of data contained in the payload (e.g. an upper layer protocol identifier like TCP or UDP).

The structure of the ESP packet given in Fig. 3.34 will be used to enable a better understanding of the protocol functioning [204]. The ESP format consists of Security Parameters Index field, which is needed to associate the packet uniquely with the related SA for proper processing. There is also a field `Sequence Number`, which increases monotonically and serves to prevent replay attacks. Next follows `Payload data` that has a variable length and contains a transport level segment in transport mode, or a complete IP packet (transport level segment plus original IP header) in tunnel mode. The original payload and a mandatory trailer are protected in both modes with encryption. In tunnel mode, the original header is also encrypted.

Another view of the overall functioning of ESP can be given from the modes perspective. In transport mode (given in Fig. 3.35), the data block is formed from a transport layer segment and an ESP trailer. The result is encrypted and the plaintext replaced by encrypted data. If required, authentication is performed, resulting in an authentication trailer being appended. The packet is then routed through the network. On receipt, the other node processes IP header and IP header extensions. Based on the `Security Parameters Index` in the ESP header, decryption (and optionally authentication) of the packet is performed.

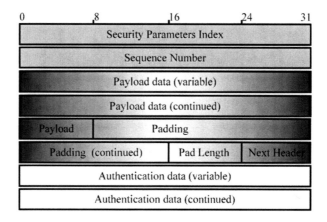

Fig. 3.34. IPSec ESP format

In tunnel mode (see Fig. 3.35), ESP functions as follows. The entire packet is encapsulated and a new header is added that provides sufficient data for routing. The basic packet, which contains the original IP header in this case, is prefixed by an ESP header and encrypted together with the ESP trailer. Note that the ESP header cannot be encrypted, because it contains processing details. Authentication data trailer is added at the end of the resulting sequence, if authentication is required. The result is prepended with a new IP header and the obtained packet is routed to the other party, usually a firewall. The firewall examines and processes the outer IP header and extensions. On the basis of `Security Parameters Index` in ESP header it identifies the related SA and the processing details for authentication and decryption. Finally, the recovered packet is delivered on a local network.

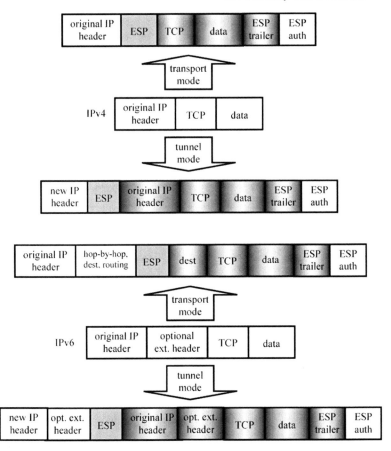

Fig. 3.35. ESP transformed IP packets - IPv4 (top) and IPv6 (bottom)

For its operation and the provision of security services, ESP uses the following symmetric cryptographic algorithms: 3DES (three keys variant), RC5 [21], IDEA [364], 3IDEA (three keys variant), CAST [4] and Blowfish [305].

IPSec is not intended to protect only the end hosts. Its enhancements can also be used to address routing. Routers constantly exchange data that enable them to route packets from source to destination. In this case, incorrect route advertising is a security threat, which can be also prevented by IPSec. For example, when a new router is added to the network, IPSec can be used to authenticate it.

IPSec is specified in an extensive set of standards that can be grouped as follows (the most important ones are referenced):

- Architecture group that covers concepts with definitions, security requirements, and mechanisms [202].

- AH that covers the packet format and issues related to packet authentication [203].
- ESP that covers the packet format and issues related to packet encryption and (optionally) authentication [204].
- Encryption Algorithm group that describes the use of various encryption algorithms for ESP.
- Authentication Algorithm group that describes the use of various authentication algorithms for AH and for the authentication option of ESP, e.g. [226].
- Domain of Interpretation (DOI) that contains the values needed for management of SAs like identifiers for cryptographic algorithms and security protocols (an example is [274]).
- Key Management that covers key management protocols for IPSec, e.g. [231].

For its operations, IPSec requires key management services, provided by Internet Key Exchange (IKE) specification [150]. IKE is particularly dependent on two protocols: OAKLEY [266] and ISAKMP [231]. These serve basically for automated key exchange with IPSec. Although the whole IKE specification contains also "some sprinkles of salt" in terms of SKEME key exchange technique [208], we will focus on its standardized ingredients - OAKLEY and ISAKMP.

OAKLEY Key Exchange Protocol

OAKLEY is a generic key management protocol, which means that the principles of operation are described without imposing exact implementation details like packet formats. It provides two authenticated parties with means for secure exchange of secret material for derivation of keys. OAKLEY is based on Diffie-Hellman key exchange, but it also enables derivation of a new key from an existing one, and distribution of an externally derived key by encrypting it. Further, OAKLEY uses additional mechanisms to counter DH weaknesses. It authenticates DH to prevent man-in-the-middle attacks, it uses nonces (nonces are one-time used identifiers) to disable replay attacks, and cookies to prevent exhaustion of resources (cookies denote bit strings).

Let us stop for a moment at the above mentioned attacks, first the man-in-the-middle attack. It was shown in section 3.3 that, with DH, two parties agree on a public component, while each of them chooses also personal secret value. Afterwards, they merge this private value with the public component in a way that prevents derivation of private value from this merged value. On receipt, each party uses the private value to compute a session key by applying it to the received merged value. Although it is not possible to calculate the private value from the merged one, an attacker can jump into communication and start impersonating the other communicating party by doing the

following. She chooses two secret values, merges them with the public component and sends one result to one party, and the other result to another party.
Because the exchanged merged values are not authenticated, initial parties
send their merged values to the attacker. Initial parties assume that the other
communicating party is the right one, while the truth is that there now exist
two session keys. One is used by the attacker to communicate with the first
initial party, while the other one serves for communication of the attacker
with the second initial party. The attacker thus intercepts the complete communication between the initial entities, exploiting the fact that exchanged
merged values were not authenticated.[8] OAKLEY ensures authentication of
exchanged merged values.

With regard to use of nonces, they serve to disable an attacker who reuses
a message that may be confidential or digitally signed, but has no unique
identifier. This creates an opportunity for a replay attack. An attacker simply
copies the message and later puts it on the wire to cause harm, even if she does
not have a possibility to cryptographically manipulate the data. The receiver
may easily recover the plaintext or check the signature and act in line with
the message. For many scenarios this is a real concern - in the case of money
transfer order, twice as much money would be transferred as requested by
sender. This vulnerability is cured by incorporation of unique identifiers into
messages, which may be nonces (i.e. non-repeating values like large random
values), timestamps or sequence numbers.

To understand the exhaustion of resources attacks, also referred to as
clogging attacks, one should know that for each communication a party has
to allocate certain resources. In a computationally intensive operation like DH
key exchange, an attacker can repeatedly trigger the other party by requesting
generation of DH values, and instructing it to send the results to a false
address. The victim performs these calculations and sends the results to the
false address. If the frequency of such requests is high enough, the victim will
run out of resources and collapse. To prevent this, an initial message is sent
that contains a cookie. This cookie is included in the reply, which acknowledges
the first message. DH key exchange takes place only after this step, and the
first message of DH exchange has to include the cookie. If the source address
was forged, the attacker would not be able to include cookie acknowledgment
in the request for secret key generation.

Three different kinds of authentication can be used with OAKLEY. The
first uses digital signatures, where each party encrypts the hash of exchange
parameters (user IDs and nonces) with private key. The second uses public-key
encryption, where the exchange parameters are encrypted with the sender's
private key. The third method is to use symmetric-key encryption, where a
key derived by out-of-band means is used for encryption.

To get an impression of OAKLEY protocol operation, somewhat simplified
aggressive key-exchange is described. It consists of only three messages:

---

[8]The exact details of this attack are given in subsection 6.2.5.

- The initiator A sends a cookie, a group (groups are abstract mathematical structures that DH relies upon), and its own DH public key to entity B. The initiator A also proposes public-key, hash and authentication algorithms, includes identifiers (IDs) of A and B, and a nonce for this step. With her private key A signs the identifiers, the nonce, the group, DH public key, and the offered algorithms.
- On receipt, the responder B verifies the signature using A's public key. B acknowledges the message by sending back A's cookie, ID, nonce and group. B includes her own cookie, nonce, ID, her own DH public key, and the selected algorithms. B further signs both identifiers, both nonces, the group, the two DH public keys and selected algorithms.
- Entity A verifies the signature of the received message with B's public key and checks the nonces that prevent replay. After these checks, A sends the last message to assure B that the message with B's public key was received. This message is similar to the first one, except that instead of offered algorithms, it contains the selected ones. In addition, it contains the responder's cookie and nonce, and the signature of both identifiers, both nonces, group, both public keys and selected algorithms.

After these steps, entities are able to calculate the session key. Thus only three steps are needed for authenticated key exchange (that is why the procedure is called aggressive). However, identities are not protected.

OAKLEY provides support to ISAKMP protocol. This latter protocol is needed to manage security associations for IPSec, and, with appropriate resolution procedures, it is defined how OAKLEY data are mapped and transferred in ISAKMP messages.

Internet Security Association and Key Management Protocol

Internet Security Association and Key Management Protocol (ISAKMP) defines procedures and packet formats to manage security associations. SA is established through payloads for exchange of key generation and authentication data. Payload formats are independent of any particular key exchange protocol, encryption algorithm and authentication protocol. In order to get an insight into functioning of the protocol, the structure of the messages of the protocol will be studied, because this structure reflects its functionality (Fig. 3.36).

Each ISAKMP message consists of a header that is followed by at least one payload. The following fields define the format of the header [231]:

- Initiator Cookie - cookie of the entity that initiated establishment, notification or deletion of SA.
- Responder Cookie - cookie of the responding entity, null in the first message from the initiator.
- Next Payload - indicates the first payload type in the message.

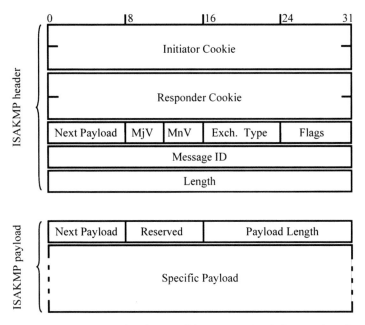

Fig. 3.36. ISAKMP header (top) and ISAKMP payload (bottom) - the generic payload header is the first row of the payload

- Major and Minor version - indicator of major and minor version of currently used ISAKMP (in Fig. 3.36, MjV denotes Major Version and MnV denotes Minor Version).
- Exchange Type - indicator, which means how keys will be exchanged and how identity of parties will be managed (examples include base type, identity protection, authentication only, and aggressive type).
- Flags - indicators of specific options, e.g. the encryption bit is set if all payloads are encrypted, or the commit bit may be set to ensure that encrypted material is delivered only after the completion of SA establishment.
- Message ID - unique identifier of this message.
- Length - the total length of the message, header plus payloads, in bytes.

All payloads begin with the generic payload header, which has the following fields [231]:

- Next Payload - this value is 0 for the last payload in the message, while other values define the type of the following payload.
- Reserved - as implied, this field is reserved for future use.
- Payload Length - this field indicates the length of this payload including the generic header (the length is given in bytes, i.e. octets).

After the generic payload header follow payloads that are of several types:

- Security Association Payload is used to prepare conditions for negotiation of security attributes for an SA. The DOI parameter identifies the domain of interpretation. In case of IPSec, this domain is, of course, IPSec.
- Proposal Payload is used in the SA negotiation phase and indicates whether ESP or AH is going to take place with this SA. The payload contains sender's SPI and the number of transforms, i.e. cryptographic algorithms.
- Transform Payload is used to offer transforms and the responder must choose one of these transforms or reject them. Transforms are identified with IDs and attribute fields, which also describe completely the intended use of a transform, e.g. 3DES for ESP.
- Key Exchange Payload serves to support various key exchange mechanisms, be it pure DH, OAKLEY, or RSA based key exchange.
- Identification Payload is used for identification (an example is IP number). This identification may further serve to support authentication.
- Certificate Payload is used for transfer of certificates and CRLs, specification of types of certificates, CRLs and their encoding. Besides X.509 certificates, PGP certificates [50] or SPKI certificates [103] may be used.
- Certificate Request Payload provides means to request certificates. It specifies the type of certificates and acceptable CAs.
- Hash Payload is used to contain hash values of the message or ISAKMP state, which assures integrity of the message data or serves to authenticate the entities during negotiation.
- Signature Payload is similar to hash payload using the same data as above, except that the data is signed, and therefore non-repudiation is assured.
- Nonce Payload contains data that serve to protect against replies.
- Notification Payload serves to transmit informational data, e.g. error report or SA status.
- Delete Payload serves to indicate SAs that the sender has deleted from its database and are therefore invalid.
- Vendor ID Payload contains a vendor defined constant to recognize its own implementation in order to enable experiments with new features.

The above payload types are used to construct messages that are exchanged between entities. ISAKMP provides five exchange types [231, 323]. The first is Base Exchange that allows simultaneous exchange of key and authentication material. The first two messages use cookies and establish an SA with agreed protocol and transforms, where both parties use nonces to prevent replay attacks. The last two messages exchange keys and user IDs with the payload for authentication of keys, IDs and nonces from the first two messages. This exchange provides no identity protection, but requires only four exchanges.

The second type of ISAKMP exchange is Identity Protection Exchange that upgrades the Base Exchange through protection of users' identities. The first two messages establish the SA. The second two messages perform key exchange, where prevention of replays is achieved by use of nonces. After computation of the secret session key, encrypted messages are exchanged that enable authentication (containing e.g. digital signatures and optionally certificates).

The third type of exchange is Authentication Only Exchange, which provides mutual authentication, but no key exchange. As with the former two types, the first two messages establish the SA, where the responder in the second message transfers its ID - this message is authenticated. Finally, in the third message the initiator transmits its authenticated ID.

The fourth type is Aggressive Exchange that provides key exchange with minimal number of exchanges, but does not provide identity protection. In the first message the initiator proposes an SA with offering protocol and transform, begins the key exchange, and provides its ID. The responder indicates in the second message its acceptance of the SA with a particular protocol and transform, completes the key-exchange and authenticates the transferred data. Finally, the initiator transmits an authentication result of the previous data, which is encrypted with the session key.

The last type of key exchange is the simplest one. This is Informational Exchange, which serves for one-way communication to convey data for SA management.

3.4.4 Secure Sockets Layer and Transport Layer Security

Secure Socket Layer Specification (SSL) defines a family of protocols that is intended for secure Web communications, but it can also protect other applications. SSL was developed by Netscape in the mid-nineties. The first version was developed in 1994. But after bugs were eliminated it reached a stable specification in 1996 with version 3, which is now the most widespread one [126].

SSL is a de facto standard, but it has reached only draft status at IETF. Its successor is Transport Layer Security (TLS) that can be seen as a variant of SSL v3. TLS is the de jure standard. But it is not so widely accepted and appears to be incomplete, because flaws are still being discovered [191]. Thus SSL will be described.

SSL provides authentication, confidentiality and integrity to upper layer protocols. It consists of four protocols: SSL Record Protocol, SSL Handshake, SSL Alert and SSL Change Cipher Spec Protocol (see Fig. 3.37). It ensures end-to-end security for applications, being positioned below the application level and above the transport level.

The philosophy of SSL is based on a client - server paradigm and notions of sessions and connections. Each connection belongs to a certain session and a connection is identified by its cryptographic parameters. These parameters can be shared among multiple connections within a session, which enables more efficient deployment. Negotiation and creation of cryptographic param-

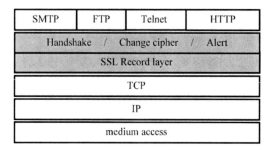

Fig. 3.37. SSL and its placement within TCP/IP protocol stack

eters are resource consuming tasks, thus a possibility to share them between connections within a session gives important advantages.

To identify a session state, SSL uses the following attributes [126, 323]:

- an arbitrary byte sequence chosen by a server that identifies a session;
- a peer certificate, which is an X.509 v3 certificate;
- a compression algorithm for data, which is optionally applied before encryption;
- a cipher specification for bulk data encryption, and calculation details for MACs;
- a 48 bytes long master secret that is shared between client and server;
- a flag that indicates if a session can be used to initiate new connection.

An SSL connection is stateful and, for identification of connection state, the following attributes are used [126, 323]:

- random sequences chosen by the server and client for each connection;
- the secret key used by server for computation of MACs (this is sent by the server to the client);
- the secret key used by client for computation of MACs (this is sent from the client to the server);
- the symmetric bulk data encryption key, used by the server for encryption;
- the symmetric bulk data encryption key, used by the client for encryption;
- initialization vectors for block ciphers that are used in a chaining mode;[9]
- sequence numbers between 0 and $2^{64} - 1$, which are started anew when an entity sends or receives a change_cipher_spec message.

The basic SSL operation is actually the one with server authentication. It is presented in Fig. 3.38 and discussed here (authentication of both parties can be provided by SSL, too). The whole SSL starts with SSL Handshake Protocol. It enables authentication and negotiation of cryptographic algorithms and keys before their operational deployment on application data. In the first

---

[9]In chaining mode the output of a currently processed block is processed with a new block before encryption, thus for the first operation some pre-defined initial values have to be used.

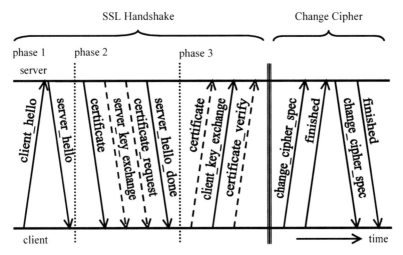

Fig. 3.38. SSL start-up procedure with server authentication (dashed lines denote optional steps)

phase a logical connection is initiated that defines the security properties of this connection. Properties are assigned through parameters that cover the protocol version, nonces for prevention of replays, a unique identifier of the session, a compression method and cryptographic algorithms. They are sent in the client_hello message. In addition, a random value is generated and it is also included in this message. The client_hello message is followed by a server_hello message, with the same kind and number of parameters as the first message, except that these are assigned by a server.

The second phase is intended for server authentication and starts with four messages. The first one transfers the server's X.509 certificate(s), while the second communicates the parameters for the key exchange method (which may be, for example, an RSA encrypted session key or DH based). The server_key_exchange is sent by the server in cases where the latter has no certificate, or has a certificate only for signing. The third message is intended to request the client's certificate from the authenticated server. There is a fourth, mandatory message sent from the server to the client (server_hello_done), which concludes this phase.

In the third phase client sends its certificate if this was requested in phase two (in case of no suitable certificate, client sends alert). This phase thus provides client authentication. Further, obligatory parameters for the selected key exchange are sent. The third message follows that provides explicit verification of the client's certificate (sending its certificate implies that client has signing capabilities). This message prevents misuse of a certificate by a third party, because of inclusion of a MAC that is calculated using the master secret and preceding handshake messages.

The whole start-up procedure is completed by the phase in which the Change Cipher Spec protocol is taking place. This is the simplest protocol in the SSL family. It copies the pending state into the current state by sending a single message that consists of a single byte with value 1. So the client sends its `change_cipher_spec` message and copies the pending cipher specification into the active, current one. The client then sends the `finished` message. Afterwards, the server sends its `change_cipher_spec` message, followed by `finished` message. This concludes the initiation of a secure session and SSL Record protocol takes place to securely exchange the application data. Besides serving at the end of handshake procedure, Change Cipher Spec protocol can also be used immediately after the `hello` message to resume the previous session. Generally, with this simple protocol the pending state is activated.

Based on work done by the Handshake Protocol, SSL Record Protocol provides operational confidentiality and message integrity, where the secret key for confidentiality and the secret key for MAC are used. The protocol first fragments the application data and, optionally, applies compression that has to be lossless. Next, MAC is calculated over the shared secret key, some padding bits, the sequence number of the current message, the current higher level protocol that is being served by SSL, the length of compressed fragment, and the compressed fragment itself. Following this, the encryption is performed. Finally, to enable inverse processing, instructions are prepended in SSL Record header. This header contains fields with major and minor versions of SSL protocol, the higher level protocol that is being served in the current step, and the length of the fragment. If the fragment is compressed, then this denotes the compressed length. The complete structure as shown in Fig. 3.39 is transmitted in a TCP segment.

The last member of the family is SSL Alert Protocol. It is used to signal alerts to the peer entity and these messages are compressed and encrypted as specified by the current state. Each message consists of two octets and defines alerts, which may be warnings (receipt of unexpected message, decompression failure, etc.), or fatal errors. In the case of the latter, SSL immediately terminates the connection. Other connections may go on, but new ones within this session are not allowed.

For SSL operations, the following block encryption algorithms are used: IDEA, RC2 and DES with 40 bits keys, ordinary DES, 3DES and Fortezza (FORTEZZA is a crypto-card based technology that presents one major component of the US National Security Agency's MISSI program). Among stream encryption algorithms, RC4 [306] with 40 or 128 bits keys can be used.

In brief, what are the implications of SSL application for management of ISs security and privacy? SSL is a very wide-spread protocol. It is available by default in browsers and many servers. So protecting Web based traffic is not hard and should be implemented wherever possible. Although SSL is not completely invisible to a user, because it requires some basic understanding of digital certificates and their use, it does not require excessive training. Further, it is stable, has been around for years and it is one of major security

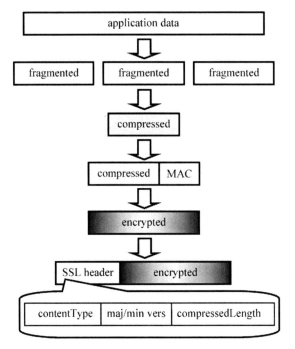

Fig. 3.39. SSL Record protocol operations

protocols in the internet. Further, it is not designed for Web only, but can be used with other applications like file transfer protocols, or e-mail.

By offering a common security basis to all applications, its universality certainly has some drawbacks. In the case of e-mail, it makes more sense to deploy a document oriented security protocol, especially considering digitally signed documents that are self-contained objects, linked to a uniquely identifiable person. SSL protects connections that may be used by many applications, which in turn, may be used by many users.

3.4.5 Secure/Multipurpose Internet Mail Extensions

Together with the Web, electronic mail is one of the most widely used internet services. The basic e-mail standards for the Internet are RFC 821 [280] and RFC 822 [81].

While RFC 821 defines the protocol for exchange of e-mails, RFC 822 defines their structure. Due to technological limitations in the early eighties, both specifications are simple, but nevertheless effective. An e-mail consists of two major parts, one being a header and the other a body. Common fields in the header are DATE, FROM, TO, and SUBJECT. A blank line separates the body from the header and the complete message is ended with a dot in a separate (last) line. Besides simple e-mail structure, mailers use a simple protocol that is not designed to transfer messages with long lines. Moreover, messages may not contain control characters or other non-printable ASCII[10] characters, or any non-ASCII alphabet. This basic mail gives the possibility of transferring only short lines with certain characters, roughly described as printable characters of the English alphabet (7-bit ASCII characters). Transfer of other kinds of messages may result in rejection or unpredictable behavior. This poses severe limitations on the use for languages with different alphabets or different kind of data, like programs, music, graphics and video.

To solve the problem, IETF standardized Multipurpose Internet Mail Extensions (MIME) - the basic standard is [125]. With additional fields in the header, new content formats were defined. These new content formats should coexist with the limitations of the infrastructure described above. It was not reasonable to assume that old mailers would be replaced at once with new, more capable ones. The large existing infrastructure base of RFC 821 conformant mailers was a factor that had to be taken into account.

To assure the coexistence of these new formats with the installed mailers, new kinds of data have to be re-coded before transmission to obtain conforming characters. This process is called Base-64 or Radix-64 conversion and produces a character set that is universally representable at all computers. The set consists of sixty-five printable characters, one of which is used for padding (=). Thus sixty-four characters, which require six bits for their unique representation, are used for transformation. The mapping goes as follows:

- Suppose there is an input "11100010 01011101 01000001". Using extended ASCII coding, this sequence corresponds to "Γ]A".
- This input is rearranged into six-bit groups "111000 100101 110101 000001". The decimal values denoted by these groups are 56, 37, 53 and 1.
- Translation follows using a Radix-64 table, where the fifty-seventh symbol is "4", thirty-eighth is "l", and so on (numbering starts with 0). Thus the result is "4l1B".
- Using ASCII code table, bits that represent characters in the sequence "4l1B" are obtained. For "4", ASCII code is "00110100", for "l" ASCII code is "01101100" and so on. The final result of conversion is "00110100 01101100 00110001 01000010" (blanks are included only for clear presentation). The price to be paid for general compatibility is expansion of data by one-third.

Base-64 encoding is not the only allowed kind of encoding for MIME, but we have focused on it because of its importance for security enhancements. MIME constitutes the basis for upgrading e-mail functionality with security services, which is referred to as Secure MIME (S/MIME).

S/MIME provides authentication, confidentiality, integrity, and non-repudiation. It is defined in over twenty standards that cover message structure,

---

[10] ASCII stands for American Standard Code for Information Interchange that assigns bit sequences to alphabet and other characters.

application of particular cryptographic mechanisms, electronic signature policies, etc. A starting point that reveals a lot about S/MIME as a whole is the
standard concerning its message structure [287]. The rest of this subsection
will be based on this standard.

Encryption transformations are not performed on a header, but on the
body, be it the entire body or its subparts only. Therefore security services are
provided through the following possible kinds of mail processing: Enveloped
Data, Signed Data, Clear-signed Data and Signed and Enveloped Data.

With Enveloped Data, any kind of content can be encrypted, where encrypted decryption keys for one or more recipients are included in the message
(this is the digital envelope principle).

With Signed Data, a digital signature is formed by the signer which is
Base-64 encoded together with the original message. With Clear-signed Data,
a signature is generated and only this signature is Base-64 encoded, while
the original message is transmitted as if it was not S/MIME processed. In
contrast to Signed Data, Clear-signed Data thus enables a reader without
S/MIME capabilities to read the message.

Signed and Enveloped Data denotes nesting of encrypted and signed parts,
i.e. encrypted data may be signed and signed data may be encrypted.

When an S/MIME program for creating e-mails[11] wants to send an
S/MIME message to a recipient, it first has to determine if the recipient
is able to decrypt a message using a given encryption algorithm. The precise procedure for determining encryption capabilities goes as follows. When
the sender has a list of preferred decrypting algorithms from the recipient, it
should choose the first possibility. If the sender has no such list, but has already received a trusted signed message from the recipient, then it should use
the same algorithm that was used in the last signed and encrypted message.
If there is no knowledge about recipient capabilities, then it should use 3DES,
if the sender accepts the risk that the message may not be understood by the
other party. If this is an unacceptable risk, the sender should use RC2 with a
40-bits long key.

Each content type of S/MIME data is specific due to the nature of these
data and has its local representation that depends on the local environment
(operating system). Before being cryptographically processed, it is converted
to so-called *canonical form that is a standardized representation of data, independent of local representation.* Canonical data are used for exchange between
the systems to avoid peculiarities of particular environments. After cryptographic processing, of course, the result has to be transformed again to assure
proper transfer encoding (by use of e.g. Base-64 conversion).

Figs. 3.40 and 3.41 illustrate the processing of Signed Data and Enveloped
Data. Signed Data can be used with one or more signers. First, the sender
selects a one-way hash function for computation of MACs (also referred to

---

[11]These programs are also referred to as user agents, and mailers are referred to
as message transfer agents.

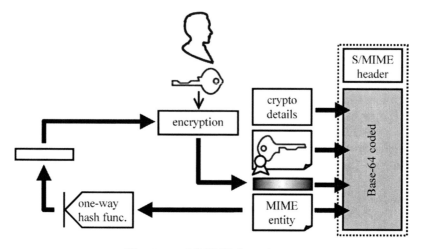

Fig. 3.40. S/MIME Signed Data

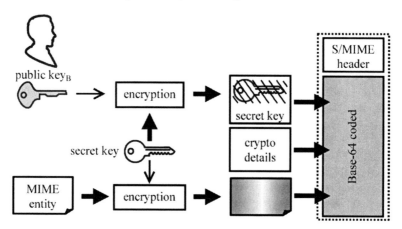

Fig. 3.41. S/MIME Enveloped Data

as message digests or MDs). In the second step, the content that is to be exchanged is hashed. With his private key, the sending entity encrypts the hash to obtain a digital signature that is added to the content. The signer's public key certificate (or chain of certificates) together with the ID of hash algorithm, the ID of the signing algorithm, and the signature itself, is appended to the original message. Thus the original message, digital signature, certificate(s) and crypto-details are Base-64 encoded before sending, and only an S/MIME capable user agent (recipient) can read this message. Below is an example of the signed data option, as given in the original standard mentioned above:

```
Content-Type: application/pkcs7-mime;
              smime-type=signed-data; name=smime.p7m
```

```
Content-Transfer-Encoding: base64
Content-Disposition: attachment; filename=smime.p7m
```

567GhIGfHfYT6ghyHhHUujpfyF4f8HHGTrfvhJhjH776tbB9HG4VQbnj7
77n8HHGT9HG4VQpfyF467GhIGfHfYT6rfvbnj756tbBghyHhHUujhJhjH
HUujhJh4VQpfyF467GhIGfHfYGTrfvbnjT6jH7756tbB9H7n8HHGghyHh
6YT64VOGhIGfHfQbnj75

In the above example, the header extensions state that the content is MIME of type PKCS7-MIME, which belongs to S/MIME. The next element states more precisely that this is the signed data option of S/MIME and that MIME extension for this kind of message is p7m. In the next line of the header, transfer encoding is specified. The last header line specifies the file name of this S/MIME message, which is sent as an attachment (and also presented as an attachment by user agent without S/MIME support). Let us compare this with an example for Enveloped Data, also given in the original S/MIME standard:

```
Content-Type: application/pkcs7-mime;
              smime-type=enveloped-data; name=smime.p7m
Content-Transfer-Encoding: base64
Content-Disposition: attachment; filename=smime.p7m
```

rfvbnj756tbBghyHhHUujhJhjH77n8HHGT9HG4VQpfyF467GhIGfHfYT6
7n8HHGghyHhHUujhJh4VQpfyF467GhIGfHfYGTrfvbnjT6jH7756tbB9H
f8HHGTrfvhJhjH776tbB9HG4VQbnj7567GhIGfHfYT6ghyHhHUujpfyF4
OGhIGfHfQbnj756YT64V

Except that the keyword signed-data is replaced by enveloped-data, there is no immediately noticeable difference. The difference is hidden in the processing of the body part (see Fig. 3.41). The sending entity first generates a pseudorandom session key for a particular symmetric encryption algorithm. For each recipient, the entity encrypts the session key with the recipient's public key. Further, crypto details are prepared for each recipient: ID of recipient's public key certificate, ID of the algorithm used for encryption of the session key, and the encrypted session key. The result, that also includes encrypted MIME entity, is then Base-64 encoded by sender. This has to be first Base-64 decoded by the recipient. Afterwards, the recipient uses the appropriate private key to decipher the session key to further decipher encrypted content. The proper algorithm for decryption is taken on the basis of its ID in the S/MIME header.

For user agents that are not able to read S/MIME messages, a message can still be signed for separate processing, while the content is sent unprocessed and can thus be directly displayed. This is the Clear-signed Data option. S/MIME offers additional options related to certificate management. The first one is a Registration Request that is used by a user to apply for a certificate at a CA. The second is a Certificate-only Message that provides only certificates or CRLs.

There are many cryptographic algorithms that can be used with S/MIME, including Digital Signature Standard (DSS) [248] (this is a public key signature standard developed by NIST), DH, and RSA from public key algorithms. Symmetric algorithms include 3DES, 40-bit RC2, while hash functions include 160 bit SHA-1 and, for backward compatibility, 128 bit MD5.

In brief, what are the implications of S/MIME for managing ISs security and privacy? Besides SSL and IPSec, S/MIME is the most stable and widely used security solution. It provides complete protection for organizations' e-mails. In addition, as the legal status of digitally signed e-mail backed with qualified certificates (which means that certificates have to be issued by accredited CAs) is becoming equal to a hand-signed mail, the importance of S/MIME is gaining momentum.

However, one should be careful to store (back-up) the complete data that reside in the incoming directory of an e-mail user agent program. In the case of legal disputes, the representation of a secure mail by a user agent program is not likely to be enough. The basic Radix-64 encoded message with S/MIME header, certificates and CRLs, constitute the only proper raw material for thoroughly proving security properties of an e-mail.

3.4.6 One-time Password Systems

With the introduction of open systems communication, cryptography became a general practice, and exchange of plain passwords was no longer sufficient. Cryptography can also be used to realize *one-time passwords, i.e. unpredictable passwords that change with each use.* Thus an attacker who gains access to one password, cannot use it later to attack the system.

More than two decades ago the idea of one-time passwords was introduced by L. Lamport [212]. It was based on one-way hash functions. The method deploys the fact that these functions are easy for computations in one direction, while in the opposite direction computations are not feasible. An entity chooses a secret string and produces its hashed value, which is again submitted to hash function, and its output is hashed again. This procedure is repeated, say, n times. The last hashed value is then given to a server that the entity wants to authenticate with.

When authenticating for the first time, the entity sends the $(n-1)$-th value, which is hashed by the server to obtain the n-th value. This value is compared with the stored value and if they match, authentication is successful, because the $(n-1)$-th value can be produced only by an entity that knows the initial seed. The server then stores the $(n-1)$-th value. For the next authentication, entity sends the $(n-2)$-th value, and so on. A well known implementation that explored this idea some ten years ago is S/Key [147].

Other methods exist for one-time password systems, e.g. synchronized clocks or challenge-response techniques. With the latter, a server sends a sequence that is input to a smart card, which does some cryptographic processing and returns an output that is used for authentication. The server performs the same cryptographic operation like the smart card and, knowing all the input parameters, it can produce appropriate output that is compared with the received value.

3.4.7 Firewalls

A firewall is a specialized computer system that is positioned between an organization's internal network and the internet to permit or block incoming and outgoing traffic in line with a security policy. The basic work in this area is [64], while a more advanced treatment is in [355]. The aim of the firewall is to protect the internal network from any kind of intruders. In order to achieve this, access points to the internal network have to be controlled and reduced to a single point.

There are two general philosophies to implementing firewall security policy. The first is "everything is allowed that is not explicitly forbidden", while the second is "everything is forbidden that is not explicitly allowed". The second approach is the most restrictive one and is recommended for majority of organizations, while only very liberal environments may stay with the first philosophy.

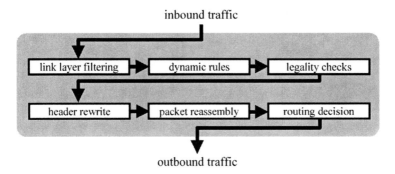

Fig. 3.42. A typicall firewall architecture

To understand firewalls, the details of their operations will be given (see Fig. 3.42). Not all firewalls offer all these functionalities but, in principle, processing goes as follows. First, a packet may be filtered at the link layer, and it may later be the subject of a dynamic rules check. These rules temporarily record accepted computers with which one has initiated connections, and these computers are allowed to pass their responses back. Next, the packet undergoes legality checks (filtering) to determine if the particular kind of traffic and IP addresses with port numbers are allowed or not. Address translation may follow, where rewriting network and port fields in the header is done. Further, advanced firewalls also reassemble packets to make an analysis at the application level (which application is in question and what kind of attack may be underway). If the result of analysis is positive, the packet is routed further according to the firewall's decision.

Firewalls are usually divided into three groups (see Fig. 3.43). The first are packet-filtering firewalls. Their main characteristic is inspection of packets at the network layer and making a decision whether to pass them or not (such functionality can be achieved also within routers). This judgement can be on the basis of source and destination addresses, source and destination ports, type of protocol being transferred in payload fields of packets, and on the basis of the physical port where a traffic enters or leaves the network.

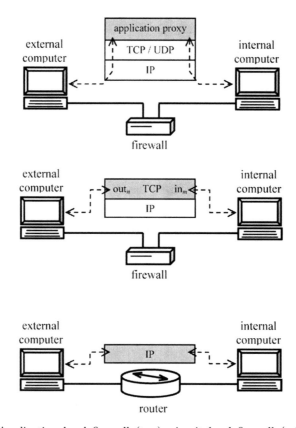

Fig. 3.43. Application level firewall (top), circuit level firewall (middle), packet filtering firewall (bottom)

Packet filtering firewalls have advantage of being simple and can thus perform operations very fast. They can also be used for network address translations (NAT) [322]. This process maps IP numbers for outgoing traffic and re-maps them for incoming traffic, which conceals the details of the internal network and makes it harder to attack. However, because these firewalls operate at the network layer, good granularity of authentication cannot be provided. Further, the complete understanding of the upper layer scenario is hidden from them and they cannot react accordingly, e.g. to certain harmful commands of an application. But even at the IP level, firewalls can be spoofed, i.e. provided with falsified addresses. For example, an attacker may generate packets with the source address being set to an internal network address in order to get access to inside resources. This can be remedied by allowing certain IP addresses only on certain physical interfaces. Further, it is possible to intensively fragment transport layer data which prevents a complete insight of a firewall into an ongoing attack, thus insufficiently long fragments should be discarded [323].

The second kind of firewall is the circuit level firewall. These systems operate at the transport layer by setting up two TCP connections and relaying the traffic between them. They decide which TCP traffic will be and which will not be allowed to pass. Before providing the relaying function, authentication can be performed. Afterwards, the proper execution of TCP traffic is monitored. These firewalls are state aware and can interpret properly the whole TCP connection (flags, sequence numbers). Their drawback is limited suitability for UDP which is, by its nature, connectionless. Further, circuit-level firewalls may slow down communications, and may interfere with some applications.

The third kind of firewall is the application level firewall, and is often called a proxy server.[12] These firewalls operate at the application level, and thus control the whole context of communication, not only IP and port numbers. They consist of proxy applications, i.e. agents, which start communication with the outer world on behalf of the corresponding application that resides on the internal network. The agents then remain in-between and monitor what is going on between the initiator and responder. Agents usually require authentication, which can be focused at the user level. This authentication can be an ordinary user ID with password approach, backed with source IP address filtering, or any other method that is appropriate for a certain application. They can also analyze communication at the level of executed application commands. Agents can thus provide fine granularity of logging events that are essential for prevention and study of unwanted events. This kind of processing is very resource consuming, which is the main disadvantage of such systems.

There are various topological possibilities for deployment of firewalls. The most common deploy a router and a firewall for the following topologies: single-homed, dual-homed and screened subnetwork [323]. They are illustrated in Fig. 3.44. With single-homed topology, an outside router performs packet

---

[12]Proxies also denote caching systems that are used to reduce Web traffic by locally storing frequently required documents. Clients access these documents indirectly by first contacting proxy and, only if the required document is not in a cache, is the request sent over the internet.

filtering for the incoming traffic, which is forwarded to a firewall for additional application level examination before entering the local network. This combination requires an intruder to bypass two devices to successfully penetrate the local network, while allowing an organization to flexibly implement its security policy. In essence, single homed configuration logically implements a *demilitarized zone (DMZ), which denotes a network that is not a part of the internet, nor it is an integral part of the internal network, but is administered by an organization.*

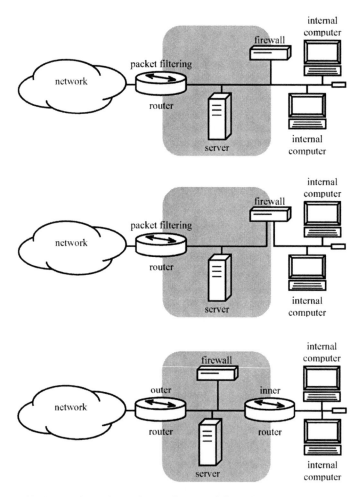

Fig. 3.44. Variants of topological installation of firewalls: single-homed at the top, dual-homed in the middle, screened subnetwork at the bottom (shaded region denotes DMZ)

The physically split DMZ is achieved with dual-homed topology, which enables network layer examination with the addition of application level proxy agents. The benefit of this configuration is automatic close of connection if something goes wrong with the firewall. Other benefits are similar to the single-homed topology. Both topologies use DMZ for placement of various information servers or modem pools.

The third topology, screened subnetwork, deploys an additional router for DMZ. This separates DMZ physically from the inner and outer networks. Only the DMZ addresses are announced to the outer network. The equivalent holds true for the inner network, where only DMZ is announced by the inner router. This configuration prevents establishment of direct routes to the internet, since the internal network remains hidden to internet, and the internet to the internal network. At the same time, the inbound and outbound traffic are monitored at the application, transport (i.e. circuit) and network level.

Let us summarize the implications for management of ISs security and privacy. Firewalls have been around for more than a decade, and constitute a stable and proven technology. Thus it is not a question whether to use it or not, but how to do so most effectively. A topology should be chosen that best meets an organization's security requirements. The highest level of security demands a state aware firewall with application proxies [247]. Firewalls, together with anti-virus software, are really successful products for security, because they do not require user intervention and interfere very little with day-to-day operations [213].

3.4.8 Intrusion Detection Systems

Intrusion detection systems (IDSs) are systems that provide real-time detection and reporting of attempts to misuse resources. Their development started in the nineties and they have been significantly improved since then [198]. The typical architecture of IDS comprises three modules (see scheme in Fig. 3.45) [260, 298] :

- A monitoring component that captures packets and submits them to an inference component.
- An analyzing component that infers from captured data whether an activity is regular or not.
- An alerting component that reacts to detected irregular events in a passive way (e.g. by writing a warning into a log file) or active way (e.g. by reconfiguring an appropriate device like a firewall).

Reliable operation of IDSs depends strongly on having complete data about the system activity. One should first determine what information to log and where to get it. Because of the distributed nature of modern ISs, information is logged at different places, and analyzing only logs of a particular host will not reveal the real picture. Thus it is recommended to collect log information at a central and well protected location.

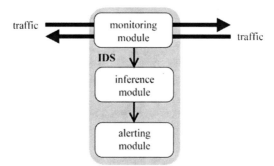

Fig. 3.45. IDS architecture

Then, one should decide between two basic technological approaches. These are anomaly detection and misuse detection:

- Anomaly detection uses patterns of normal behavior and detects patterns of acts that differ from these. The advantage of these systems is that they can detect previously unknown attacks, but they produce high false-positive alarms.
- Misuse detection systems are based on definitions, also called signatures, of wrong behavior. This is similar to the functioning of anti-virus and anti-spyware[13] software, which are actually a kind of IDSs. Audited data are compared with the signatures and, in the case of a match, an alarm is generated. The advantage of these systems is the low rate of false positive alarms, while the drawback is that they can detect only known attacks.

At the beginning of IDSs development, the majority of IDSs were signature-based. But rule-based IDSs are becoming more and more widespread due to their ability to recognize unknown attacks. To obtain the best of both worlds, it is not uncommon to use hybrid techniques.

When mentioning hybrid IDSs, this often refers to the placement of IDSs monitoring modules. If they are placed on a host to protect that particular host, these IDSs are host-based IDSs, but if they are placed over the network, they are a network-based IDSs.

The benefits of the latter are overall protection of the network and provision of a global picture of suspicious activities. On the other hand, the problem is when encryption is used at the network layer, which disables their operation. Further, switching technologies are increasingly deployed at the link layer to optimize traffic, which gets directed only to certain lines as required by addresses, and not broadcast to all wires. This means that IDS has to sensor all lines in order not to miss some suspicious activity.

Contrary to network based IDSs, host based IDSs also have access to plaintext data and can be tailored to specifics of a certain host. This is the

---

[13]Spyware refers to software that gathers user information without her knowledge.

main advantage of the host based approach, but its main drawback is extensive use of a host's resources. Thus, using host-based monitoring with network-based one results in an optimal set-up, which is called a hybrid configuration.

The benefits of employing IDSs for management of ISs security and privacy are numerous. IDSs are a mature technology that belongs to the golden arsenal of security infrastructure solutions together with IPSec, SSL, S/MIME, one-time password systems and firewalls. In general, they interfere very little with business processes, and quality open source solutions are freely available on the internet [298].

3.4.9 Extensible Markup Language Security

Extensible Markup Language (XML) is probably the most revolutionary technology to be invented after the creation of the World Wide Web. XML is based on Standard Generalized Markup Language (SGML) [167] that serves as a framework for defining text based markup languages. Thus *XML is human-readable and tagged (meta)language for support of various data manipulation needs.* These needs range from data transfer, through presentation of these data to various kinds of its processing. XML is standardized by W3C Consortium. The basic and most recent standard is [40].

XML Basics

XML is becoming so essential that some background has to be given in order to understand contemporary solutions like Web services, which are dependent on XML.

Historically, XML is not the first initiative for open exchange of data. First efforts started at the end of the seventies with the introduction of Electronic Data Interchange (EDI). *EDI means exchange of highly structured and standardized business documents through electronic communication means.* The basic idea of EDI was to reduce paperwork and consequently improve related business operations with faster and cheaper data processing that was less prone to errors. The main player behind EDI in the US was ANSI that specified X.12 family of standards, and the main player in Europe was the UN Economic Commission for Europe that was specifying EDIFACT family of standards.

EDI was concentrated on structuring documents and transfer encoding. As far as transfer is concerned, EDI efforts were very limited - they were really only about message transfer. They were not aimed at the discovery of other EDI applications, business protocols were not automated (from requests to invoices), etc. Clearly, the original EDI standards were tied to the technology that was available at that time. This was probably one of the main reasons why the idea of EDI did not take off, although it was strongly supported by governments. Another reason was that these standards were insufficiently flexible to meet various business needs. Further, EDI documents were hard to understand by humans. This all resulted in a situation where classical EDI applications played a minor role, except in some segments for business-to-business communications.

With the birth of the Web a widely available, accepted and open infrastructure for transfer of documents appeared. But at the beginning, only static HTML documents could be exchanged, which certainly did not cover many business needs. Nevertheless, the transport infrastructure was there and only lacked a flexible data description framework. That is where XML came in and started to take over the efforts of the EDI community. Today, XML is not only a synonym for EDI, but much more.

Referring to an XML document means actually referring to a set of documents. It all starts with a basic XML document, where the data intended for exchange are contained. This basic XML document has to fulfill a minimal set of requirements concerning proper structuring, which go as follows: Each starting tag has to be closed by a matching ending tag. Further, only proper nesting of elements is allowed. This means that when an element contains a sub-element, this sub-element has to have an ending tag before an ending tag of its superior element takes place. Further, the document must have a single root element that contains all other elements. All attribute values must be enclosed in quotation marks and cannot contain the < character, while elements cannot have more than one attribute of a particular name.

These are some of the most important requirements (the full set of requirements can be found in the basic XML standard [40]). A properly structured document that meets these requirements is called a *well-formed* document, and an example of a well-formed document is given below:

```
<?xml version="1.0" encoding="ISO 8859-1" standalone="no"?>
<!DOCTYPE alarmsystem SYSTEM "alarmsystem.dtd">
<alarmsystem>
    <sensor deviceid="A33f">
        <size height="30" width="60" depth="30"/>
        <type>AD</type>
        <location> Main door </location>
        <status>on</status>
    </sensor>
    <sensor deviceid="A33g">
        <size height="45" width="45" depth="45"/>
        <type>Noname</type>
        <location> Level 8 </location>
        <status>off</status>
    </sensor>
</alarmsystem>
```

The first line is an XML declaration that is defined by a sequence <?xml. In this line, the version of XML is given next, and the second part specifies

the type of encoding, which is a Latin-1 encoding in this case, defined in ISO 8859-1 [171]. The last part of the declaration states whether external entities can be included, such as those being part of some other file. The sequence ?> ends the XML file declaration.

A quick look at tags reveals that they consist of a keyword between sharp brackets. The only difference between the starting and the ending tag is that the ending tag contains a slash after the opening bracket. Under the top level element, which is alarmsystem, there has to be proper nesting. A sensor element is formed with attribute deviceid, which has values A33f for the first sensor and A33g for the second. Dimensions are also specified with attributes, but other sub-elements that further specify the sensor, are given as standalone elements type, location and status. Element type has value AD for the first sensor and value Noname for the second sensor. Further, element location has value Main door for the first sensor and Level 8 for the second. Finally, element status has value on for the first sensor and off for the second.

The above well-formed example is a simple alarm system database. But for applications, a well-formed structure is usually not enough. Additional constraints have to be imposed on the structure of the basic XML document by stating the number of repetitions of a certain element, its type, etc. Thus refined syntax requirements are put in place. If they are followed, one obtains a *valid document* that is structured exactly as required for a particular application. There are two possibilities to achieve valid structuring: the first, the older one, is through document type definition (DTD) [37], and the second is through XML Schema [114].

The second line in our XML example specifies an external file, called alarmsystem.dtd that contains the structuring details against which the basic document is checked. This alarmsystem.dtd file is given below:

```
<!ELEMENT alarmsystem (sensor+)>
<!ELEMENT sensor (size, type, location, status)>
<!ATTLIST sensor deviceid CDATA #IMPLIED>
<!ELEMENT size (#PCDATA)>
<!ATTLIST size height CDATA  #IMPLIED
              width  CDATA  #IMPLIED
              depth  CDATA  #IMPLIED>
<!ELEMENT type (#PCDATA)>
<!ELEMENT location (#PCDATA)>
<!ELEMENT status (#PCDATA)>
```

Each ELEMENT declaration in the above DTD is followed by the name of an element in the basic XML file. The first declaration is about the root element alarmsystem which has one or more children elements sensor (this is denoted by +). Each sensor element consists of four child elements: size, type, location and status (the order is important). The lowest level elements are defined with their names and types of data. Some of the most common types are PCDATA that denotes parsed character data, and CDATA that denotes character data that are not parsed (i.e. analyzed by an XML parser). The cautious reader has probably noticed that attributes are declared with a keyword ATTLIST, followed by the name of an element, the name of its attribute, type and options. Two options are IMPLIED and REQUIRED. The first one means that the attribute may be left out completely, while the second means the opposite - the attribute must be present.

Besides DTDs, XML schemas can be used for validating of XML documents. The main difference between DTDs and schemas is that schemas are native XML documents, while DTDs are not XML by their structure. Further, schemas enable better granularity of specification in terms of available types and ranges of values.

The third important part of XML language is transformation capability, be it for presentation of the basic XML file, or its conversion to a format required by another system. This is achieved with Extensible Stylesheet Language Transformations (XSLT) [69]. For the particular case of WWW, the conversion of basic XML file into a HTML form (that can be displayed by a browser) is often achieved by Cascading Style Sheets (CSS) [220]. Roughly, for transformations, CSS has a similar relation to XSLT as that of DTD to schemas for validity.

The fourth important part of XML is XPath [68]. XPath provides the means to specify the selected part of an XML document, and means to manipulate data. XPath is implemented on top of Document Object Model (DOM) that has been developed to provide programmers with unified capabilities to access and manipulate XML documents [218]. With DOM, documents and their elements are treated as objects and DOM defines interfaces to access these objects through programs (programming languages). The document is represented as a tree with nodes, where the document itself is a node, while document elements with their children, TEXT nodes, are subordinate nodes. With programs, document elements can be read, changed, added to, or deleted.

Using DOM requires writing a program parser, while XPath enables a more straightforward way to process XML document elements at "plain-vanilla" XML level with scripts. Because XPath processes documents, it is functionally similar to XSLT.

The fifth important part of XML is XPointer [141]. XPointer has its roots in World Wide Web and its uniform resource identifiers (URIs) [29]. URIs provide unique standardized identifiers for objects existing in the network, and also the means to access these objects. An example of URI is

```
http://www.host.net/objectdir/myobject
```

In this URI, http presents a protocol to access the object myobject on a server www.host.net, which resides in a directory objectdir. All this is aimed at preventing name clashes in XML applications. Every element belongs to a certain name space and, within this name space, it has a unique name. Thus for example, when two documents use the same element name for two different kinds of data, the concept of namespaces prevents ambiguities and assures proper processing in case of, e.g., merging documents. So XPointer is the syntax that is used for the most general addressing of parts of XML documents (objects) [98], and in fact builds on XPath [59].

There are other parts of XML, but these ones are a sufficient basis to start dealing with the XML security.

XML Signature

Although XML security is based on standard security services and mechanisms, it is almost a security area in its own right. Thus it is not easy to cover it briefly.

Two basic standards in this field are XML Signature Syntax and Processing (XML Signature for short) [23] and XML Encryption Syntax and Processing (XML Encryption for short) [165]. Starting with XML Signature - a compliant document is itself an XML document, a text based, human readable document that has to conform to rules of well-formedness. It can be self-sufficient, i.e. it may contain all the processing rules and information within itself that are needed for security processing. But this is not a must [95].

An important concept with XML Signature is manifest, which contains digests of resources that are signed. These resources can be simple documents, Web resources, or even references [95]. Manifest is designated by a `SignedInfo` element. This element contains one or more hashed values of resources that are subject to signing, and actually, the signature is done over these hashes in the manifest, and not over the original resources. With XML Signature the manifest of the XML document is hashed again before signing. In the manifest, each hashed value is given together with an URI of the resource and the identification of the hash algorithm. For all the resources a common signature algorithm is used and referenced within the manifest [95]. Below is a simple example of an XML Signature document:

```
<Signature>
 <SignedInfo>
  <CanonicalizationMethod
   Algorithm="http://www.w3.org/TR/2001/REC-xml-c14n"/>
  <SignatureMethod
   Algorithm="http://www.w3.org/2000/09/xmldsig#rsa-sha1"/>
  <Reference
   URI="http://somehost.somedomain.com/FileToBeSigned.txt">
   <DigestMethod
    Algorithm="http://www.w3.org/2000/09/xmldsig#sha1"/>
   <DigestValue>qaTROOt++43sdfefsDdjtgfdDs6=</DigestValue>
  </Reference>
 </SignedInfo>
 <SignatureValue>
```

fj4rdwQ8cUHGepsfgAF554qdASfasddgkscu59
KO98W233L199kli+oizDkkcbGpscf4XCF45875
. . .
oiOIUrtfncDafwsdw34=
</SignatureValue>
</Signature>

The parent element `Signature` contains the subordinated, nested elements `SignedInfo` and `SignedValue`. Further, `SignedInfo` contains the element `SignatureMethod` with a URI referencing RSA with SHA-1 to be used for signing. The next level elements contain one-way hash function identification and a hashed value that was produced with this function on the above referenced resource. Here the manifest ends and the signature itself starts. An output of encryption can be an arbitrary string of bytes that is not acceptable for XML text oriented documents. Thus this output is Base-64 encoded to produce a unique and printable representation of binary ciphertext.

But this is not the only encoding that is performed on the basic XML document before signing. The element `CanonicalizationMethod` was intentionally overlooked above. It serves to sort out problems that may arise out of XML files that are semantically equivalent, but have a different representation. These problems may be system/editing software specific or caused by a user. In the first case, assume that a user creates an XML file with a standard editor on a UNIX operating system, while another user uses MS Windows with some other editor. Although the visual appearance of the very same file at both operating systems may seem the same, different local coding is taking place, despite the fact that both systems may be ASCII based. For example, in the first case bytes that are used to signal the end of one line and the start of another will contain only LF ASCII characters, while in the second case this will be a sequence of LF and CR characters. But it is not only the visual indistinguishability that causes problems - a user may also use more than one space character between attributes instead of only one.

In all these cases, digital signatures will differ, because hashing will produce different digest values. To prevent such situations, canonicalization takes place before any cryptographic operation is done on the file. With canonicalization of XML data that have more than one possible representation, a standard representation is achieved that is independent of local peculiarities. The `CanonicalizationMethod` element defines the procedure for performing this task. This is similar to S/MIME processing.

XML Signature documents optionally contain additional elements, the first being `KeyInfo`. This element provides details of information for verification of a signature. This can be a public key alone, its X.509 certificate, a chain of certificates and CRLs, etc. The next element is `Object` element that further supports signature functionality. For example, it may include a timestamp or other form of unique ID to prevent the re-use of a digitally signed XML document like a money transfer order. This is far from being exhaustive description of all elements in XML Signature files, but the ones covered should be sufficient.

In the above example, it can be seen that the signature actually wraps the complete document, and this kind of XML Signature document is called enveloping signature. There are two additional possibilities: The original text can wrap the signature (called enveloped signature), and the signature as such exists without any wrapping (called detached signature).

Certainly, XML Signature files have to be not only well-formed, but also valid. Because of the general applicability of digital signatures, related schemas and DTDs cannot be left to users for specification. Thus W3C has standardized DTDs and schemas for XML Signature [23].

The main advantage of XML Signature is its flexibility, which allows multiple users to sign a document. In addition, the signature can be applied only to certain elements, or to resources that reside somewhere on the network [95].

XML Encryption

The main advantage of XML Encryption over ordinary document security is again flexibility. It allows multiple users to encrypt a document. Further, the encryption can be applied to certain elements, by encrypting only the values of these elements, or encryption can also include tags. This provides even better confidentiality. Further, encrypted resources do not have to be contained in the security file, but may reside somewhere on the network.

All this is achieved by a process for encrypting data and representing the result with XML syntax. The fundamental element here is the **EncryptedData** element. It contains other child elements that specify the encryption method and information about the key, which may be included in encrypted form, obtained by means like DH, or retrieved from some place over the network.

As with XML Signature, the output of the encryption process is an arbitrary sequence of bits, and these have to be encoded in the text form, for which Base-64 encoding is used. This Base-64 encoded result resides between the starting and ending tags for the **EncryptedData** element. A notion that is related to this element is plaintext replacement - the **EncryptedData** element with its attributes and child elements represents replacement. This can be explained through an example of an XML cheque:

```
<XMLCheque>
 <ChequeId> 123456789 </ChequeId>
 <Payer> John Reed </Payer>
 <Payee> Ivan Novak </Payee>
 <SensitiveData>
  <SourceAccountNo> 987654321 </SourceAccountNo>
  <TransferAmount> 100,000.00 </TransferAmount>
 </SensitiveData>
</XMLCheque>
```

The above fictitious example shows an XML document with sensitive part (`SensitiveData` element), which is cut, cryptographically processed, converted to XML form and pasted back as a new value of `SensitiveData` element:

```
<XMLCheque>
 <ChequeId> 123456789 </ChequeId>
 <Payer> John Reed </Payer>
 <Payee> Ivan Novak </Payee>
 <SensitiveData>
  <EncryptedData
   xmlns:ds="http://www.w3.org/TR/xmlenc-core/"
   Type="http://www.w3.org/2001/04/xmlenc#Content">
   <EncryptionMethod
    Algorithm="http://www.w3.org/2001/04/xmlenc#aes128-cbc"/>
   <ds:KeyInfo>
    <ds:KeyName> ProtectionKey </KeyName>
   </ds:KeyInfo>
   <CipherData>
    <CipherValue>
    ikdFRdFdck454k1LK981lkdKDDS78
    1kLOKJdh7rPOLdsfRfh89iueszsjn
    ...
    1sS72jD38sh
    </CipherValue>
   </CipherData>
  </EncryptedData>
 </SensitiveData>
</XMLCheque>
```

XML Security element `EncryptedData` has two attributes that define the namespace and type of encryption, which is the content of the element. Further, sub-elements specify encryption algorithm, and encryption key name. This means that this reference to a key is sufficient to decrypt the content. The last two elements, `CipherData` and `CipherValue`, embrace the actual Base-64 encoded crypto output.

Of course, XML security documents have to be well-formed and valid, which requires checking them against schemas.

Finally, a few words about management of keys with XML. Key management specification referred to as XML Key Management Specification (or XKMS for short) is currently at the stage of candidate recommendation. Therefore it is not yet an official standard. XKMS is in fact an XML-based protocol that helps to manage public key operations, like location of public keys, their registration and revocation. PKI operations are thus required for XKML and they affect XKMS.

Security of XML Itself

XML is becoming a core technology for most organizations, therefore its own security is of utmost importance. Unfortunately, it was not designed from scratch with security in mind, thus XML processing tools may pose severe risks. They may be prone to attacks on the DTD level, document corruption, single-node or multi-node attacks and back-end system attacks [34]:

- DTD based attacks exploit the possibility that an XML document can contain DTD definitions within the basic XML file, which override external DTD. In this case an attacker can create a document that will invoke a kind of processing that the original DTD would not allow. For example, internal DTD may allow specification of an XML document of virtually infinite length. It is not hard to imagine that its parsing would require so much resources that a computer got stuck. The majority of parsers build DOM trees in the active memory, and large data structures can easily use all the resources.
- Document corruption attacks exploit the fact that DOM based processing tools do not assume that a comment can occur within meaningful data. Thus processing will be completely corrupted.
- Single node attack exploits the fact that certain data in an XML document may perfectly satisfy corresponding DTD rules, but may be in fact false, because an intruder has modified it within the limits, allowed by DTD definition. This can be cured with XML Encryption and XML Signature. A variant of single node attacks are multi-node attacks that exploit more than one element of an XML document, for example when a value of an element implicitly contains a value that is a result of using values of two other elements.
- Back-end system attacks use extracted data from an XML document in a way that may cause improper functioning of the application, to which this data are submitted. For example, a part of extracted data can be an SQL query that exceeds planned operations by e.g. deleting and not just inserting some values in the database.

3.4.10 Smart cards

Smart cards started to penetrate the world markets in the last decade, but it took almost thirty years to see these wheels really turning. Smart cards were introduced in Japan back in 1970 and patented in Europe in 1974 [152]. Areas of applications range from identification and access control systems, through electronic payment systems, (mobile) telephony, to logistics and transport. They are becoming increasingly important also in healthcare applications, even on a nation-wide basis [195, 340].

What are smart cards? *Smart cards are standardized plastic cards with an embedded micro controller.* They are used primarily to store data securely (e.g. biometrics data, secret encryption keys) and to enable local secure computations related to these data (e.g. digital signature calculations). For secure storage and secure computation, tamper resistance of smart cards is considered to be their vital property.

These cards can be with or without contacts. For those with contacts, the main family of standards is [181], and for those without contacts, the main family of standards is [182]. Smart cards contain a central processing unit, random access memory, read only memory for storage of the card operating system, and electrically erasable and programmable read only memory for permanent storage of data. In addition, they may contain coprocessors to speed up dedicated computations, and they, of course, contain input and output systems. All card components are linked one to another with a local bus. Although smart cards are active devices, they only become operational when in contact with a reader, because the reader supplies the operating power. Cards without contacts are powered through inductive electromagnetic coupling with a reader.

One important limitation of smart cards is their processing inferiority compared to other computing devices. Being limited to a small area allows only a relatively small number of transistors to be packed into the integrated circuit. Thus, for example, desktop systems inherently have an advantage of having more processing power. This limitation turned out to be critical for smart cards when deploying asymmetric cryptography, which is computationally intensive. Luckily, efforts to reduce the complexity of asymmetric key cryptosystems resulted in elliptic curve based cryptosystems, which provide comparable strength with significantly shorter keys (see subsection 3.1.4).

For management of ISs security and privacy the positive implications are that these cards offer high protection for the most sensitive data, like private keys. In this sense, these cards are real e-business and PKI enablers. The most sensitive computations can be performed on cards. They are also mature technology with an expanding range of applications, e.g. for management of digital content rights. They are practical for use and they present a technology that users are familiar with. Further, their processing inferiority is still a factor, but less important than it used to be in the early days of their introduction. This is not only thanks to elliptic curve cryptography, but also due to Moore's law and natural limits of certain kinds of data. For example, high quality digital handling of voice requires a certain frequency of samples, where each sample takes a certain number of bits. These two factors do not need to exceed limits, defined by physiological limitations of a human ear.

An important issue with smart cards is ensuring their tamper resistance. Various counter-measures are taken into account to preserve this tamper resistance: scrambling of memory addresses, content encryption, proper positioning of memory layer within integrated circuit and inclusion of dummy components. Further, to prevent attacks based on variations of voltage or clock frequency, sensors are incorporated in the integrated circuit. Despite this, a seminal work in this area shows how these devices can be effectively attacked without requiring a lot of man-power or money [14].

Further, at the end of the nineties non-invasive attacks were discovered like simple power analysis and differential power analysis. With these techniques one can analyze power consumption of a smart card and on this basis obtain secret keys [206]. This shows that tamper resistance should not be taken for granted [261].

Smart cards are technical devices subject to various possible failures and these are not security specific in the sense of being a consequence of intentional security threats. But they are nevertheless security related - if a card chip fails, secure applications remain inoperational. To quantify these failures, reliability engineering defines a mean time between failures (MTBF) for a product. From this value it is possible to derive a failure probability, which serves to determine risk, and as such presents a constituent part of risk management.[14]

Smart cards are becoming almost a synonym for biometrics, but they present only one (although important) piece in the mosaic of each biometrics system.

3.4.11 Biometrics Based Technology

Biometric technology has been gaining momentum, especially during the last few years, due to the events of 9/11. But the fact is that this technology is still in its early stages [65].

What is biometry? Based on [65], *biometry denotes computer based authentication techniques that rely on measurable characteristics of an individual.* There are various kinds of characteristics that can be used for this purposes, e.g. face, voice, fingerprint, iris, retina, handwritten signature, and, of course, DNA. Which kind of characteristic is chosen for a particular application is a matter of requirements and trade-offs like costs vs. required accuracy, or speed of processing vs. required accuracy.

Other factors that are considered in these trade-offs include user acceptance and ease of use. Further important factors are false accept rate (FAR) and false reject rate (FRR). But we prefer to talk about crossover error rate (CER). The reason is that, for biometrics systems, FRR and FAR are interdependent. Lowering sensitivity increases false acceptance rate and decreases false rejection rate - the situation is the reverse when the sensitivity of a device is increased. The point where both rates are equal is the CER; thus systems with lower CER are better. This is clarified in Fig. 3.46.

Other important issues with biometrics technology are security of the technology itself and long-term stability. Long term stability relates to maturity of the technology, which is reflected usually in its acceptance and standardization. In some cases, a factor can also be the amount of information required to perform biometrics. For example, a finger scan requires 300 to 1200 bytes, iris

---

[14]MTBF definitions vary, thus one should rely on an accurate source like [253].

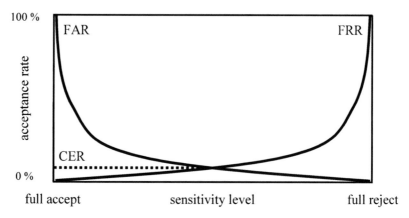

Fig. 3.46. Crossover error rate example

recognition approx. 500 bytes, face recognition 500 to 1000 bytes and voice verification 1500 bytes [115]. The table in Fig. 3.47 summarizes the major factors for some technologies that should enable better decision making about the deployment of biometrics [221].

	fingerprint	retina	iris	face	signature	voice
ease of use	high	low	medium	medium	high	high
accuracy	high	very high	very high	high	high	high
user acceptance	medium	medium	medium	medium	medium	high
security level	high	high	very high	medium	medium	medium
long-term stabiltiy	high	high	high	medium	medium	medium

Fig. 3.47. A comparison of some biometric technologies (adapted with permission from Liu S., Solverman M.: A Practical Guide to Biometric Security Technology, http://www.computer.org/itpro/homepage/Jan_Feb/security3.htm, © 2001 IEEE)

A model of a biometrics system is given in Fig. 3.48.[15] With each biometrics system raw data is first collected and then processed to extract the required features, i.e. patterns. These extracted patterns are next compared with those in a database. The system has to make a decision if these two patterns match or not. In case of a positive decision, the identity stored in the database is submitted to the application and this authenticates the entity.

---

[15]Reproduced from Biometric Technology Today, Vol 11, Issue 2, Wirtz B., Biometric system security - Part 1, pp. 6-8, ©2003, with permission from Elsevier.

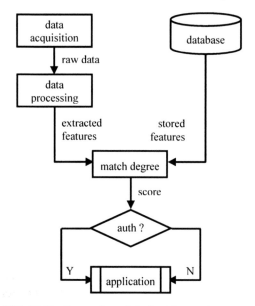

Fig. 3.48. General model of a biometric system

The model reveals an important property of biometrics systems. In essence, these systems are statistical, pattern recognition systems, thus their evaluation has to be based on statistics [358].

Briefly summarized implications for the management of ISs security and privacy are the following. The basic positive properties of biometrics technology are user friendliness, efficiency, decreasing costs for implementation and non-intrusiveness. But there are also drawbacks. Biometrics data are certainly the most sensitive kind of data regarding privacy concerns. Further, biometrics technology is far from being immune to attacks. There exist some bizarre examples of identity theft by exploiting vulnerabilities of biometrics technology shortcomings [123]:

- Face substitute was accepted by biometrics technology that was produced by capturing a person's images in motion.
- A similar experiment was successfully applied to fingerprint.
- A printed copy of an iris image was presented to biometrics system and access to protected area was granted.

Further sources of vulnerability can be identified from the model of a biometrics system. These include possible attacks on a database and associating different identity strings with biometrics data, capturing the data on the communication lines, etc. Thus a biometrics system has to be treated holistically, and should be built by taking into account security engineering approaches.

3.5 Security Services as the Basis for e-Business Processes

Many contemporary e-business services are, in their essence, cryptographic protocols, or strongly depend on them. Cryptographic protocols in turn depend on security mechanisms that include cryptographic algorithms, also called cryptographic primitives. All these elements are at the heart of e-business services, that is why so much attention is paid to them in this chapter.

This subsection will be no exception. It will concentrate on technologies that are coming to the front line as state-of-the-art technologies. The approach will be based not only on low-level insight issues, but also on a birds eye perspective of this field. Simultaneous top-down and bottom-up approaches should give a more unbiased view.

3.5.1 Electronic Payment Systems

Having a virtual digital world everywhere around us, it is logical to think about possibilities to use it for electronic payment systems. We will define *an electronic payment system as one that enables financial transactions by deploying digital technology*. Thus electronic payment systems include solutions that can exist within ordinary computer communications networks, e.g. digital money and electronic money orders. The definition is general enough to cover other payment systems like those based on mobile telephony, which is nowadays digital.

Some ten years ago this subsection would probably start with many promising words about digital money, which was just about to become a reality. Further, digital money would compensate for many undesired properties of classical money (cash) that is impractical for storage and carrying around, and that can be stolen or lost. Further, significant costs are associated with classical money to produce it, transport it, distribute it and destroy it. And further, all this should be done in a secure manner - thus the idea of digital money would be very appealing.

The first proposals for digital money appeared in the literature in the eighties [60, 61, 63, 62]. Research in this field spawned practical implementations in the first half of the nineties, when the first patents were issued. In the mid nineties, the main player on this promising market was the Dutch company DigiCash. DigiCash owned the majority of related patents at that time. In 1999 it succeeded in selling its technology to Deutsche Bank that made an operational service that was based on its e-Cash technology. However, Deutsche Bank stopped the service in 2001. In the US, e-Cash was used by the Mark Twain Bank roughly at the same time. This bank also gave up its trials soon after their beginning.

To cut a long story short, in 1998 DigiCash filed for bankruptcy. It was bought by eCash Technologies. But in 2002, eCash was bought by a provider of software and application services, called InfoSpace.

Another player on this market was First Virtual Holdings, which also left the digital money market and moved to messaging business [356]. Similar fate befell CyberCash company, another DigiCash competitor. CyberCash pulled out and was later acquired by Verisign Inc. There were some other players, but until now, no real success has been achieved with digital money.

Digital money is just one kind of electronic payment system, and there are other forms of electronic payments. Another one are the credit or debit card transaction supporting technologies. The one that gained a lot of attention in the second half of the nineties was Secure Electronic Transactions (SET) [299]. This specification was jointly developed by MasterCard and Visa in collaboration with IBM, Microsoft, RSA Laboratories, Netscape, Terisa, and Verisign. The work started in 1996 and the first specification was finished in 1997.

SET enabled various security services for plastic cards based transaction over the Web. It enabled authentication of cardholder and merchant. It also provided data integrity for orders and payment instructions. The most interesting feature was a dual signature mechanism that enabled confidentiality and non-repudiation for orders and payment instructions in a special way. Payment details and order details were bound in such a way that a merchant could see order details, but no payment details. Similarly, a bank could see payment details, but no order details. Despite this, it was not possible to claim that the payment was not related to the corresponding order and vice versa.

SET grew and its third version was almost thousand pages long. In fact, SET became over-specified, its implementations were expensive, and it also required X.509 compliant PKI. It did not really take off and at the turn of the century it was quietly dismissed.

There is another kind of electronic payment system, called micropayments, which belongs partially to the domain of digital money. Micropayments are intended as a replacement for small amounts of money. They therefore do not require high security. Logically, the more security one wants, the higher the costs. With micropayments, transaction costs have to be kept at a minimum in order for micropayment technology to be a success.

There are examples of micropayment systems, which deploy one-way hash functions using the following principle. One takes a seed and produces its hashed output. This output is hashed again, and so on, until the n-th output is generated. This n-th output is shared between a merchant and a customer and each step in the hashing chain is associated with a certain amount of money. When a customer wants to buy goods, the $(n-1)$-th output is sent to the merchant that hashes this value and compares it with the n-th output. If they match, the merchant knows that only the customer in question could produce that value. She charges the customer for an increment of money that corresponds to each step of the above protocol. Basically, this is the same idea as deployed for one-time password systems. To make such hash values more suitable for business use, the n-th iteration can be digitally signed. An example of a micropayments system that is based on this idea is PayWord [294].

However, these kinds of micropayments did not take off. Some authors claim that "micropayments are the technology of the future, and always will be." [263, 219]. But, referring to our definition of digital payment systems, this claim seems to be premature. There are micropayments systems that are really becoming accepted. They do not exist within the internet (yet), but they use a parallel channel. These systems deploy a mobile telephone network. To effect a micropayment, a user calls a certain number, which has a special charge rate, and the call lasts for the time increments needed to cover the cost. A similar approach is to use the short messaging service (SMS), where sending an SMS to a particular number charges the user's account for a certain amount of money.

In brief, the present situation is that organizations should keep an eye on micropayments. But for other financial transactions, ready-to-use solutions already exist and they have been discussed in details: S/MIME and SSL. With recent changes in national legislations, these technologies, combined with one-time password systems, are "full-blown" technologies, ready for e-business with complete legal coverage. And they can be used in ways that fall within the scope of our definition for electronic payment systems.

3.5.2 Web Services

Web services are a new approach to a decades old paradigm of distributed computing. The main difference between Web services and other approaches is that the former rely mainly on two kinds of widely accepted standards - XML for documents processing, and the internet with its Web infrastructure. For Web services this infrastructure can also be e-mail, more precisely MIME. Thus it is not easy to define Web services. Our definition will be derived from the one given in [59]: *A Web service is an XML oriented application that is available to other applications over the internet by using a predictable means for sending input and receiving a reply, if there is one.*

Because of the widespread presence and acceptance of Web infrastructure, it is likely that the Web services approach to distributed computing will be a success. Distributed computing means primarily that Web services are designed for machine-to-machine communication, and not human-to-machine interaction. The difference is essential. With ordinary use of Web, a user issues instructions directly through a browser, and drives interaction with a server by a browser that can be seen as a kind of a passive interface to resources on the Web. On the other hand, with Web services, a user can instruct the system about the desired service and provide the system with the appropriate details. The local system then autonomously searches the Web for the appropriate server, performs the necessary negotiations, executes the core task and returns the results to the user.

The glue that binds together elements of Web services is XML. XML provides a common base to clients and servers for their interactions. The machine-to-machine interaction takes place with exchange of messages, which are defined by Simple Object Access Protocol (SOAP) [362].[16] SOAP protocol uses XML messages and relies on some transfer protocol, most often Hypertext Transfer Protocol (HTTP) [119]. Therefore a SOAP/HTTP pair is a de facto couple for provision of Web services.

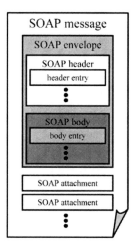

Fig. 3.49. The structure of SOAP message

The structure of SOAP message is given in Fig. 3.49 [245]. The message consists of envelope and attachments. Within the envelope, which is mandatory, there are a body and a header with zero or more entries, while the body may contain one or more entries. Thus, while the envelope and body are mandatory, the header and attachments are optional. It is worth emphasizing that SOAP does not support DTDs, but only XML schemas [245].

In the following example a temperature is measured at some distant location. At this location, all sensors are connected to a computer that reports the temperature by deploying Web services. Our example consists of two messages, the first being a request for current values, and the second response with current values. The first line of the first and the second message is an XML file declaration. In both cases, the envelope element follows next with attributes that define namespaces and aliases for more easily referencing the defined namespaces (an example of a namespace in the first message is http://schemas.xmlsoap.org/soap/envelope/, which is for the SOAP envelope, and its elements are specified by prepending them

---

[16]Gone are the days when SOAP was simple. It is also hard to claim that it deals with objects - nowadays it more frequently deals with components, which are aggregates of objects.

with alias `soap-env`). In the body part of the first messages the required method (`getLocalTemperature`) and location (`hall` with value G) are specified. The body of the second message analogously contains the method `getLocalTemperatureResponse` and a returned value 25. Attention should be paid to the total extent of both messages - all body elements are wrapped into additional declarations that are needed because of namespaces issues to prevent clashes with element names. The request is given below:

```
<?xml version="1.0" encoding="UTF-8"?>
<soap-env:Envelope
 xmlns:soap-env="http://schemas.xmlsoap.org/soap/envelope/"
 xmlns:xsd="http://www.w3.org/2001/XMLSchema">
 <soap-env:Header/>
 <soap-env:Body>
  <tns:getLocalTemperature
  xmlns:tns="urn:TemperatureMeasurement"
  soap-env:encodingStyle=
  "http://schemas.xmlsoap.org/soap/encoding/">
   <hall
   xmlns:xsi="http://www.w3.org/2001/XMLSchema-instance"
   xsi:type="xsd:string"> G </hall>
  </tns:getLocalTemperature>
 </soap-env:Body>
</soap-env:Envelope>
```

And this is the response to the above request:

```
<?xml version="1.0" encoding="UTF-8"?>
<soap-env:Envelope
 xmlns:soap-env="http://schemas.xmlsoap.org/soap/envelope/"
 xmlns:xsi="http://www.w3.org/2001/XMLSchema-instance"
 xmlns:xsd="http://www.w3.org/2001/XMLSchema">
 <soap-env:Body>
  <ns1:getLocalTemperatureResponse
  xmlns:ns1="urn:TemperatureMeasurement"
  soap-env:encodingStyle=
  "http://schemas.xmlsoap.org/soap/encoding/">
   <return xsi:type="xsd:int"> 25 </return>
  </ns1:getLocalTemperatureResponse>
 </soap-env:Body>
</soap-env:Envelope>
```

In order for SOAP to be usable in real environments, it has to support application specific data types, which is achieved with SOAP Encoding specification [362]. This specification contains encoding rules for mapping specific data types to XML elements and vice versa. Finally, XML RPC conventions must be mentioned, because they are actually what Web services are all about. These conventions specify a simple and portable way to enable calls of remote procedures (RPC stands for remote procedure call). This means the sequence and the structure of requests and responses between a client and server, where the client wants to have some service performed by a server, accessible over the Web.

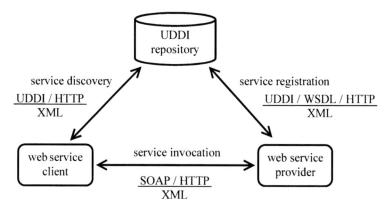

Fig. 3.50. Operational model of Web services

The complete model of Web services is given in Fig. 3.50. From this model it can be seen that SOAP is not the only key component. SOAP is actually the last step in the whole Web services deployment scenario.

Before a service is made available to the outer world, it has to be registered with some directory where it can be found by other applications. The specification that enables this description (and later support the discovery of available services) is Web Services Description Language (WSDL) [66]. WSDL is a schema based XML specification for describing Web services through operations and formats of data input and output. Moreover, WSDL provides the necessary details for binding with the actual transport protocol.

The third essential specification of Web services is Universal Description, Discovery and Integration (UDDI) [70]. This specification is concerned with operations of Web services registries. It helps to manage data about service providers and available implementations, and by means of UDDI providers can advertise their services, while consumers can find them. The exact details about a particular service, however, are provided with the WSDL document.

An example of the WSDL document is given below.[17] The first part after the XML file declaration consists of definitions, devoted to namespaces. The second part deals with the type of data, which, in our case, is intentionally represented as a complex type to show how flexibility is provided by schemas. Types define information that is sent to and received from the Web service.

---

[17]This and the following example are adapted and revised from [259].

The third part deals with description of the messages to be exchanged. The fourth part describes the port's type that gives available input and output methods (operations) - it is also wise to specify here operations for the case when input or output operations fail. The binding describes the actual transport means, which is HTTP in this case, and is specified in the fifth part. Finally, the sixth part describes the service location, i.e. the address.[18]

```
<?xml version="1.0" encoding="UTF-8"?>

<definitions name="TemperatureMeasurementServiceDefn"
 targetNamespace=
 "http://localhost:8080/soap/wsdl/TM-service.wsdl"
 xmlns="http://schemas.xmlsoap.org/wsdl/"
 xmlns:tns=
 "http://localhost:8080/soap/wsdl/TM-service.wsdl"
 xmlns:soap="http://schemas.xmlsoap.org/wsdl/soap/"
 xmlns:binding=
 "http://localhost:8080/definitions/TMRemoteInterface">

<types>
 <xsd:schema
 elementFormDefault="qualified"
 xmlns:xsd="http://www.w3.org/2001/XMLSchema">
  <xsd:element name="getLocalTemperature">
   <xsd:complexType>
    <xsd:sequence>
     <xsd:element
     minOccurs="0"
     maxOccurs="1"
     name="hall"
     type="xsd:string"/>
    </xsd:sequence>
   </xsd:complexType>
  </xsd:element>
 </xsd:schema>
</types>

<message name="getLocalTemperature">
 <part name="parameters" element="tns:getLocalTemperature"/>
</message>
<message name="getLocalTemperatureResponse">
 <part name="result" type="xsd:double"/>
</message>
```

---

[18]Where needed in this example, TM stands for TemperatureMeasurement to fit on the page.

```
<portType name="TemperatureMeasurementJavaPortType">
 <operation name="getLocalTemperature">
  <input name="getLocalTemperature"
  message="tns:getLocalTemperature"/>
  <output name="getLocalTemperatureResponse"
  message="tns:LocalTemperatureResponse"/>
 </operation>
</portType>

<binding
 name="TemperatureMeasurementBinding"
 type="tns:TemperatureMeasurementJavaPortType">
 <soap:binding
 style="rpc"
 transport="http://schemas.xmlsoap.org/soap/http"/>
 <operation name="getLocalTemperature">
  <soap:operation soapAction="" style="rpc"/>
  <input name="getLocalTemperature">
   <soap:body use="encoded"
   encodingStyle="http://schemas.xmlsoap.org/soap/encoding/"
   namespace="urn:TemperatureMeasurementInformationSystem"/>
  </input>
  <output name="getLocalTemperatureResponse">
   <soap:body
   use="encoded"
   encodingStyle="http://schemas.xmlsoap.org/soap/encoding/"
   namespace="urn:TemperatureMeasurementInformationSystem"/>
  </output>
 </operation>
</binding>

<service name="TemperatureMeasurementService">
 <documentation>
 Our temperature measurement service.
 </documentation>
 <port
  name="TemperatureMeasurementPort"
  binding="binding:TemperatureMeasurementBinding">
  <soap:address
  location="http://localhost:8080/soap/servlet/rpcrouter"/>
 </port>
</service>
</definitions>
```

To complete the Web services example, the fourth part of the mosaic has to be added. This is the UDDI file given below with fictitious codes for certain key element values (the file should be self-explanatory). By UDDI we announce the created services and enable others to find them. Note that WSDL and UDDI operations are using SOAP.[19]

```xml
<?xml version="1.0" encoding="UTF-8"?>
<businessEntity
 businessKey="00000000-1111-2222-3333-123456789abc"
 operator="www.somews.com/services/uddi"
 authorizedName="ABCDEFGHIJ">
<discoveryURLs>
 <discoveryURL useType="businessEntity">
 http://www.somews.com/services/uddi/uddiget?businessKey=BK
 </discoveryURL>
</discoveryURLs>
<name>XMethods</name>
<description xml:lang="en">
 Some-WS Web services provider
</description>
<contacts>
 <contact>
  <personName>Sam Johnson</personName>
  <email>samj@somews.com</email>
 </contact>
</contacts>
<businessServices>
 <businessService
 serviceKey="444abcde-5555-6666-7777-123456789abc"
 businessKey="00000000-1111-2222-3333-123456789abc">
  <name>Remote Temparature Meassurements Reports</name>
  <bindingTemplates>
   <bindingTemplate
   bindingKey="444abcde-5555-6666-7777-123456789abc"
   serviceKey="444aaaaa-5555-6666-7777-123456789abc">
    <description xml:lang="en">
    WS Based Remote Temperature Meassurements Reports
    </description>
    <accessPoint URLType="http">
    http://services.somews.com:80/soap
    </accessPoint>
    <tModelInstanceDetails>
     <tModelInstanceInfo
```

---

[19]Where   needed   in   this   example,   BK   stands   for
00000000-1111-2222-3333-123456789abc to fit on the page.

```
    tModelKey="uuid:D9ABBD80-E120-6666-7777-123456789abc"/>
    </tModelInstanceDetails>
   </bindingTemplate>
  </bindingTemplates>
 </businessService>
</businessServices>
</businessEntity>
```

By now the service has been created, described, and offered within XML world. Putting all these pieces into operation requires some programming with languages like Java, C++, or PHP. There is no need to explore further the programming details in order to understand the functionality of Web services. Because this book is not about manipulation of bits and bytes, the above explanation should be sufficient.

If an organization wants to provide Web services, the most straightforward approach is to use a Web server, which has some additional components that enable Web services operations. Through these components the server is locally linked with business applications that perform the actual service, while the server acts as a front-end system towards the outer world. It translates Web-services requests to local ones and results of local operations back to the Web services world. The question that now arises is: "What about security?"

In order to get security things right, Microsoft, VeriSign and IBM jointly developed a new framework called WS-Security, and the first basic standard in this framework is [205]. The framework that has been handed over to OASIS provides the means whereby various security protocols and models can fit in to provide security: authentication, authorization, multiple trust domains, and end-to-end message security. Put another way, WS-Security is a specification that describes how to secure Web services by adding extensions to SOAP documents that enable combinations of encryption and signing. WS-Security depends on XML security standards, i.e. XML Signature, XML Encryption, and the yet to be born XKMS standard.

But WS-Security goes further with Security Assertion Markup Language (SAML) [52], which provides an XML-based framework[20] for exchange of security relevant data, with emphasis on authentication and authorization. SAML does not mandate or build on a particular implementation of authentication or authorization. It enables a standardized exchange of relevant data so that the actual implementations can openly exchange this data across various security domains. This would, for example, support single sign-on implementations. When accessing resources over the network, the security details are handled automatically without the need for additional signing, which is also the goal of the authentication and authorization infrastructure efforts, mentioned earlier in this chapter.

---

[20]Saying framework usually implies a set of standards, which is also the case with SAML, so [155] is just one of them, being the most relevant within the current context.

Descriptions of documents are not enough, thus the family of WS-Security standards also addresses mapping of SAML message to the actual transfer protocol and security considerations for SAML itself [155].

Finally, WS-Security family includes XML Access Control Markup Language (XACML) [242]. This XML based extension is used to express access control policies for Web services and is a complement to SAML. SAML is more communication oriented, while XACML is a security policy description that is handled back and forth over the network through SAML.

Instead of looking at security issues from Web-services out, it is worthwhile changing the point of view and looking at them from outside in. Firstly, WS-Security is a very recent framework. It is based on another framework, XML Security, which is also recent. Further, XML Security is not complete as far as key management is concerned. But XKMS is complemented by PKI, which has been around for more than a decade, and many issues remain unresolved. Furthermore, XML and WS-Security include numerous complex interactions, enhanced with cryptographic primitives. But cryptographic protocols (what in essence we are dealing here with) are prone to errors even in their simplest forms. Many cryptographic protocols were known for decades before flaws were discovered, some of them being standardized and found to be flawed afterwards. The antidote for such cases are formal methods, discussed in the appendix. Some authors claim that Web services remain inherently insecure, because they rely on SOAP protocol that was not designed with security in mind [205]. Moreover, security services mainly use HTTP port, which passes through firewalls. Therefore these service requests are allowed to get into the heart of organization's IS and start various services there. Accordingly, threats include unauthorized access, network eavesdropping, disclosure of configuration data, message replays and parameter manipulation [205].

In brief, what are the implications for management of ISs security and privacy? Firstly, organizations should be conservative. Only the smallest part of IS should be opened to offer the absolutely necessary set of Web services. And this should be done after a careful risk analysis that will make proper risk management attitude more likely. Secondly, organizations should not be over-conservative, as they may miss an important opportunity. A recent case of SSL is very descriptive.

The essential part of every SSL based transaction is the ability to check the certificate against the CA's CRL. The author of this book conducted a survey of internet banking services security at the end of 2001. Among others, it was not possible to obtain CRLs of two biggest European banks. Today, this is usually possible, but only experienced users are aware of the fact that CRLs have to be checked. In cases when this test fails to be done automatically, one should know what certificate extensions mean to manually download CRLs and check the certificate. Without these checks (including checks of fields in a certificate), using SSL means using it in a handicapped way that can hardly be considered as proper for internet banking. Yet internet banking based on SSL has gained a wide acceptance during recent years, because it enables lower operating costs for the banks, while offering flexibility to users. Can one imagine the destiny of a bank that is still waiting for PKI issues to be sorted out before entering internet banking services?

3.6 Privacy Enabling Technologies

Privacy is such an important category that it is seen as one of the key-stones of civilizations. Some authors even claim that a society cannot function without it [76].

Assuring privacy is a two stage process: The first step is the awareness of users that they have to pay attention to privacy. The second step is that there have to exist means that enable them to protect and control data about themselves. Appropriate means are of a technological and legislative nature. The legislation view will be covered in the fourth chapter, while we will concentrate on technology in this chapter.

Privacy in this case is assured through deployment of security services and mechanisms. Their principles of operation have already been described. It is just another field of application, but tools of the trade remain the same, be it IPSec, S/MIME, intrusion detection systems (including anti-virus and spyware detectors), SSL, firewalls, or some XML based application. These technologies can provide privacy in the following ways:

- IPSec can provide confidentiality at the network level against attacks from intermediate nodes. However, at the other end of IPSec connection, the identity of the originating party is disclosed as well as content of communication. So if one wants to remain anonymous to the peer communicating party, IPSec alone is not the answer.
- SSL sits on top of TCP and is a common security layer for all applications, similar to IPSec. Thus, in principle, it hides the identity of a user of an application on the network, but again not from the peer communicating party. In contrast to IPSec, the disclosure of identity of a machine (IP number) cannot be prevented.
- The same holds true for S/MIME with notable difference that S/MIME also discloses an e-mail sender's identity. E-mail headers have to remain readable to be delivered to the other party, so that the traffic flow analysis at least can be performed (who communicates with whom at which time). Of course, it is assumed that the content in this case is encrypted.
- Firewalls can perform NAT function and thus protect network level identity, similarly to tunneling mode of IPSec. Furthermore, they prevent unauthorized access to local computers and thus leakage of sensitive data.
- Anti-virus and anti-spy software are complements to the above technologies, because they ensure privacy by detecting injected code that can reveal privacy related data.

There are some specific issues that have to be covered where privacy is concerned. Starting from scratch, one already knows that each device in a network has its unique identification - in internet, this is the IP number. Further, computers are grouped into domains, which imply organizational or geographical relationships associated with a certain computer. Identification of a computer through domain names is more user friendly than through IP numbers. It is much easier to remember identifier like `www.springeronline.de` compared to identifier like `62.156.147.57`. But computers can only use numbers, therefore translation between domain names and IP numbers has to be provided. This is the task of Domain Name System (DNS) [241], and through this system a lot of data can be collected about a computer. Further, each user at a certain computer has a unique system identification, and through log files every communication can, in principle, be traced back to the originating system and originating user at the local system. Computers can log virtually all activities that take place on them.

To prevent IP number and DNS based tracking of activities, proxies and firewalls can be used. As already described, these devices initiate a new connection on behalf of its users. Thus the original IP number is not disclosed to the outside world, ensuring network level anonymity. In addition to network level anonymity, application level anonymizers exist for e-mail and Web browsers. For e-mails, the easiest way is to register a bogus username with no link to real identity at some free e-mail service provider. Another option relies on remailers that re-pack an e-mail in a way that does not disclose true identity, and transmits it to the final recipient. This is the principle of using an intermediate server (proxy) that hides the originating party, and which is also used to support anonymous Web surfing.

To enable more effective Web communication, cookies are used. In case of HTTP protocol, which is stateless, cookies are needed to keep track of previous interactions to make communication more effective. They may contain various kinds of information, most often related to recent activities at a certain site, e.g. Web-pages visited, time spent there, personal information submitted to the servers, passwords used, etc. Although cookies enable better interactivity and customization, they can easily be exploited to violate users privacy. Therefore they should be disabled by users. But this may lead to situation where a requested service will be unavailable, because accepting cookies may be required by a server. Thus cookies should be regularly cleaned from a computer with software tools.

There have also been some efforts to standardize privacy enabling technologies within W3C. The result of these efforts is a specification called Platform for Privacy Preferences (P3P) [80]. This specification is intended to support privacy in P3P agents ensuring the following principles: information privacy, choice and control, fairness and integrity, and security [190]. Briefly, P3P provides an automated means for users to control their personal information when surfing the Web. It standardizes a set of questions that address privacy policies of Web sites. P3P compliant sites provide this information in a machine-readable form, and a browser (agent) can automatically decide what to do on the basis of user selected preferences. P3P is already included in the latest versions of the most popular browsers.

Besides the pioneering W3C efforts, some other endeavors in this field should be mentioned: the Roadmap for Privacy Incorporated Software Agent (PISA) [276] and project GUIDES [187]. GUIDES was aimed at specifying guidelines, i.e. best practices to assure privacy, by deploying privacy enhancing technologies in line with relevant EU directives. PISA, on the other hand, is a more technology oriented project aimed at developing privacy supporting solutions for intelligent agents.

What does all this say about personal privacy? It is important to change one's state of mind and pay attention to privacy. The above mentioned tools should be deployed to protect one's privacy while using computer communications. Further, one should think about encryption of all the data that reside on the local hard disk (and back-ups). This functionality is now available in many operating systems by default. Thus even in case when one's computer gets physically stolen, one is fairly safe. The necessary tools exist, so by far most important act is for users actually to pay attention to privacy.

3.7 A Different Paradigm - Wireless Networking

Wireless issues were intentionally left until the end of this chapter. Not only due to the fact that wireless computing is a rather recent paradigm, but it is also very different from the wired computing with regards to security. What are wireless communications? *Wireless communications are the process of communicating information in electro-magnetic media over a distance through a free-space environment* [269].

Wireless data, carried by electromagnetic radiation, can be intercepted by an attacker in a much larger space than with ordinary networks, where access to wires has to exist. Electromagnetic radiation can be focused, but this still requires an incomparably larger space to be controlled than within a wired environment. A large portion of wireless communications takes place in the radio-frequency (RF) part of the electromagnetic spectrum. Thus to catch a passive attacker in the act is like having to catch a listener to a radio station. But things change if an attacker starts transmitting. In this case data packets are sent, which results in electromagnetic emission from attacker's device and makes the discovery easier (provided that the attacker does this for sufficiently long time).

Further, wireless products have to be portable and thus smaller, which results in limited space for implementation of a processing device and its power consumption. Therefore cellular phones, personal digital assistants and all other mobile devices remain inferior to other computing devices in the network (this should remind the reader of smart cards).

Summing up, widespread radiation and limited space due to dimensions of portable devices are factors that make wireless devices inherently less secure than their wired counterparts [258]. These facts are essential for security related issues.

Wireless communications is actually a term that covers two traditional paradigms. The first is ordinary voice telephony, the other one is computer communications. Voice telephony moved to wireless by using analog technology in the beginning of eighties.[21] This is referred to as first generation (1G) wireless communication technology, and a European representative was Nordic Mobile Telephony (NMT). The second generation (2G) of mobile telephony was already partially digital with the most outstanding standard being Global System for Mobile Communications (GSM). This technology was upgraded into pre-third generation (pre-3G) technology, with a representative being General Packet Radio Service (GPRS). Currently, upgrades into full 3G technologies are taking place with a typical technology in Europe being Universal Mobile Telecommunications System (UMTS) [285].

Before getting into security details, the concept of switching has to be discussed. When a connection between a sender and receiver is established, some kind of switching has to be deployed. Two types of switching technologies are circuit switching technology and packet switching technology. With circuit switched technology, a physical circuit is established between communicating parties and cannot be shared with other parties during communication. A fixed data rate is dedicated to a particular communication channel, whether this channel is used or not. With packet switched technology, the same wires are shared among many parties during communication. Data in this case is fragmented and packed into packets that simultaneously use the transmission medium. Based on addresses, data packets are routed as required from sender to receiver, where they are reassembled and delivered. This enables better utilization of available data rate for the majority of applications, which is proven by the success of Internet technology that is based on packet switching. Packet switching is tied to digital technology.

What are the main characteristics of the above wireless telephony evolution? The oldest, 1G technology was purely analog, with low capacity of channels, and was circuit switched. The next generation, 2G, already introduced a large proportion of digitalization. Bandwidth was increased, and the process is continuing with 3G. The 3G systems are becoming fully digital, with packet switching being a norm, with larger data transfer rates and ready for IP core [285]. Once data are treated completely digitally, there is no need to think in terms of mobile telephony. In such networks not only voice, but any

---

[21] Mobile telephony is also referred to as cellular telephony, because base stations transmit low-power signals that cover regions, which are typically of a few kilometers in diameter (this also depends on the frequency). Each cell is covered with a certain frequency, and the layout of these cells is such that it enables reuse of the same frequencies in non-adjacent cells. This prevents interference and better utilization of electromagnetic spectrum.

kind of data can be transferred, thus this network is functioning essentially as a computer network.

So IP is also here to stay in the cellular world, which is getting integrated with its sister paradigm - wireless local area networks (WLANs). WLANs are originally IP based and their operations are similar to cellular telephony. The exception is that they use higher frequencies in the RF part of spectrum, and also in the infrared (IR). Higher frequencies make the space propagation much more limited (smaller cells) than with mobile telephony.

The difference between the wired and the wireless paradigms has important implications for management of ISs security and privacy. The main differences are concentrated at the medium access level. And because of them, wireless has many advantages, but remains inherently more vulnerable from the security point of view than wired networks.

Wireless communications are exposed to eavesdropping, unauthorized access, interference and jamming [258]. With cryptography, eavesdropping and unauthorized access can be prevented. IEEE 802.11 standards [332], which are the basic WLAN standards, addressed security with Wired Equivalent Privacy (WEP) protocol. Not long after its specification, WEP was broken. There are already WEP replacement initiatives underway like WiFi Protected Access (WPA) [255, 289] - when they are available, they should be deployed. Physical layer access security can be further improved by registering physical addresses[22] of all devices that are allowed to use wireless access points. From the network level up, wireless networks can be treated as ordinary TCP/IP networks. Thus a golden arsenal of weapons like IPSec and SSL should be applied to compensate for possible flaws at the physical and link layer, or to complement future enhancements there. Further, monitoring of rogue stations should be performed in real-time to discover intruder's stations or access points. It is important to know that WLANs can be attacked, leaving very little forensic evidence. Last but not least, local area networks are becoming interconnected via satellites to complement existing terrestrial public access networks in remote regions [16].

Taking into account all the above mentioned concerns, it is common to put wireless access points outside the organization's firewall [143].

*   *   *

There is nothing that can replace hands-on experiences. Thus employees should have a possibility to learn techniques of attackers in as realistic way as possible. Because operational environments cannot serve for such purposes, it is becoming a common practice for organizations to set-up so-called honeynets. These serve as a playground to watch attackers in action and learn their tactics. An extensive overview of such approach for a nation-wide network is given in [291].

---

[22]Besides IP address, each device has also a unique physical address - IP address identifies an entity at the network layer, physical address at medium access layer.

4

Legal Aspects of ISs Security and Privacy

Ignorantia legis neminem excusat.[1]

Without a doubt, legislation related to ISs security and privacy is becoming very broad and detailed. But being unfamiliar with it does not absolve ISs users from their actions and gives (almost) no protection from being sued in case of illegal activities (of course, when being subject of a lawsuit, the final judgement is based on one's intentions and the actual damage caused). But it is far better to avoid troubles by anticipating them, and by minimizing their impact if (and when) they occur. This requires at least basic familiarity with this field.

Getting an insight into the historical evolution of a field enables to better understand the current situation and to predict future trends. Such approach will be used in this chapter. It should be emphasized that this chapter is not intended to provide all the details in this area. Rather, it presents an evolutionary view in order to understand the driving forces and the levers in the background, and to enable the reader to be oriented appropriately in a particular situation. Last but not least, we will not deal with practices that a common-sense person would avoid, e.g. misuse of systems (unauthorized penetration into systems, making them inoperational), dissemination of illegal content (hosting child pornography, posting racist messages), etc. The chapter concentrates on more sophisticated legal issues that are not transparent to many ISs managers, not to mention ordinary users.

4.1 Cryptography in General

Cryptography can be used in many ways - the algorithm can serve for completely different purposes. This is best understood through the concept of security services. The average user first thinks of confidentiality when discussing ISs security and privacy, but there are other important applications.

---

[1]Ignorance of the law is no excuse.

These are, for example, authentication and digital signatures. While the latter two are usually treated quite similarly in various legislations, this is not the case with confidentiality. When confidentiality becomes a subject of discussion, a major confrontation between privacy issues, national security and business policies appears. This has resulted in two typical approaches - on one hand we are facing key escrow efforts, while on the other we are facing controls with limits on cryptography use and import or export.

A historical overview of this field will be given first [7]. Export controls of cryptography were internationally covered for the first time in the Coordinating Committee for Multilateral Export Controls (COCOM) that was established in 1949. COCOM maintained international munitions lists and international industrial lists, in which crypto products were included.[2] In 1991 COCOM relaxed its restrictions on cryptography export by allowing export of mass-market and public domain crypto products. But the US decided to stick with their own policy, which was more restrictive. In 1995 COCOM was succeeded by the Wassenar Arrangement and its Export Controls for Conventional Arms and Dual-use[3] Goods and Technologies. This agreement was signed in 1996 by 31 countries.[4] Basically following the COCOM heritage, the Wassenar Arrangement brought two further revisions. Free to export were symmetric key products with key length up to 56 bits, asymmetric with key length up to 512 bits, and subgroup based systems with keys up to 112 bits. Mass market crypto products, along with public domain products, were free for export.

An additional international framework for cryptography regulation was set up by the Organization for Economic Co-operation and Development (OECD), stimulated by the fact that cryptography had become a common practice in the business environment. In 1997 OECD announced its Cryptography Guidelines [264]. These guidelines support privacy. They reject key escrow approaches, although cryptography policies may allow lawful access to plaintext, or cryptographic keys of encrypted data. Additionally, it is required that cryptographic methods should be trustworthy to generate confidence, and that they should be developed in response to the needs, demands and responsibilities of users and governments. Users should have the right to choose any cryptographic method, subject to applicable law. Further, the liability of individuals and entities that offer cryptographic services, or hold or access cryptographic keys, should be clearly stated. Finally, criteria for related methods should be developed on the national and international level.

---

[2]COCOM consisted of 17 permanent members, Australia, Belgium, Canada, Denmark, France, Germany, Greece, Italy, Japan, Luxembourg, Netherlands, Norway, Portugal, Spain, Turkey, UK and USA.

[3]Dual use refers to military and civil use.

[4]Argentina, Australia, Austria, Belgium, Canada, Czech Republic, Denmark, Finland, France, Germany, Greece, Hungary, Ireland, Italy, Japan, Luxembourg, Netherlands, New Zealand, Norway, South Korea, Poland, Portugal, Romania, Russian Federation, Spain, Sweden, Switzerland, Turkey, UK, Ukraine and USA.

All these are only guidelines, not a must for actual national implementation. Moreover, the above guidelines are of a general nature and deal only partially with many important issues. In case of the Wassenaar Arrangement, only export controls are addressed, while in national legislation additional restrictions may exist. For example, there are import restrictions in Russian Federation, restricted development and commercialization of crypto products in Russian Federation and China, etc. [7].

Going back to the Wassenaar Arrangement it has to be added that US (supported by the UK) failed in 1998 to enforce key-escrow solutions. This is probably one important point where their position in favor of strong regulation of cryptography started to melt. This relaxed treatment was additionally influenced by a booming digital economy and strong civil resistance. The first liberal changes in US crypto regulations were made in 1996, when crypto products were no longer considered as munitions, and thus fell under the supervision of the Department of Commerce. The explicit exceptions for any export were Cuba, Iran, Iraq, Libya, North Korea, Sudan and Syria. New changes followed in 1998 with further relaxed export regulations for 45 countries (a so-called financial list). They allowed export of any key length if used in client-server architecture for on-line merchandize, elimination of key recovery requirements, etc.[5] The additional relaxation took place in the year 2000 [334]:

- Any cryptography, without key length limitations, could be exported under a license exception, after a technical review, to non-government end users in any country except Cuba, Iran, Iraq, Libya, North Korea, Sudan and Syria. Exports to governments required a license.
- Under a license exception, retail encryption products of any key length could be exported to any recipient in any country except to Cuba, Iran, Iraq, Libya, North Korea, Sudan and Syria.
- After a technical review, export of 56 bit products and 64 bit products was allowed if products met the mass-market requirement of the Wassenaar Arrangement. After being exported, reporting was necessary for any product with keys above 64 bits (this allowed a reduction of the licensing requirements and assured compliance with the regulations).
- Non-US citizens no longer needed licenses to work for US companies on encryption, while any cryptography could be exported to foreign branches of US companies without technical review.
- Source code (public domain code and publicly available commercial code) could be exported to any end-user under a license exception without a technical review. The exception countries were, again, Cuba, Iran, Iraq, Libya, North Korea, Sudan and Syria.

---

[5]Key recovery may be very useful in commercial environments, therefore research in this area is still quite intensive [135].

In the EU, the main legal activities that followed the Waasenaar Arrangement can be summarized as follows [106, 107, 109, 334]:

- The transit of dual-use items was liberalized within the EU. The exceptions were sensitive products such as cryptanalytic software.
- Export of dual-use products to Australia, Canada, Czech Republic, Hungary, Japan, New Zealand, Norway, Poland, Switzerland and the US was subject to Community general export authorization.[6]
- Mass-market cryptography could be exported without key-length limitations.
- Export to other countries required an individual authorization, granted by the Member State in which the exporter was established, and valid for a particular country only.
- A Member State could establish further controls on export of dual-use items for reasons of public security or human rights.

The general trend in the field of cryptography is towards liberalization. Nevertheless, organizations should be cautious and evaluate situations on a case by case basis. For this purpose a quality and up-to-date on-line survey of cryptographic legislation can be found at [207].

4.2 Digital Signatures

In the field of digital signatures, the United Nations Commission on International Trade Law (UNCITRAL) defined an international framework for the derivation of national implementations in 1996. More precisely, UNCITRAL adopted model laws for electronic commerce and electronic signatures [346, 347]. Many countries have already defined their national legislation and implementations are often based on these model laws.

EU set up a general framework in 2000. This framework states the following basic principles [108, 334]:

- Legal recognition of electronic signatures, which means that an electronic signature cannot be legally opposed solely because of being in electronic form.
- Free circulation of all products and services related to electronic signatures, which are only subject to the legislation and control by the country of origin.
- Supply of digital certificates to the public for identification of communicating entities.
- Liability of certificate issuers for the validity of a certificate's content.
- Legal recognition of electronic signatures irrespective of the technology used.

---

[6]Recent enlargement of the EU has certainly affected this decision.

- Promotion of global e-commerce through mechanisms for cooperation with third countries on the basis of mutual recognition of certificates.

The area of digital signatures is still changing for many reasons, e.g. current legislation may be overly dependent on technology, or new general practices are being introduced, like free market competition between providers of CA services. A comprehensive reference to relevant legislation, [20], includes international directives, enacted and pending regulation with summaries, and related resources. Another quality reference, i.e. an extensive survey about digital signatures, can be found on-line [354].

4.3 Privacy Issues

Security services present technical means for enabling and supporting privacy. Clearly, these services alone are not sufficient, and the additional, complementary support of legislation is needed.

There is a quite strong consensus among cryptography experts that limitations on the use of cryptography should be banned (see e.g. [295, 308]). These views are also supported by various organizations in the field of privacy rights on the internet, e.g. Electronic Privacy Information Center (EPIC) and Electronic Frontiers Foundation (EFF).[7] It is common to all these activities that regulating cryptography is not an appropriate answer to security concerns, but is primarily an endangerment of rights of individuals [7].

A notable difference exists between US and EU in the field of privacy. In contrast to US, EU considers privacy not to be an interest, but a fundamental, inalienable right [27]. This has roots in the European Convention for the Protection of Human Rights and Fundamental Freedoms, where the right to privacy is explicitly stated. Not surprisingly, this is another consequence of World War II. Later, the evolution of interpretation of this statement resulted in its application to state-to-individual as well as individual-to-individual relations. Moreover, the modern understanding of privacy refers not only to negative obligations, but also positive ones, which means that resources have to be provided so the individuals can effect privacy rights [27].

The EU Commission has been working on privacy issues since the late eighties. Its work was backed by OECD Guidelines on the Protection of Privacy and Transborder Flows of Personal Data from 1980 (these guidelines were signed by European countries and the US) [237, 265]. Its work was additionally backed by the Council of Europe Recommendations on the Protection of Personal Data Used for Employment Purposes from 1989 [78]. In 1995, EU enacted the Directive 95/64/EC, called also the Data Protection Directive

---

[7]An extensive list of such organizations can be found on-line at http://www1.umn.edu/humanrts/links/internet.html.

(DPD) [104]. This directive became effective in 1998 and established a framework for protection of individuals with regard to manipulation of personal data.

In DPD, *personal data are defined as any information relating to an identified or identifiable person (data subject).* This includes direct and indirect identification by referencing one or more factors that include physical, physiological, mental, economic, cultural or social identity. Regarding the processing of personal data, this includes any operation or set of operations which is performed upon personal data, be it automated or not. Further, the DPD introduces the notion of *data controller, which is a natural or legal person, public authority, agency or other body which alone or jointly determines the purposes and means of the processing of personal data.* Another notion is *data processor, which is an entity that carries out the processing on behalf of the controller.* This clearly identifies the responsible entity in personal data processing.

Some important obligations imposed by the DPD are:

- Organizations must inform individuals about the purposes of collecting and using data about them.
- For sensitive data like racial or ethnical roots, medical status, etc., individuals must give an explicit consent to collect such data.
- Organizations must offer individuals the opportunity to opt out if use of their data differs from the one planned.
- Each organization must take reasonable steps to ensure security and integrity of personal data, while the data may be conserved only for a limited period of time.[8]
- Individuals must have access to their personal data, and be able to correct it.
- There exists liability for damages caused by misuse of data.
- Personal data of EU citizens may be transferred only to those countries that provide adequate protection for the data.[9]

The last requirement led to confrontation with the US. As US have no general data protection laws, it is not allowed to transfer EU citizens' data to the US. US, with the exception of some particular laws, relies on self-regulation and limited legislation. US legislation is fragmented, it is a kind of "patchwork legislation".[10] There are examples of privacy federal laws in the commercial sector that are about cable TV and video store records [324], while in the

---

[8]Leaving confidential personal data on disposed computers may lead to prosecution under the DPD [153].

[9]In many legal documents adequate security is mentioned. This may sound clear at the first glance, but the reality is that semantics of this word is very dependent on the context of application [49].

[10]This holds true for the private sector, while there is a privacy statute that applies generally to the federal government [228].

health care sector there is the Health Insurance Portability and Accountability Act from 1996 [153]. Additionally, the US Federal Trade Commission produced in 1998 fair practices for commercial Web services that collect users' data where the following is proposed [324]:

- organizations should use clear notices about collecting data and what this data is used for;
- users should be enabled to choose whether data can be used beyond the purpose for which it was provided;
- users should be given access to data about them, so that they can correct them or even delete them;
- organizations should use security measures for handling collected data.

It is thus evident why confrontation between US and EU appeared in the field of data privacy. To resolve it, US and EU started negotiations and reached a so-called Safe Harbor Arrangement in the year 2000. This arrangement enabled US companies doing business in EU to accept a code of business practices that basically leads to conformance with the EU Directive. However, sanctions are based on the US principle - if a company does not adhere to this agreement, it will be subject to prosecution because of deceptive business practices. Safe Harbor does not seem to resolve this dispute. It imposes additional costs on organizations, and US companies often see it as an unfair practice because it protects EU customers to a higher degree than US ones. There are certainly additional reasons, but the bottom line is that very few US companies have joined the agreement.

It is interesting to note that EU style legislation is becoming the preferred international standard [228].

4.3.1 Privacy and Electronic Communications

Privacy issues were further elaborated because of specifics dictated by technology. In 1998, OECD updated its Privacy Guidelines by adding an emphasis on the internet with inclusion of the following principles [265]:

- transparency regarding the collection of personal data, which requires informing people when data about them are being collected - such example are cookies, where users are usually not aware of their exchange;
- transparency regarding the use of personal data, which implies allowing people to prevent spamming and prevent the use of information about them, e.g. data-mining;
- control of personal data and access to these data by the individual, which requires enabling people to check the accuracy of consumer data and to restrict their transfer, sale or distribution.

Additional directives were also enacted by the EU. The first was Telecommunications Data Protection Directive 97/66 [105], which was later replaced and extended by Privacy and Electronic Communications Directive 02/58 [111]. Some important IT specific issues in this directive are:

- If necessary and legally authorized, communications can be recorded to serve as evidence of a commercial transaction, but parties should be informed about this in advance. Recordings should be erased by the end of the period during which the transaction can be lawfully challenged.
- Entering data into users' computers like cookies and spyware should be allowed only for legitimate purposes and with their knowledge. Users should have the possibility to refuse such mechanisms.
- The data relating to subscribers (processed within electronic communications networks to establish connections and to transmit information) may only be stored to the necessary extent for the provision of the service, and for a limited time.
- Owners of directories of services subscribers should inform the subscribers about inclusion of their data, and about the purposes of the directory.
- Unsolicited communications for direct marketing purposes by means of faxes, e-mails, SMS messages, etc. is allowed only with the prior and explicit consent of the recipients.

4.3.2 Workplace Privacy

In 1997, the International Labor Organization (ILO) adopted a Code of Practice on the Protection of Workers' Personal Data [166]. This code defines fair information practices for public and private sector employees. Some most important requirements are the following:

- employees should receive a notice on data collection processes, which should be collected only from the employee and used lawfully and fairly;
- employers should collect and use the minimum necessary data required for employment, and only for the purposes for which the data were originally collected;
- all data should be held securely and workers should have access to data;
- the data should not be transferred to third parties without consent, except to comply with a legal requirement;
- data such as sex life, political and religious beliefs should not be collected, while medical data are confidential;
- certain collection techniques, such as polygraph testing, should be prohibited;
- all data should be held securely and workers cannot waive their privacy rights.

Workplace privacy legislation in a particular state is, of course, tied to the rest of the relevant national privacy legislation. Therefore workers in the US have few privacy protections - as a minimum standard, they can count on a reasonable expectation of privacy. Based on what has been said in the previous subsection, one can expect quite a different situation in the EU - employees are well protected by data protection legislation.

However, translation of these directives to workplace conditions is not a straightforward task. An interesting case can be seen in the UK [318]. In 2003, the UK Information Commissioner published a Code of Practice for the use of personal data obtained by employers as a result of workplace monitoring. The Code recognizes that employers have a primary obligation to comply with the Data Protection Act (DPA).[11] The DPA distinguishes between two types of monitoring, systematic and occasional, where the former type of monitoring is likely to be the most problematic. Next, the key to compliant monitoring is the implementation of an impact assessment procedure, where a study of negative impacts and consideration of alternatives should be done. According to the basic principles of the Code, workers have legitimate expectations about keeping their personal lives private. If employers wish to monitor them, they should clearly state the purpose and benefits. Last, but not least, workers should be informed about the nature, extent and reasons for monitoring. Finally, the Code includes a number of good practice recommendations. But business interests succeeded in Parliament's passing of the Lawful Business Practice Regulations. These Regulations enable employers to bypass employees' privacy rights for commercial purposes.

An extensive coverage of workplace privacy at the international level can be found in [101].

4.3.3 Spamming

Spamming is referring to receiving unsolicited (mostly commercial) e-mail and has become a real concern for internet users during the last years. Spammers usually use open SMTP relays, proxy servers and free commercial Web based e-mail services. The imagination of spammers is almost unlimited and it is not hard to anticipate use of viruses to set up proxy servers for spamming [327]. But spamming is not limited to e-mails only. It also uses other means of electronic communications like faxes and SMS messages.

Besides technology based counter-measures, legislative basis is essential to stop spamming. The basis against spamming in the EU was established in 2002 by the EC Privacy and Electronic Communications Directive [111]. This directive addresses spamming for all kinds of electronic communications. A soft opt in applies to e-mail in case of an existing customer relationship. Corporate subscribers are not protected, even if the marketing is directed at individuals within organizations. But using e-mail for direct marketing, where the identity or address of the sender is disguised or concealed, is strictly prohibited [148].

US has recently adopted similar anti-spam steps with the Controlling the Assault of Non-Solicited Pornography and Marketing Act [353]. This act,

---

[11]DPA is a UK implementation of the EU DPD.

which took effect in January 2004, requires labeling of unsolicited commercial e-mail messages, inclusion of opt-out instructions, and the sender's physical address. Further, it prohibits deceptive subject lines and false headers in messages. Last but not least, the Federal Trade Commission is authorized to establish a registry of users that want to be excluded from spamming [353].

4.3.4 Electronic Tracking Technologies

Electronic tracking devices include primarily cookies and spyware. Cookies enable effective implementation of World Wide Web sessions, because its protocol (i.e. HTTP) is connectionless. Besides, they are usually used to gather statistics on the Web and to access behavior patterns of Web users. However, spyware and cookies (usually) operate in the background and remain invisible to users, who are therefore unaware of monitoring. This places serious concerns on privacy.

EU legislation addresses electronic tracking technologies in EC Privacy and Electronic Communications Directive [111]. Their use is prohibited unless the user opts in. When submitting cookies for the first time, clear and comprehensive information about the purpose of their use must be provided. The exception is when cookies are used strictly to enable transmission of the Web site or other content, which cannot be provided without it [148].

US legislation is also addressing these issues. According to [54], several initiatives exist that would establish civil penalties for using deceptive software practices. Some of them even propose prison sentences of up to five years for certain spyware-related crimes. It is likely that US will establish relevant legislation in the very near future.

4.3.5 Identity Theft

With regard to privacy, identity theft is becoming a real concern. In the US it is expected that 500,000 to 700,000 Americans become its victims every year [154]. This issue has very tangible consequences that are primarily related to credit card fraudulent usage.

Users themselves should care about data in the first place. Whenever disclosing sensitive personal information, one should know to whom it is disclosed, for what purpose, and how it will be protected (especially in terms of confidentiality). Further, as personal computers enable financial transactions, people should treat them not only as a kind of identification device, but also as electronic wallets. Thus users should protect computers accordingly, and detailed recommendations, given by McAffee, can be found in [154].

4.4 ISs and Software Liability

The increasingly important issues of security and privacy are resulting in emphasized liability with regard to manufacturing, and not only administering and using ISs in appropriate, security and privacy assuring ways. One of the most problematic pieces in the liability mosaic is software. It is a fact that security flaws exist in software, and these flaws are cured with patches, installation of additional software like anti-virus products, and use of firewalls.

Efforts for improved ISs security and privacy have resulted in the situation where "the issue of liability is lurking beneath the surface and is waiting to be addressed" [234]. But liability is a chained category and is usually attributed to software producers. Of course, an important part of it goes on the account of software producers, especially as "any smart software producer will talk big about security but do as little as possible, because that is what makes most economic sense" [309].

Nevertheless, there is a chain of responsibility, which starts with software producers, continues with those who have to properly install and maintain it, and ends with those that have to use it properly. In other cases, the chain starts again with the software vendor, continues with the person that wrote an attack tool, goes to the person who has used the tool to penetrate an IS, and goes further to those that were in charge of protecting the IS.

Therefore there exists a split of liability. To cope with it, appropriate models would be very helpful. In [201] a two stage approach is suggested:

- In the first stage, ISs administrators use a worksheet to set up a liability diagram that identifies penetrations, the means (technical cause) that have been used (exploited), and possible entities that might be liable in connection with a certain penetration. For example, the penetrations can include Web site defacement, data stealing and internet access disruption. The means can include software bugs, insecure network configuration, lack of security policies, and so on. Finally, possibly liable entities include vendors, service providers, etc.
- In the second stage, administrators link the above elements in a diagram or a matrix to identify the relationships for determining liability. For example, Web site defacing may be linked to software bugs and this further to the vendor, or to insecure network configuration, and this further to service provider and so on.

This makes for a complex mix, but one that definitely needs to be resolved. The first step will be legally enforced liability. The next step will allow parties to transfer liability, while in the third step mechanisms will be provided to reduce risk [309]. Thus being initiated by legislative levers, they will then be driven by the market.

But how can one successfully cope with liability in ISs? Key elements are adherence to standards like Common Criteria and licensing (certification) of data and software engineers and administrators. Software vendors will certainly face harder times and will have to invest much more into security of their products. But the fact that there is no 100 % security is strongly in their favor.

4.5 Intellectual Property Rights

Intellectual property rights (IPR) cover copyrights, patents, design rights and trademarks - the main international body in this area is the World Intellectual Property Organization (WIPO), which regularly issues publications about IPR [361].

From the IPR point of view, software copyright issues are a major concern for the majority of organizations. Thus, organizations should have copyright compliance statements and employees should be aware of them. This requires defined procedures for acquisition, installation and use of new software products. They should have registers of copyrighted assets and they should implement procedures to control compliance with licensing agreements [178].

A copyright legislation act that is tailored to specifics of internet is the US Digital Millenium Copyright Act (DMCA) from 1998 [352]. It is a result of the 1996 WIPO Copyright Treaty that required member states to adopt measures that would prevent the circumvention of technological protection for copyrighted works, and to protect the integrity of rights management information [344]. DMCA applies to text and non-text copying, i.e. graphics, videos, music. It defines procedures for copyright owners to contact service providers when encountering other subscriber's improper use of their copyrighted materials. Service providers are obliged to remove such materials if they can reasonably assume the violation of copyrights. In the case where the subscriber protests, the materials have to be re-posted until the copyright claimant files a lawsuit [284].

WIPO Copyright Treaty was also the basis for improving EU copyright legislation, which adopted the Directive on the Harmonization of Certain Aspects of Copyright and Related Rights in the Information Society in 2001 [110]. As with DMCA, this directive addresses the rights of copyright owners with regard to electronic reproduction and dissemination of their work. It defines acceptable practices and exceptions, e.g. for pure technical purposes like caching, for non-commercial activities, etc. [303]. However, it is expected that after final implementations are made (by the beginning of the year 2004 only half members states actually implemented the directive), these will not result in such powers that DMCA has given to the recording industry to sue individuals involved in peer-to-peer (P2P) exchange of files [304].

As far as patents are concerned for ISs security and privacy, they used to be of concern mainly for US users. However, also in this field the situation is becoming more complicated, not only in the US, but also in the EU. The latest examples were initiatives on software patents. In the US, the trend is towards support of software patentability despite strong opposition from software advocates and economists [239]. Also in the EU, recent software patents initiative resulted in a sharp debate, as it was expected that software patents would influence open software initiatives, hinder further research in this area, result in side-effect anomalies like being included in standards, etc. Nevertheless, the decision about this initiative has been made and the European Parliament voted strongly against it in July 2005.

The last issue to be addressed under IPR concerns trademarks. While it is more or less clear to the majority of users that trademarks have to be considered carefully, one should note that trademark infringements can happen in many surprising forms. For example, careless use of meta-tags in Web documents may easily lead to violation of trademarks. Similarly, trademark issues need to be addressed when registering domain names.

Also other issues exist that are hard to categorize. For example, use of Web based services, where users post various contents on servers of providers, should be carefully studied to avoid the liability of providers for unlawful content. Similarly, linking of Web documents can cause troubles if deep-linking is used, i.e. a frameworked page inside one's own page [284].

4.6 Computer Forensics

Although extensive treatment of computer forensics is outside the scope of this book, some words about this area have to be given. Because courts cannot rely on questionable evidence from an IS, such circumstances are likely to weaken the chances of an attacked organization getting legal satisfaction [283].

Generally, *forensics means use of scientific methods to solve criminal acts.* Computer forensics is thus a sub-area of computer science and other forensics sciences. More precisely, "forensic computing refers to the methodologies used to capture and authenticate data at a source, analyze that captured data for evidence relevant to the case at hand, produce an understandable report that can be introduced into evidence in a court of law, and testify as to the authenticity of evidence presented" [360].

The above sequence must be followed to prevent failure of the entire investigation process. Thus, collecting evidence in appropriate ways plays a pivotal role in computer forensics. It is suggested that relevant standards are followed in this area, particularly RFC 3227 for collection of evidence [42], and US Department of Justice Guide [350].

The reader might quibble that an experienced attacker can get away without a trace. But the truth is that evidence will very likely exist. A golden rule of forensics is Locard's exchange principle [223], which states that it is impossible for a criminal to act, especially considering the intensity of a crime, without traces of presence. Because the basic psychology of human beings remains unchanged, Locard's principle remains valid also in the digital age.

One of the first formalized computer forensic practices is Practice Guide for Computer Based Evidence, published by the Association of Chief Police Officers for England and Wales [18]. Its main points are as follows:

- No action taken by police or their agents should change data on a computer or other media which may subsequently be relied upon in court.

- In exceptional circumstances where a person finds it necessary to access original data held on a target computer, that person must be competent to do so and to give evidence explaining the relevance and the implications of his/her actions.
- An audit trail or other record of all processes applied to computer based evidence should be created and preserved. An independent third party should be able to examine those processes and achieve the same result.
- The officer that is in charge of the case is responsible for ensuring that the law and these principles are adhered to. This applies to the possession of and access to data contained in a computer. Anyone accessing the computer, or any use of a copying device, must comply with laws and these principles.

Historically, computer forensics started with simple tools and soon, two distinct branches arose [82]: network investigation, which dealt with the inspection of the data packets being transmitted over the network, and forensic investigation, which dealt with (physical) inspection of the storage media.

In the beginning, acquisition of digital evidence included also seizure of the suspect systems and the inspection of its long-term storage media. But recently, these practices changed, mainly due to technology. Modern society is becoming dependent on computer ISs even at the level of strategic systems like power plants and air-traffic communications. In such cases, forced downtime for computer investigation is not acceptable. Therefore efforts are going in the direction to enable investigation without making dependent systems non-operational [82]. There now exist such tools, i.e. servlets (daemons) that monitor bit streams between hardware and operating systems. Future trends in computer forensics will certainly be determined by the development of technology.

Those interested in more detailed coverage of these topics can find an extensive treatment in [301], while a classical reading that presents the beginning of computer forensics is [328]. And the most relevant formal international framework related to computer forensics should be mentioned. This is the Council of Europe CyberCrime Convention [79].

*   *   *

Finally, the reader is warned that the information provided in this chapter should by no means be treated as legal advice. The chapter serves as an integral part of the methodology of this book and is for informational purposes only. Whenever applying legally relevant steps, a lawyer or a field expert should be involved.

5

Where Are We Headed?

Per aspera ad astra.[1]

What more is there to say at the end of this book? By now the reader has probably become convinced that ISs security and privacy has to be played "hard and soft", and that a single approach is not sufficient. So if reader's origin is from traditionally "hard sciences", that's fine. If reader's origin is from traditionally "soft sciences", that's fine too.

Managing ISs security and privacy is not just a science, but also an art. With regard to science - the results that are already applicable and present proven solutions, these have been described in the first four chapters using a moderate, reader friendly approach. But some harder parts of (ongoing) scientific research in this field will be given in the appendix.

We try to make things scientific and practically applicable at the same time. It is an experience based fact that one should rely on scientific approaches as much as possible. When this kind of homework is done, intuition and other ingredients should come in. Of course, science can not provide answers to every question.

So where are we headed from technological point of view? As far as the basis of security technology is concerned, it is known that current cryptography is largely based on two disciplines. The first is Shannon's theory of information, while the second is the theory of computational complexity that rests on Turing machines. But radical shifts in computing paradigms are on the horizon. These are bio-computing and quantum computing.

Quantum physics research has led to quantum information theory with surprising new properties [275]. For example, factoring of certain composite numbers that is computationally hard on classical computers, becomes easy using quantum computers. Moreover, some completely new concepts and new cryptographic primitives can be introduced, e.g. it follows from the quantum no-cloning theorem that quantum keys exist, which cannot be copied. Further,

---

[1]Through the thorns to the stars.

there are other important properties of quantum cryptography with relation to key exchange. They are based on the physical law that one cannot obtain information about a particle's quantum state without interfering, and thus disturbing its state. Which means that an attempt to obtain a shared secret key is likely to be detected. Therefore quantum key exchange is not subject to the basic constraint of classical computation, where shared secret keys have to be regularly changed in order not to become accessible due to faster computers or new code-breaking algorithms. More than this, with quantum techniques exchanged secret values are exposed to an attack only during the life time of the transmission. With public key cryptosystems one half of a key pair is resting for years in a some directory, being exposed to accumulation of additional information, which can end with a successful attack [162]. At the moment, however, one fundamental issue that has to be solved in quantum computing is how to manipulate quantum information reliably. Another issue is a bit older - transmission of information encoded in particles properties is inherently prone to transmission errors [162]. Surprisingly, this leads to a marriage of classical cryptosystems with quantum ones by use of error detecting and correcting codes. Nevertheless, the real application of this important research to information security has yet to be seen.

Further directions in technology can be anticipated in the area of applications, where trends are towards network-aware and autonomous computing, e.g. global computing [286]. It is characteristic of this kind of computing systems that entities are mobile and move freely around the network, that they are not centrally controlled, and that their configuration varies over time. Finally, these computing entities have to operate with incomplete information about their environments. A programmatic case of the global computing paradigm is mobile intelligent agents. It is clear that such computing introduces many additional security concerns, some of them being completely new, like how to protect the code against the host, where the code is executed.

There are also changes in management on the horizon that are driven by ISs security and privacy. Management is facing a great diversity of factors and their relationships. These factors come from multiple domains. The human factor is something that management is basically familiar with. But due to their wide range of influences, ISs are gaining importance and the management will likely have to become familiar with their technology - at least conceptually [192]. It is further anticipated that appropriate decision support systems will have to be introduced [144]. They will have to be specific and probably different from the traditional ones. Methodologies that are promising to provide the basis for such systems are systems dynamics and agent based technologies.

Finally, where are we headed from the legal point of view? Unfortunately, evidence suggests that courts and legislation may not always be about justice and fairness, but sometimes about strange ways of reasoning and about interests of certain lobbies. An often cited example in case of the latter is the US Digital Millenium Copyright Act. DMCA is a very strict implementation of WIPO measures, and is stated that it violates privacy rights and inhibits computer science research [344]. Based on DMCA, further extensions of legislation seem to be on the way, where even use of firewalls and proxies could be illegal. The reason given is that these technologies could hinder the identification of a final recipient of a certain content and prevent this person from being tracked. The main actors behind DMCA are assumed to be movie and music industry giants.

On the other hand, an example of reasoning that is hard to understand is the following. A programmer in the UK has been arrested for producing and offering a tool that could be exploited to attack systems, while the very same programmer has not performed any kind of attack [313]. The reasonableness of this legal action can be challenged by making an analogy with producers of classical weapons. Moreover, many attacks on ISs begin with port scanning, which necessitates the use of tools that can be used to break into a system. It is at least as likely to assume that the intention of port scanning is to illegally access a system, as it is to assume that certain software is produced for the same reason. But there exists a case in the US where it has been judged that port scanning is legal [99], while the writer of such software in the EU has been sentenced.

*   *   *

It is possible that the above cases are over-sensitive reactions to events that are taking place in the world, which was not legally covered until recently. Thus it is likely that in the long run, fair practices will prevail. Until then, what remains for us to do is to stimulate the development in the above mentioned directions of ethical and moral practices in all areas related to ISs security and privacy. This will further improve our coexistence in the new world that has been brought into being thanks to modern technology, for the benefits of humankind.

6

Appendix

Omnis scientia requirit mathematicam.[1]

This appendix is intended to serve two purposes. Firstly, it presents the basics that are necessary for in-depth understanding of contemporary security mechanisms and services. It is structured and written in a way that a reader with graduate-level knowledge of mathematics should be able to follow it. Secondly, it presents methodologies that improve security from a technological point of view (formal methods) and from an organizational, management point of view (business dynamics and agent technologies based simulations).

Thus it is not necessary for every reader to read this appendix. The main body of the book should be sufficient to enable the reader, independently of the background, to get an insight and understanding of the ISs security and privacy tools.

The appendix is partially focused on the most advanced work in this area. This includes business dynamics and agent technologies. But generally, it uses a moderate approach, focused on established and widely deployed methods that have been around for years. This includes SHA-1, Triple DES, RSA, and DH in order to communicate to the reader the details of some core mechanisms. If we would concentrate also on AES, this would require more complicated explanations and, besides, 3DES is expected to remain (de facto and de jure) standard for quite some years to come. Similarly, concentrating on elliptic curve based cryptography, which is gaining importance, would again require extensive additional explanation. Again, RSA is the most widely accepted de facto and de jure asymmetric standard.

Those readers that are more interested in details of AES and elliptic curve based cryptography can find good explanations in [323, 189]. Readers with deeper interest in the whole field of cryptography are advised to look in the bible for this field [236].[2] For the majority of readers, this bible will be prob-

---

[1] All sciences depend on mathematics.

[2] This book is freely available on the internet at the following URI: http://www.cacr.math.uwaterloo.ca/hac/.

ably too hard to read, and an excellent alternative is [306]. A bit older, but still very good option is [85].[3] The approach of the appendix has its roots in the above mentioned works, but it takes a different path and perspective to meet the objectives of this book.

6.1 Brief Mathematical Preliminaries

In this appendix, algorithms will be frequently mentioned and we will stay with the definition that *an algorithm is a well-defined computational procedure that takes a variable input and halts with an output.* Algorithms are the essence of computation (or programs in a broader sense), thus their properties are fundamental for this field. Before getting into details of cryptographic computation, some insight into Shannon's information theory is required [317].

6.1.1 Information Theory

Shannon based this theory on very formal mathematical grounds. One of the central issues of this theory is the problem of quantity of information in a message and consequently, optimal coding. Besides these issues, information theory also addresses the problem of a noisy communication channel, through which an original transmitted message P is received as a distorted message P'. The question is how to restore the original message. This is achieved by using redundant bits, known as error checking and correcting codes.

The problem is analogous to that of sending an encrypted message over a communication channel, where "noise" is introduced by a cryptographic algorithm, used by sender. For an attacker the recovery of received message P' should not be feasible, while the intended recipient is able to recover the message with computationally feasible procedures, because of knowing the keys.

The amount of information in a message is measured by the entropy of the message, which is a function of the probability distribution over the set of all possible messages.[4] More formally, this is stated as follows.

Let $A = \{x_1, \ldots, x_n\}$ *denote n possible messages occurring with probabilities* $p(x_1), \ldots, p(x_n)$, *where* $\sum_{i=1}^{n} p(x_i) = 1$. *The entropy is then defined by the weighted average*

$$H(X) = -\sum_{i=1}^{i=n} p(x_i) \lg p(x_i), \tag{6.1}$$

where random variable X takes on values from A (notation "lg" stands for base-2 logarithm). This can be rewritten into an equivalent form:

---

[3]Unfortunately, this book has been out of print for years.

[4]Information as defined by Shannon is not related to the definition of information that was given in the first chapter.

$$H(X) = -\sum_i p(x_i) \lg p(x_i) \text{ or}$$
$$H(X) = \sum_i p(x_i) \lg(1/p(x_i)).$$

The number of bits needed to encode message x in an optimal way (which minimizes the expected number of bits to be transmitted) is given by the term $\lg(1/p(x))$. Term $(1/p(x))$ decreases with increasing $p(x)$, therefore shorter codes are assigned to more frequent messages, while longer codes are assigned to less frequent ones. Thus the weighted average $H(X)$ gives the expected number of bits in optimally encoded messages.

For example, let $n = 3$, and let three messages be a, b and c, where $p(a) = p(c) = 0.25$, and $p(b) = 0.5$. Then $\lg(1/p(a)) = 2 = \lg(1/p(c))$ and $\lg(1/p(b)) = 1$. Therefore

$$H(X) = (1/4) \lg 4 + (1/2) \lg 2 + (1/4) \lg 4 = 0.5 + 0.5 + 0.5 = 1.5.$$

Thus it is optimal to assign 1-bit code to b and 2-bit codes to a and c. One possibility for optimal coding would be to assign 1 to b, 00 to a, and 01 to c. Then a sequence *bbaccbba* would be encoded as 110001011100. Note that a or c cannot start with 1, because this would cause overlapping with the code for b. Thus when a receiver gets 1, it knows it is b. If the receiver receives 0, it has to check the next bit to properly assign a symbol.

Entropy has many interesting properties, e.g.:

- Having n messages, entropy is maximal for $p(x_1) = \ldots = p(x_n) = 1/n$. This describes the case where all messages are equally likely, thus $H(X) = n((1/n) \lg n) = \lg n$. Therefore $\lg n$ bits are needed to encode each message in such system.
- The probability distribution in the above case is uniform, and it results in maximal entropy. Logically, it is expected that $H(X)$ decreases, if the distribution of messages becomes more skewed. It can be checked that this indeed happens, and, going to the extreme, entropy reaches a minimum $H(X) = 0$ at $p(x_i) = 1$ for some message x_i.
- Entropy as a measure of uncertainty of a message states the number of bits of information that must be obtained to recover this message when it has been distorted by noise or enciphering.

With this formal apparatus, one can perform useful kinds of analysis on a certain language, because cryptography is primarily about hiding language based communication [85]:

- Suppose the set of all messages in a certain language that are N characters long is formed. Then the rate of language r is defined by $r = H(X)/N$, which gives the average number of bits of information in each character. This value varies for different languages - for English language this value is 1.0 to 1.5 bits/letter for large values of N.
- Let us assume that all possible sequences of characters are equally likely. Then the absolute rate of the language is defined to be the maximum

number of bits of information that could be encoded in each character. If there are L characters in the alphabet of a language, then the absolute rate is given by $R = \lg L$, the maximum entropy of the individual character. For English, this is $R = \lg 26 = 4.7\text{bits/letter}$.

- Considering the above observations, it follows that human languages are "inefficient". True, they contain a lot of redundancy. For example, writing "This s suny dy" instead of writing "This is a sunny day", everyone can recognize the original, undistorted message. More formally, the redundancy of a language with rate r and absolute rate R is defined by $D = R - r$. For the English language, where $R = 4.7$ and $r = 1$, the redundancy is $D = 3.7$ (all units are bits/letter). In relative terms, the ratio D/R is approximately 79%.

Such statistics are useful for cryptanalysis. To successfully attack a ciphertext, additional information can be used. This additional information, reduces entropy, i.e. the uncertainty of message.

Suppose an attacker knows that a ciphertext $8\&\$K8s$ denotes a value of field in a database denoting a sex, then the uncertainty is just one bit. Depending on the cipher, e.g. padding mechanism, an attacker needs to determine only a certain character, for example the first one.

Suppose further that this attacker intercepts a message about a person, knowing that it contains the sum on the bank account of this person. This clearly narrows the uncertainty interval. Using the reasonable assumption that this sum does not exceed CAD\$ 2,000,000 this interval is between 1 bit and 21 bits (binary presentation of two millions requires 21 bits).

Such additional information leads to vulnerability of public key cryptosystems when they are used for confidentiality [85]. Let $P' = \{P\}_{K_{pub}}$ denote an encrypted message with the public key K_{pub}. Even if the private key is not known and computationally not feasible to obtain, it is possible to attack the system. An attacker has to perform (in the worst case) two million encryptions to find the matching plaintext, i.e. $P' = \{P_i\}_{K_{pub}}$ for $P_i = 1, \ldots, 2000000$. To prevent this kind of attack, a random bit string can be added to plaintext before encryption.

To formally handle such additional information, conditional probabilities have to be included. So given a message $y_i \in \{y_1, \ldots, y_m\} = B$, where $\sum_{j=1}^{j=m} p(y_j) = 1$, let $p(x_i \mid y_j)$ denote the conditional probability of message x_i given message y_j, and let $p(x_i, y_j)$ be the joint probability of message x_i and message y_j, thus $p(x_i, y_j) = p(x_i \mid y_j)p(y_j)$. Using conditional probabilities, the conditional entropy can be obtained as follows:

$$H(X \mid y_j) = -\sum_i p(x_i \mid y_j) \lg p(x_i \mid y_j).$$

This can be rewritten as

$$H(X \mid y_j) = \sum_i p(x_i \mid y_j) \lg(1/p(x_i \mid y_j)).$$

When taken over all y_j, *the equivocation, i.e. the conditional entropy of X given Y, is defined by equation*

$$H(X \mid Y) = \sum_{j=1}^{j=m} p(y_j) \sum_{i=1}^{i=n} p(x_i \mid y_j) \lg(1/p(x_i \mid y_j)). \qquad (6.2)$$

What is the purpose of equivocation? It is a measure of entropy for cases where an attacker succeeds in getting some additional information. Let us assume a case where $n = 4$ and $p(x_i) = 1/4$ for each message in set A. The entropy is $H(X) = \lg 4 = 2$. Assume further that $m = 2$ and $p(y_i) = 1/2$ for each message in set B, and that each message from B limits the choice of message from A from four to two messages: y_1 limits the choice to x_1 or x_2, and y_2 limits the choice to x_3 or x_4.

Thus for each y, $p(x \mid y) = 1/2$ for the two x's and $p(x \mid y) = 0$ for the remaining two x's. The equivocation is calculated as follows:

$$
\begin{aligned}
H(X \mid Y) = p(y_1)[\; & p(x_1 \mid y_1) \lg(p(x_1 \mid y_1))^{-1} + p(x_2 \mid y_1) \lg(p(x_2 \mid y_1))^{-1} + \\
& p(x_3 \mid y_1) \lg(p(x_3 \mid y_1))^{-1} + p(x_4 \mid y_1) \lg(p(x_4 \mid y_1))^{-1}] + \\
p(y_2)[\; & p(x_1 \mid y_2) \lg(p(x_1 \mid y_2))^{-1} + p(x_2 \mid y_2) \lg(p(x_2 \mid y_2))^{-1} + \\
& p(x_3 \mid y_2) \lg(p(x_3 \mid y_2))^{-1} + p(x_4 \mid y_2) \lg(p(x_4 \mid y_2))^{-1}]
\end{aligned}
$$

Taking into account that

$$p(x_1 \mid y_1) = p(x_2 \mid y_1) = p(x_3 \mid y_2) = p(x_4 \mid y_2) = 0.5$$

and that all other conditional probabilities are 0, one can calculate that the equivocation is $H(X \mid Y) = 1$ (when $p(x)$ is 0, the term $p(x) * \lg p(x)$ is also 0). Thus knowledge of the element from B reduces the uncertainty of the element from A to one bit. Comparing this to an initial two bits, when X was not related to Y, a gain is evident.

With cryptosystems, three classes of information have to be considered [317, 85]:

- plaintexts P occurring with prior probabilities $p(P)$, where $\sum_P p(P) = 1$,
- ciphertexts C occurring with probabilities $p(C)$, where $\sum_C p(C) = 1$,
- and keys K chosen with prior probabilities $p(K)$, where $\sum_K p(K) = 1$.

This provides the basis for the definition of perfect secrecy (PS), i.e. an unbreakable cipher [85]. Let $p(P \mid C)$ denote the probability that message P was sent given that C was received. *PS is defined by $p(P \mid C) = p(P)$, which assures that ciphertext gives no additional information to attacker. Further, let $p(C \mid P)$ be the probability of receiving ciphertext C, given that P was sent. Then $p(C \mid P)$ is the sum of the probabilities $p(K)$ of the keys K that encipher P into C:*

$$p(C \mid P) = \sum_K p(K), \qquad (6.3)$$

where $E_K(P) = C$, and where E denotes encryption.

A necessary and sufficient condition for PS is that for every C, $p(C \mid P) = p(C)$ for all P. This is interpreted as follows [85]: The probability of receiving a particular ciphertext C, given that P was sent (encrypted under some key), is the same as the probability of receiving C, given that some other message P' was sent (encrypted under some other key). Perfect secrecy requires that the number of keys is equal to or greater than the number of possible messages. Otherwise there would exist some message P, such that for a given C, no K would provide mapping of C into P, which would imply $p(P \mid C) = 0$. This enables exclusion of certain plaintexts, and the chances to break the cipher are increased.

Using random keys, which are at least as long as the messages they encipher, PS can be obtained. A one-time pad is a kind of PS, which achieves its total secrecy by deploying a non-repeating random key stream that is as long as the message stream is. The message and the random key are XORed to produce the ciphertext, while XORing the ciphertext with the key recovers the original message (XOR operation assigns "1" to a pair of different bits, while two equal bits are assigned value "0"; the symbol for this operation is $\oplus$).

The important requirement for one-time pad is that every key must be replaced with a new one after being used. The reason can be seen from the example in Fig. 6.1:

plaintext	1	1	1	1	0	0	0	0	XOR
radnom key	**0**	**1**	**1**	**0**	**0**	**1**	**1**	**1**	
ciphertext	1	0	0	1	0	1	1	1	

plaintext	1	1	1	1	0	0	0	0	XOR
ciphertext	1	0	0	1	0	1	1	1	
random key	**0**	**1**	**1**	**0**	**0**	**1**	**1**	**1**	

Fig. 6.1. Example of use of a one-time pad

If just one pair (P, C) is obtained, the key can be calculated and all other messages decrypted.

It follows that statistical analysis is at the heart of cryptanalysis. To make cryptanalysis as hard as possible, Shannon suggested the following [85]:

- Remove redundancy of a language before encryption (use e.g. file compression).
- Apply confusion, which means application of substitutions to make the relationship between the key and ciphertext as complex as possible.
- Apply diffusion, which means application of transformations to dissipate the statistical properties of the plaintext across the ciphertext.

6.1.2 Complexity Theory

Computational complexity provides the basis for many contemporary crypto-systems. The strength of a cipher is determined by the computational complexity of the problems, which are used to produce ciphers and reverse them into plaintexts. Algorithms that are solutions to these problems are computationally feasible, provided that one knows the keys. Without knowing these keys, inverse transformations are not computationally feasible.

The computational complexity (of an algorithm) is measured by the required number of steps, expressed as a function of its input, i.e. bits. Since we do not count the number of steps precisely, this function is expressed as an asymptotic upper bound (the "big O" notation). This means that no input will cause the algorithm to use more resources than the bound [31]. Besides asymptotic upper bound, asymptotic lower bound is also used (the "big Ω" notation), meaning that no algorithm can use fewer resources than the bound [31].

More formally, $f(n) = O(g(n))$ *if there exists a positive constant c and a positive integer n_0 such that $0 \leq f(n) \leq cg(n)$ for all $n \geq n_0$.* To clarify the above definition, let $f(n) = 5n + 5$. Then $f(n) = O(n)$ because $5n + 5 \leq 6n$ for $n \geq 5$, thus $g(n) = n, c = 6$, and $n_0 = 5$. Now let $f(n) = a_m n^m + a_{m-1} n^{m-1} + \ldots + a_0$. For a given m it follows that $f(n) = O(n^m)$. If $m = 1$, linear complexity $O(n)$ is obtained, if $m = 2$, quadratic complexity $O(n^2)$ is obtained, and so on. Consequently, a polynomial-time algorithm is an algorithm whose worst-case running time is $O(n^m)$, where n is the input size and m is a constant. Algorithms with running time exceeding this bound are called exponential-time algorithms with a running time $O(m^{h(n)})$, where m is some constant and $h(n)$ is a polynomial. An example of exponential complexity is $O(2^n)$.

The most universal formal model of computation is Turing Machine (TM). It has a finite control, a tape with a leftmost cell, which is infinite to the right and is divided into cells. A head scans one tape cell at a time, and each of these cells holds exactly one symbol from a finite set of symbols. Initially, the n leftmost cells hold the input symbols, which represent a program, and the remaining cells hold the special symbol, called blank. In one move, defined by the scanned symbol and the state of the finite control, TM changes the state, prints a symbol to replace the previous one, and moves its head left or right. Besides this basic TM, which is called deterministic TM, there exists also non-deterministic TM (NTM). In contrast to the former, non-deterministic TM has a finite number of choices for the next move for a given state and scanned tape symbol [157].

Now *problems that are solvable in polynomial time on a TM are tractable (computationally feasible).* Further, *problems that cannot be solved systematically in polynomial time are called intractable (computationally hard).* In addition, *problems for which it is impossible to write an algorithm to solve them are undecidable.*

The above definition introduces an interesting notion - undecidable problems. These are a kind of problems for which we cannot always find solutions by computation, whatever resources we use. Such problems provably exist, but for the purpose of cryptosystems they are not important. However, the following problems are important: *The class* **P** *consists of all problems solvable in polynomial time on deterministic TM. The class* **NP** *(nondeterministic polynomial) consists of all problems solvable in polynomial time on non-deterministic TM.*

In line with the interpretation of the definition, the class **NP** includes the class **P**. Any problem polynomial solvable on a deterministic TM is polynomial solvable on NTM. Further, a problem is in **NP** if a correct solution can be proved in polynomial time, which means that knowledge of the computational path enables verification in polynomial time. So it seems intuitively correct to assume that **P** $\neq$ **NP**, but no one has proved this yet. The problem whether **P=NP** remains unresolved, but it is a widely accepted belief that it does not. Further, it should come as no surprise that systematic (deterministic) solving of certain problems in **NP** appears to require exponential time [85].

This leads to another important distinction within **NP** problems. *A problem is* **NP-hard** *if it cannot be solved in polynomial time unless* **P=NP**. *Further, a problem is* **NP-complete** *if it is in* **NP** *and* **NP-hard**.

Known algorithms for systematically solving **NP-complete** problems have exponential worst case complexities. Thus in 1976 Diffie and Hellman suggested applying computational complexity to the design of crypto-systems [90]:

- **NP-complete** problems are suitable because they cannot be solved systematically in polynomial time using known algorithms. Information is enciphered by encoding it in an **NP-complete** problem, while knowing a secret key enables a "perfect guess", which enables deterministic computation with polynomial complexity.
- More complex problems are not suitable for use because crypto transformations would exceed polynomial time complexity.

Some typical hard problems that are used for crypto-systems include factorization of large primes composites and discrete logarithm.

6.1.3 Abstract Algebra

In order to realize certain public key cryptosystems that are based on the idea of Diffie and Hellman, appropriate algebraic structures are needed.

Let binary operation $\circ$ on a set S perform a mapping from $S \times S$ to S. That is, $\circ$ is a rule which assigns to each ordered pair of elements from S an element of S. This definition is interpreted as follows. Assume a set, defined by elements a, b and c, and suppose there exists a mapping $a \circ b \to c$. Then a and b present an ordered pair that maps to c, which also is an element of the same set.

A group $(G, \circ)$ *denotes an abstract structure consisting of a set* G *with a binary operation* $\circ$ *on* G *that satisfy the following axioms* [236]:

- *The group operation is associative, meaning that* $a \circ (b \circ c) = (a \circ b) \circ c$ *for all* $a, b, c \in G$.
- *There exists an element* $1 \in G$, *called the identity element, such that* $a \circ 1 = 1 \circ a = a$ *for all* $a \in G$.
- *For each* $a \in G$ *there exists an element* $a^{-1} \in G$, *called the inverse of* a, *such that* $a \circ a^{-1} = a^{-1} \circ a = 1$.
- *A group is abelian (or commutative) if* $a \circ b = b \circ a$ *for all* $a, b \in G$.

With groups, their order is often mentioned. *A group* G *is finite if it contains a finite number of elements, and this number is called its order.*

Groups are often not enough, and more complex structures such as ring and field have to be used. *A ring is an abstract structure denoted by* $(R, +, *)$ *that consists of a set* R *with two binary operations on* R *denoted by* $+$ *(addition) and* $*$ *(multiplication), which satisfies the following axioms* [236]:

- $(R, +)$ *is an abelian group and the identity is denoted by* 0.
- *The operation* $*$ *is associative, which means that* $a * (b * c) = (a * b) * c$ *for all* $a, b, c \in R$.
- *There exists a multiplicative identity denoted* 1, *with* $1 \neq 0$, *such that* $1 * a = a * 1 = a$ *for all* $a \in R$.
- *The operation* $*$ *is distributive over* $+$, *which means that* $a * (b + c) = (a * b) + (a * c)$ *and* $(b + c) * a = (b * a) + (c * a)$ *for all* $a, b, c \in R$.

The ring is called commutative if $a * b = b * a$ for all $a, b \in R$. Further, special elements are often sought, called units or invertibles. *An element* a *of* R *is called a unit or an invertible element if there is an element* $b \in R$ *such that* $a * b = 1$.

The last basic structure that we will deal with is field. *A field is defined as a commutative ring where multiplicative inverses exist for all non-zero elements.* Let us consider the set of integers with respect to addition and multiplication. This set is not a field, because 1 and -1 are the only non-zero elements that have multiplicative inverses. However, rational, real and complex numbers form fields under the usual operations [236].

6.1.4 Number Theory

Additional knowledge is necessary to understand certain public key cryptosystems, thus modular arithmetic and congruencies have to be discussed. Two basic definitions have to be given first. *A prime (number) is a positive integer that has no positive integer divisors other than 1 and itself.* Further, *two integers are relatively prime if they share no common positive factor except 1.* Relatively prime integers are also called coprime integers.

The Integers Modulo n

If x is any integer and n a positive integer, then x mod n equals the integer remainder r in the range $[0, n-1]$ after x is divided by n, i.e. $x = k*n+r$ for some integer k. The divisor n is called a *modulus*. Let " $\diamond$" stand for addition, or subtraction, or multiplication. Then

$$[(a \bmod n) \diamond (b \bmod n)] \bmod n = (a \diamond b) \bmod n.$$

This means that taking the remainder of the result of operation gives the same result as taking first the remainder of arguments, performing the operation and then calculating its reminder. For example, $((7 \bmod 2) * (3 \bmod 2)) \bmod 2 = (7 * 3) \bmod 2$, and further $(1 * 1) \bmod 2 = 21 \bmod 2$.

A more complex relation is congruence. *If a and b are integers, then a is said to be congruent to b modulo n,* written as $a \equiv b \pmod{n}$, or $a \equiv_n b$, *if n divides $(a - b)$.* The integer n is again called the modulus of the congruence. For example, $22 \equiv_5 2$, because $(22 - 2) = 4 * 5$.

The *integers modulo n is the set of integers $\{0, 1, 2, \ldots, n-1\}$,* denoted $\mathbb{Z}_n$. Addition, subtraction, and multiplication in $\mathbb{Z}_n$ are calculated modulo n. It can be easily checked that the following properties within $\mathbb{Z}_n$ hold true [323]:

- Commutativity: $(w + x) \bmod n = (x + w) \bmod n$,
  and $(w * x) \bmod n = (x * w) \bmod n$.
- Associativity: $[(w + x) + y] \bmod n = [w + (x + y)] \bmod n$,
  and $[(w * x) * y] \bmod n = [w * (x * y)] \bmod n$.
- Distributivity: $[w * (x + y)] \bmod n = [(w * x) + (w * y)] \bmod n$.
- Existence of identities: $(0 + w) \bmod n = w \bmod n$,
  and $(1 * w) \bmod n = w \bmod n$.
- Existence of additive inverse: For each $w \in \mathbb{Z}_n$ there exists a z such that $w + z \equiv_n 0$.

The next definition has to do with inverse transformations of public key cryptosystems. *Having $a \in \mathbb{Z}_n$, then the multiplicative inverse of a modulo n is an integer $x \in \mathbb{Z}_n$, such that $ax \equiv_n 1$.* If such an x exists, then it is unique, and a is said to be *invertible*, or a *unit*; the inverse of a is denoted by a^{-1}. Further, *the multiplicative group of $\mathbb{Z}_n$ is $\mathbb{Z}_n^* = \{a \in \mathbb{Z}_n \mid gcd(a, n) = 1\}$,* where *gcd* stands for greatest common divisor. This means that the set $\mathbb{Z}_n^*$ consists of elements that are relatively prime to modulus. For example, if $n = 9$, then $\mathbb{Z}_9^* = \{1, 2, 4, 5, 7, 8\}$. Thus, when n is a prime, then $\mathbb{Z}_n^* = \{a \mid 1 \leq a \leq n-1\}$.

A group G is defined as cyclic if there is an element $\alpha \in G$ such that for each $b \in G$ there is an integer i with $b = \alpha^i$. Such α is called a *generator of G.* For example, the group $\mathbb{Z}_{19}^* = \{1, 2, \ldots, 18\}$ is a multiplicative group of order 18. It is also cyclic, and the generator is $\alpha = 2$. Let us check that 2 is the generator of this group, i.e. that all its elements can be obtained with exponentiation of 2: $2^0 \bmod 19 = 1, 2^1 \bmod 19 = 2, 2^2 \bmod 19 = 4, 2^3 \bmod 19 = 8, 2^4 \bmod 19 = 16, 2^5 \bmod 19 = 13, \ldots, 2^{16} \bmod 19 = 5, 2^{17} \bmod 19 = 10$. This produces all the elements of the above group. Further exponentiation of generator reproduces already obtained elements in the same order; that is why we refer to this group to be cyclic.

The following function plays an important role in certain public-key crypto-systems. This is the Euler phi function ϕ, which is defined as follows. *For $n \geq 1$ let $\phi(n)$ denote the number of integers in the interval $[1, n]$ that are relatively prime to n.* For example, $\phi(10) = 4$, and the related set is $\{1, 3, 7, 9\}$. It can be easily seen that if p is a prime, then $\phi(p) = p - 1$.

Before proceeding further, properties of congruencies have to be given. It can be checked with some examples that for all $a, a_1, b, b_1, c \in \mathbb{Z}$, the following properties hold:

- $a \equiv_n b$ iff a and b leave the same reminder when divided by n, where notation "iff" stands for "if and only if", which means equivalence.
- $a \equiv_n a$ (reflexivity).
- If $a \equiv_n b$ then $b \equiv_n a$ (symmetry).
- If $a \equiv_n b$ and $b \equiv_n c$, then $a \equiv_n c$ (transitivity).
- If $a \equiv_n a_1$ and $b \equiv_n b_1$,
  then $a + b \equiv_n a_1 + b_1$ and $ab \equiv_n a_1 b_1$.
- $a \bmod n = b \Rightarrow a \equiv_n b$, but $a \equiv_n b \not\Rightarrow a \bmod n = b$.
- $(a * b) \equiv_n (a * c) \Rightarrow b \equiv_n c$ if a is relatively prime to n (a common factor on both sides of congruence can be dropped in such cases).

There are additional important facts about congruencies, if a and n are integers, $n \geq 2$, and p is a prime:

- If $\gcd(a, p) = 1$, then $a^{p-1} \equiv_p 1$ (Fermat's theorem).
- If $a \in \mathbb{Z}_n^*$ and n as required above, then $a^{\phi(n)} \equiv_n 1$ (Euler's theorem).
- If $r \equiv_{p-1} s$, then $a^r \equiv_p a^s$ for all integers a (this enables to reduce exponents mod p-1 when working modulo a prime p).
- If n is a product of distinct primes, and if $r \equiv_{\phi(n)} s$, then $a^r \equiv_n a^s$ for all integers a (this enables to reduce exponents mod $\phi(n)$ when working modulo such an n).

The first two of the above statements are very important and we will prove them, because they are at a core certain public key cryptosystems. The last two ones are important for efficient operations with such systems.

Euler's theorem is a generalization of the simpler Fermat's theorem. Therefore the latter will be addressed first. Let us assume a prime p and an integer a, which is coprime with p. Assume further that a set $A = \{1, 2, 3, ..., p - 1\}$ is taken and used for derivation of a new set $B = \{1a, 2a, 3a, ..., (p - 1)a\}$, where all multiplications are mod p.

We will first show that B is a permutation of set A. Let $p = 5$, $a = 7$, and therefore $A = \{1, 2, 3, 4\}$. By calculating $1*7 \bmod 5, 2*7 \bmod 5, 3*7 \bmod 5, 4*7 \bmod 5$, it follows that $B = \{2, 4, 1, 3\}$.

To prove that set B is always a permutation of set A, let us assume that this is not the case. Then one can choose two elements m and n from A that should be different according to the initial assumption. If all elements in B are not different, then for some n and m we can write $ma \equiv_p na$, or equivalently $(m - n)a \equiv_p 0$. Because a is an arbitrary integer, which is relatively prime to p, it can be dropped. Thus $m = n$ should hold true. But this contradicts the initial assumption, therefore set B is a permutation of set A.

Let us now form the product of elements in A and B. These two products are congruent modulo p, because B is a permutation of A:

$$1 * 2 * ... * (p - 1) \equiv_p 1a * 2a * ... * (p - 1)a,$$

or

$$1 * 2 * ... * (p - 1) \equiv_p 1 * 2 * ... * (p - 1) * a^{p-1}.$$

The product $1 * 2 * ... * (p - 1)$ is relatively prime to p, because there is no common divisor except 1. Therefore both parts of the above congruence can be divided by this product. Thus $a^{p-1} \equiv_p 1$, which is Fermat's theorem.

Now to prove Euler's theorem, assume two primes p and q, $p \neq q$. For $n = pq$ it can be stated

$$\phi(n) = \phi(pq) = \phi(p) * \phi(q) = (p - 1)(q - 1)$$

To prove the above fact, these steps should be followed [323]:

1. The set of remainders $\bmod n$ is $\mathbb{Z}_n = \{0, 1, ..., (pq - 1)\}$.
2. The reminders that are not relatively prime to n are multiples of p, i.e. $\{p, 2p, ..., (q - 1)p\}$ (n and p are not coprimes, thus each multiple of p is not relatively prime to n). The same holds true for q and the set $\{q, 2q, ..., (p - 1)q\}$. Finally, this also holds true for 0.
3. It follows from the first statement that the number of all reminders is pq, but we have to exclude those that are not relatively prime to n (bullet 2):

$$\phi(n) = pq - [(q - 1) + (p - 1) + 1] = (p - 1)(q - 1) = \phi(p)\phi(q)$$

To illustrate the situation, assume $p = 5$ and $q = 3$, which means that $n = 15$. Thus $\phi(p) = 4$, $\phi(q) = 2$ and $\phi(n) = 4 * 2 = 8$. The total number of integers that are smaller and relatively prime to the argument of Euler's function is 4 for p ($\{1, 2, 3, 4\}$) and 2 for q ($\{1, 2\}$). For $n=15$ the value of Euler's function is 8, i.e. the corresponding set of relatively prime integers is $\{1, 2, 4, 7, 8, 11, 13, 14\}$.

This is not yet the end of the proof. For every coprime a and n the following holds true:

$$a^{\phi(n)} \equiv_n 1.$$

Proving this is straightforward, if n is a prime - in this case Fermat's theorem is obtained. But generally, for an arbitrary integer n, let the set of integers that are less than n and relatively prime to n be written as

$$\mathbb{Z}_{(\phi,n)} = \{x_1, x_2, \ldots, x_{\phi(n)}\}.$$

Multiplying each element in the above set by a modulo n one obtains

$$\mathbb{Z}'_{(\phi,n)} = \{(ax_1 \bmod n),(ax_2 \bmod n),\ldots,(ax_{\phi(n)} \bmod n)\}.$$

Again, $\mathbb{Z}'_{(\phi,n)}$ is "just" a permutation of $\mathbb{Z}_{(\phi,n)}$. The proof is similar to the proof of Fermat's theorem and goes as follows:

1. Because a and x_i are relatively prime to n, their product ax_i must also be relatively prime to n. Thus the set $\mathbb{Z}'_{(\phi,n)}$ contains integers that are smaller than n and relatively prime to n.
2. In $\mathbb{Z}'_{(\phi,n)}$ there are no duplicates - if a is relatively prime to n (which holds true according to our assumption), then $ax_i \bmod n = ax_j \bmod n$ if $x_i = x_j$, and this is a contradiction.

Therefore

$$\Pi_{i=1}^{\phi(n)}(ax_i \bmod n) = \Pi_{i=1}^{\phi(n)} x_i \qquad (6.4)$$

$$\Pi_{i=1}^{\phi(n)} ax_i \equiv_n \Pi_{i=1}^{\phi(n)} x_i$$

$$a^{\phi(n)} * \Pi_{i=1}^{\phi(n)} x_i \equiv_n \Pi_{i=1}^{\phi(n)} x_i$$

$$a^{\phi(n)} \equiv_n 1 \text{ or } a^{\phi(n)+1} \equiv_n a.$$

The last line concludes the proof and states the Euler's theorem. And here is the last fact that we will take for granted. Any integer in $\mathbb{Z}_n$ has a multiplicative inverse iff this integer is relatively prime to n. Thus, in the finite field $\mathbb{Z}_p$, where p is a prime, denoted also $\mathrm{GF}(p)$ (Galois field), for each $w \in \mathbb{Z}_p, w \neq 0$, there exists a multiplicative inverse $z \in \mathbb{Z}_p$, such that $w * z \equiv_p 1$ [323].

6.1.5 Computing Inverses and Exponentiation in $\mathbb{Z}_n$

Computing inverses in $\mathbb{Z}_n$ is done on the basis of the extended Euclidean algorithm. This algorithm takes an input of two non-negative integers a and n with $a \geq n$. It outputs a greatest common divisor $d = \gcd(a,n)$ and integers x, y that satisfy the condition $ax + ny = d$ (the notation $\lfloor x \rfloor$ denotes the largest integer that is less than or equal to x, and $\leftarrow$ denotes assignment of the value of a variable on the right to the value of a variable on the left) [236]:

1. If $n = 0$ then set $d \leftarrow a, x \leftarrow 1, y \leftarrow 0$, and return (d,x,y).
2. Set $x_2 \leftarrow 1, x_1 \leftarrow 0, y_2 \leftarrow 0, y_1 \leftarrow 1$.
3. While $n > 0$ do:
   a) $q \leftarrow \lfloor a/n \rfloor, r \leftarrow a - qn, x \leftarrow x_2 - qx_1, y \leftarrow y_2 - qy_1,$
   b) $a \leftarrow n, n \leftarrow r, x_2 \leftarrow x_1, x_1 \leftarrow x, y_2 \leftarrow y_1,$ and $y_1 \leftarrow y.$
4. Set $d \leftarrow a, x \leftarrow x_2, y \leftarrow y_2$, and return (d,x,y).

q	r	x	y	a	n	x_2	x_1	y_2	y_1
-	-	-	-	240	72	1	0	0	1
3	24	1	-3	72	24	0	1	1	-3
3	0	-3	10	24	0	1	-3	-3	10

Fig. 6.2. Example of extended Euclidean algorithm for $a = 240$ and $n = 72$

The running time of this algorithm (in bit operations) is $O(\lg^2 n)$, and an example of the use of the extended Euclidean algorithm is given Fig. 6.2.

Using the extended Euclidean algorithm with some additions, multiplicative inverses in $\mathbb{Z}_n$ can be computed. The complete algorithm for calculating of the above mentioned multiplicative inverses accepts an input $a \in \mathbb{Z}_n$ and produces an output $a^{-1} \bmod n$, provided that it exists. It goes as follows [236]:

1. Use extended Euclidean algorithm to find integers x and y such that $ax + ny = d$, where $d = \gcd(a, n)$.
2. If $d > 1$, then $a^{-1} \bmod n$ does not exist. Otherwise, return x.

Central operational procedures of RSA and DH are exponentiations in $\mathbb{Z}_n$. An algorithm for this operation is the square-and-multiply algorithm. This algorithm takes $a \in \mathbb{Z}_n$ as input, and integer $k \in [0, n)$ with a binary representation $k = \sum_{i=0}^{t} k_i 2^i$. On output it produces $a^k \bmod n$. The algorithm goes as follows [236]:

1. Set $b \leftarrow 1$. If $k = 0$ then return b.
2. Set $A \leftarrow a$.
3. If $k_0 = 1$ then set $b \leftarrow a$.
4. For i from 1 to t do:
    a) Set $A \leftarrow A^2 \bmod n$ and
    b) if $k_i = 1$, then set $b \leftarrow A \cdot b \bmod n$.
5. Return b.

6.1.6 Computational Complexities in $\mathbb{Z}_n$

To understand the complexities related discussion below, one should recall that $\lfloor \lg n \rfloor + 1$ bits are needed to present an integer n in binary notation. Once we obtain bits, these bits can be related to some time value that is necessary to computationally process them. As a consequence, the following time (bit) complexities of algorithms are obtained [236]:

- Taking into account that $(a + b) \bmod n = a + b$ if $(a + b < n)$, the number of bit operations is $\lg a$ (or $\lg b$ if $b > a$). If $(a + b \geq n)$ then $(a + b) \bmod n = a + b - n$, so the number of bit operations is twice as much as that in the previous case. Thus the asymptotic complexity is $O(\lg n)$ (analogous arguments hold true for subtraction).

- Multiplication - multiply a and b as integers, which means that $\lg n$ bits are multiplied by $\lg n$ bits. Next, divide the result by n and then take the remainder; thus the worst case complexity is $O(lg^2 n)$.
- Multiplicative inversion can be computed with the extended Euclidean algorithm - the complexity is $O(lg^2 n)$.
- Exponentiation can be computed with the square-and-multiply algorithm, which has the asymptotic upper bound $O(lg^3 n)$, because $\lg n$ loops with multiplications are executed.
- However, using appropriate modulus, the fastest known algorithm for factorization and discrete log is of the order of $e^{[(\ln n)^{1/3} * (\ln(\ln n))^{2/3}]}$ (ln denotes logarithm to base e).

And this is where the complexity gap is hidden. Knowing the secret key, decryption does not exceed $O(lg^3 n)$. Without the key, the effort is of the order of $e^{[(\ln n)^{1/3} * (\ln(\ln n))^{2/3}]}$, which is not feasible if n is large enough [323].

6.2 Cryptographic Primitives

So far mathematical tools were developed that are needed for implementation of certain cryptosystems, which will be discussed in the following sub-subsections.

6.2.1 One-way Hash Functions

One-way hash functions are essential for the whole field of cryptography. Not only that it is almost impossible to imagine digital signatures without hashing, but they are at the heart of the complexity gap that modern cryptography relies on. While one-way hash functions are being used on a daily basis, the very existence of such (idealized) functions, in the strict mathematical sense, is not yet proved. But it is widely believed that these functions exist [133].

Cryptographically strong one-way hash functions fulfil the following properties (the reasons have been discussed in 3.1.2):

- Effective computation: For any input x it is easy to compute the output $f(x)$.
- Pre-image resistance (or non-invertibility): For any output $f(x)$ it should be computationally infeasible to find x that mapped to this output.
- Second pre-image resistance: For a given x_1 it should be computationally infeasible to find x_2, $x_1 \neq x_2$, such that $f(x_1) = f(x_2)$.
- Collision resistance: For any x_1 it should be computationally infeasible to find x_2 with the same hashed value, i.e. $f(x_1) = f(x_2)$.

The simplest way of producing one-way hash function is to stack bytes one on top of another and perform XORing in each column. Assuming that bytes represent ASCII text characters, the most significant bit will always be 0, thus eight bit hashing is actually reduced to seven bit hashing. The obvious way to cure this situation is to perform rotations in the stack and this is indeed done in practical implementations. Further, in practical implementations the input is processed iteratively, one block after another, to produce an n-bit output. To ensure that a currently processed block depends on its predecessors, one input to processing of a current block is also the output of processing of the previous block [323].

The general structure of secure hash function is given in Fig. 6.3 (IV stands for initial value, CV_i for i-th chaining value, i.e. intermediate hash value $H^{(i)}$, $M^{(i)}$ for the i-th input block, f for compression algorithm, L for number of input blocks, n for hash length and b for length of input block, where $b > n$) [323]:

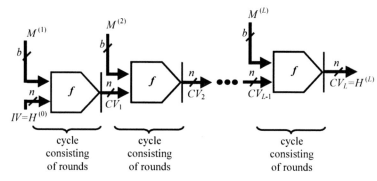

Fig. 6.3. The general structure of a one-way hash function

The complete input document is divided into b-bit blocks. The first b-bit block is used as an input, together with the starting n-bit IV, which is submitted to compression algorithm, i.e. function. The resulting output constitutes an input for the second cycle, together with the second b-bit block of input and so on. The output of the last compression cycle presents the n-bit result of the whole one way hash function. The central architectural element is compression function.

Following are the details of the currently most widely used one-way hash function, which is SHA-1 [252].[5] SHA-1 performs processing of input in $b = 512$ bits, where the input has to be smaller than 2^{64} bits, while the output represents an $n = 160$ bits digest.

The processing starts with preprocessing that includes appending padding bits, appending length to specify original length before padding, and initialization of the 160-bit buffer. Afterwards, a message is processed in 512-bit blocks. Each of these blocks is processed in a cycle that has 80 rounds. With

---

[5]This standard also specifies SHA-256, SHA-384 and SHA-512, but the basis remains SHA-1.

each of eighty rounds the new value in the buffer is calculated by using the old buffer value and two additional variables, where one variable is derived from the current input block. Finally, the buffer value after the last round is added mod 2^{32} to the initial value of the buffer of the first round of a particular cycle to produce the output of this cycle. Afterwards a new cycle is started, where the output of the previous cycle is used to initialize the buffer and the new input block is taken for processing.

A more detailed description of SHA-1 functioning goes as follows. It is started by preprocessing:

- Each document M has to be a multiple of 512 bits, which is assured by padding. Padding starts with one ("1") and is followed by zeroes ("0") until the desired length is obtained. The desired length is determined by another requirement. This is inclusion of 64 bits, which denote the binary representation of the bit-length of the original message.
- The obtained sequence is split into 512-bit blocks, and the number of resulting 512-bit blocks is denoted by L. In addition, the buffer is initialized with the following initial hexadecimal values (the buffer consists of five 32-bit words, denoted by A, B, C, D and E): $A = 67452301$, $B = \text{EFCDAB89}$, $C = \text{98BADCFE}$, $D = 10325476$ and $E = \text{C3D2E1F0}$. The concatenation of these register values presents $H^{(0)}$.

With initialization of the buffer the preprocessing phase is complete. Message processing starts with the first block and continues block by block. Blocks are processed in cycles, where each cycle consists of 80 rounds and results are stored in the buffer. The cycle i goes as follows (i runs from 1 to L):

1. Take the block $M^{(i)}$ of M and calculate variable W_r, variable K_r and logical function f_r for each round r as follows (S^k denotes k left shifts in a register by one bit):

$$W_r = \begin{cases} M_r^{(i)} & 0 \le r \le 15 \\ S^1(W_{r-3} \oplus W_{r-8} \oplus W_{r-14} \oplus W_{r-16}) & 16 \le r \le 79 \end{cases}$$

$$K_r = \begin{cases} 5A827999 & 0 \le r \le 19 \\ 6ED9EBA1 & 20 \le r \le 39 \\ 8F1BBCDC & 40 \le r \le 59 \\ CA62C1D6 & 60 \le r \le 79 \end{cases}$$

$$f_r = \begin{cases} f_r = (B \wedge C) \vee (\overline{B} \wedge D) & 0 \le r \le 19 \\ f_r = (B \oplus C \oplus D) & 20 \le r \le 39 \\ f_r = (B \wedge C) \vee (B \wedge D) \vee (C \wedge D) & 40 \le r \le 59 \\ f_r = (B \oplus C \oplus D) & 60 \le r \le 79 \end{cases}$$

Values $M_r^{(i)}$ are obtained from the current 512-bit input, which is divided into sixteen 32-bit words. Further, f_r is not calculated in advance, because it depends on values in the buffer, which change with each round r.

2. Set the buffer values to the values that are the result of the previous cycle (for the first cycle these values are prepared in the preprocessing phase).
3. Execute the 80 rounds by performing the following operations, whose results are placed back in the buffer (r runs from 0 to 79):
   a) $T \leftarrow S^5(A)(+)f_r(B, C, D)(+)E(+)K_r(+)W_r$
   b) $E \leftarrow D$
   c) $D \leftarrow C$
   d) $C \leftarrow S^{30}(B)$
   e) $B \leftarrow A$
   f) $A \leftarrow T$

   T serves as a temporary value for proper handling of calculation of values in registers, $(+)$ denotes addition mod 2^{32}, and $\leftarrow$ denotes assignment of value of a variable on the right side of the operator to the value of a variable on its left side.
4. After the 80th round perform addition mod 2^{32} using the calculated values in buffer with the initial values of this cycle to get the hash value of this particular cycle $H^{(i)}$ ("$||$" stands for concatenation):

$$initial\_content(A)(+)current\_content(A) = H_0^{(i)}$$
$$\cdots$$
$$initial\_content(E)(+)current\_content(E) = H_4^{(i)}$$
$$H^{(i)} = H_0^{(i)} \ || \ H_1^{(i)} \ || \ H_2^{(i)} \ || \ H_3^{(i)} \ || \ H_4^{(i)}$$

5. If there are additional blocks of input to be processed, i.e. $i < L$, increase i by 1, go to step 1 and use the value $H^{(i-1)}$ as the starting value in the buffer for the next cycle. Otherwise, the sequence $H^{(L)}$ represents the hashed value of the whole document M.

The compression round is shown in Fig. 6.4. Compression function requires W_r as input and its derivation is shown in Fig. 6.5. Both figures together present the complete SHA-1.

Recall that one-way hash functions map a set A with a (practically almost) unlimited number of elements into a set B with a relatively small number of elements. Thus, the number of elements of the input set far exceeds the available number of elements of the set that a one-way hash function maps to. This implies that collisions will happen - certain elements from set A will map to the same element in set B. But discovery of these collisions should be computationally infeasible.

To derive the probability of collisions, suppose there are two sets A and B, where A has an infinite number of elements, while B has a finite number of elements. Let elements in B be natural numbers from a closed interval $[1, n]$ and let each element in A map to exactly one element in B. Let the probability of an element in A being mapped to a particular element in B be equal for all elements in B (a uniform distribution of A over B). How many elements m from set A have to be chosen randomly so that at least one collision occurs in

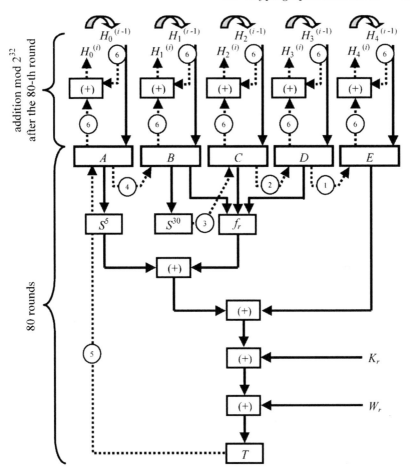

Fig. 6.4. Compression function of SHA-1 where each cycle goes first along the solid lines and then along the dashed lines as numbered, except the 6th step, which is performed after the 80th round ($H^{(i)}$ denotes an output of a cycle, which serves as an input for the next cycle in case where additional blocks have to be processed)

B with probability p? Now consider the generalizations of the two scenarios, given in subsection 3.1.2, when digital signature forgery was discussed:

- Suppose we hash the first randomly chosen element from A and get the corresponding value in B. This value of element in B is recorded and we continue with the mapping procedure. How many elements from A have to be chosen on average to obtain a collision with the first recorded value with a probability of at least 50%?
- Perform the same procedure as above, except that each mapped value in B is recorded and we are accepting any collision, not just the collision with the first recorded number. How many elements from A have to be

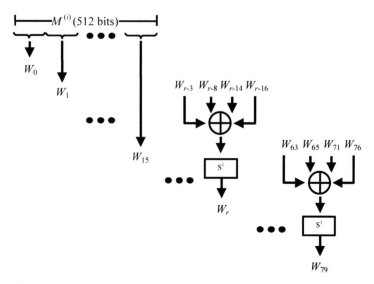

Fig. 6.5. Derivation of a 32-bit word from the current 512-bit input

processed on average to obtain a collision between any two recorded values with probability of 50% or more?

Let c stand for collision, cf for a collision-free event, and let n represent the number of elements in B. In the first scenario, when the first element is chosen, the probability of no collision event is 1. When the second element is chosen, the probability that there is no collision is $1 * [(n-1)/n]$. When the third element is chosen, the probability of no collision is $1 * [(n-1)/n] * [(n-1)/n]$, and so on. Taking into account that the sum of probabilities for collision and no collision events is equal to 1, the probability of collision after m elements are processed is $p_c(n, m) = 1 - p_{cf}(n, m) = 1 - (n-1)^{m-1}/n^{m-1}$.

In the second scenario, when the first element is chosen, the probability that there is no collision is 1. When the second element is chosen, the probability of no collision is $n/n * [(n-1)/n]$. When the third element is chosen, the probability is $n/n * [(n-1)/n] * [(n-2)/n]$, and so on. The sum of probabilities for collision and no collision events is again equal to 1, thus the probability for collision after m elements are processed is $p_c(n, m) = 1 - p_{cf}(n, m) = 1 - (n/n) * [(n-1)/n] * \ldots * [(n-m+1)/(n)] = 1 - n!/(n^m(n-m)!)$.

6.2.2 Pseudorandom Number Generators

True random number generators like a Geiger counter, coin tossing etc., are almost never used because they are impractical. They are replaced by pseudorandom number generators that can be effectively realized within computing environments. Unlike true random numbers, where bits are produced statistically independently one from another, pseudorandom numbers are obtained by algorithms. Of course, the deterministic nature of algorithms cannot produce true random numbers. Sooner or later the sequence produced starts to show statistical dependence. But under certain conditions, these sequences are sufficient to effectively replace real random sequences.

Thus *pseudorandom generators can be more precisely defined as generators that produce sequences of bits, with bits being sufficiently independent one of another*. Without giving the proof, we state the fact that pseudorandom generators exist iff one-way hash functions exist [133]. No wonder why one-way (hash) functions are often used for pseudorandom sequence generation and the principle goes as follows [236]. One chooses the seed s, and derives the sequence $s + 1$, $s + 2$, ..., $s + n$. Each of these values is used to obtain the random sequence by calculating $f(s+1)$, $f(s+2)$, ..., $f(s+n)$. A standardized way of generating pseudorandom sequences by using SHA-1 is given in [248].

Pseudorandom generators are often calculated with congruential generators. A well known example is Blum Blum Shub pseudorandom bit algorithm, which computes pseudo-random bit sequence $z_1, z_2, \ldots, z_k$ [33, 236]:

1. Generate two large, secret and distinct primes p and q and compute $n = p * q$. Each prime should be congruent 3 modulo 4.
2. Select a random integer s from the closed interval $[1, n - 1]$, which is relatively prime to n, and compute $x_0 \leftarrow s^2 \bmod n$.
3. For $i = 1$ to k do the following: $x_1 \leftarrow x_{i-1}^2 \bmod n$ and $z_i \leftarrow LSB(x_i)$.[6]
4. Output bits $z_1, z_2, \ldots, z_k$.

Quality pseudorandom sequences have to possess certain properties like uniform distribution on a covered interval, no serial correlation and a long cycle. The latter means that the repeating sequence of the stream has to be sufficiently long to prevent predictions on the basis of known sequences. In general, the following tests are performed for assuring the quality of pseudorandom bit sequences: frequency test, serial test, poker test, runs test and auto-correlation test (more details can be found in [236]).

6.2.3 Triple DES

Triple DES is implemented by applying three times the ordinary DES to a plaintext. There are two variants of 3DES: the basic one uses three different keys as shown in Fig. 6.6, while the second one uses one key for the first and the third run, and another key for the second run. The second variant has advantage of requiring only 112 bits and is popular also in key management standards [323]. It is worth adding that using decryption at the second stage has no cryptographic significance. The reason is related purely to compatibility with old DES implementations, which is obtained by setting $K_1 = K_2$, thus $C = E_{K_1}(D_{K_1}(E_{K_1}(P))) = E_{K_1}(P)$.

---

[6]LSB stands for least significant bit.

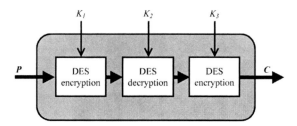

Fig. 6.6. Triple DES

At the heart of 3DES there is the ordinary DES that is presented in Fig. 6.7. It operates on 64 bit blocks, where operations are dictated by a 64 bit key. Actually, DES uses only 56 bits of the key, while the rest can be used for e.g. parity checks (see Fig. 6.10). The plaintext is first permuted and then enters sixteen consecutive rounds, which are followed by inverse initial permutation (it is easy to check that *inverse initial permutation* (*initial permutation* $(b_n)) = b_n$). The exact details of initial permutation and inverse initial permutation are given in Fig. 6.9.

Each of the sixteen rounds is affected by a key. The key is first permuted, split, then shifted left for a certain number of bits, permuted with a new permutation for the second time, reduced, and afterwards finally applied to data of a certain round. The details of permutation A and permutation B are given in Fig. 6.11. Between permutations there is always a left shifting of key bits, as defined in Fig. 6.12.

In each round a key is applied to data using function f (see Fig. 6.7). The key is split into two halves that are separately shifted left according to Fig. 6.12. These two shifted halves are then permuted and contracted to 48 bits. These remaining 48 bits are then XORed with the expanded and permuted right-part data of a particular round:

$$right-data_i = left-data_{i+1},$$
$$right-data_{i+1} = left-data_i \oplus f(right-data_i, key_{i+1})$$

The function f is shaded in Fig. 6.8, where it can be seen that the expanded data are XORed with the permuted and contracted key. Afterwards, the result is sent through so-called S-boxes (see Fig. 6.14), where contraction takes place, followed by permutation. This presents the output of function f, which is XORed with the left half of current input bits. The result presents the new right half of data that enters the next round, while the new left half of data is a direct copy of the current right half of data.

For complete functioning of the f function (see shaded region in Fig. 6.8), the operations of expansion permutation, substitution and permutation have to be given. Expansion permutation and permutation are given in Fig. 6.13, while substitution takes place in S-boxes given in Fig. 6.14.

S-boxes function as follows. Suppose that an input 011000 is submitted to box S_1. The outer two bits (00) denote the row in the box table, and the

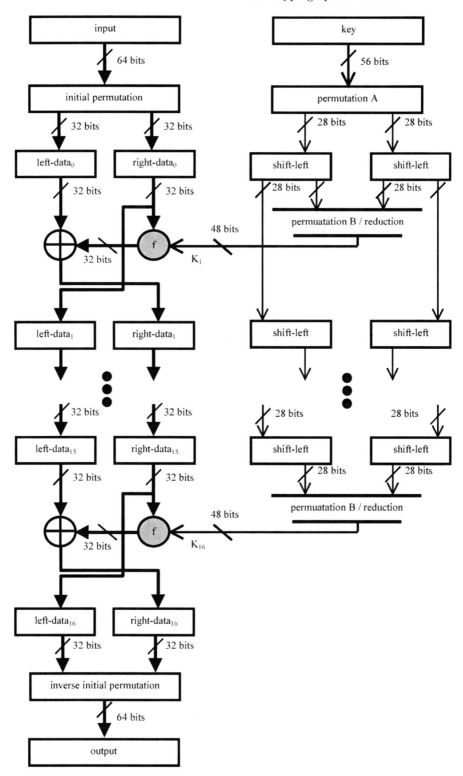

Fig. 6.7. The basic DES (a circle with a plus denotes XOR operation)

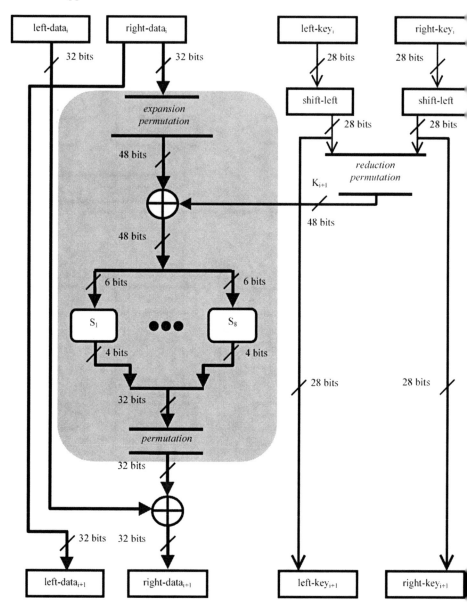

Fig. 6.8. The DES round (shaded region denotes function f from Fig. 6.7)

inner four bits (1100) denote the column. At the cross-section (0,12), the value 0101 (which is the binary representation of 5) is found. These bits constitute the output of the box. Note that this logic requires the indexing of rows and columns to start with 0.

58	50	42	34	26	18	10	2
60	52	44	36	28	20	12	4
62	54	46	38	30	22	14	6
64	56	48	40	32	24	16	8
57	49	41	33	25	17	9	1
59	51	43	35	27	19	11	3
61	53	45	37	29	21	13	5
63	55	47	39	31	23	15	7

40	8	48	16	56	24	64	32
39	7	47	15	55	23	63	31
38	6	46	14	54	22	62	30
37	5	45	13	53	21	61	29
36	4	44	12	52	20	60	28
35	3	43	11	51	19	59	27
34	2	42	10	50	18	58	26
33	1	41	9	49	17	57	25

Fig. 6.9. The initial permutation at the top, and the inverse initial permutation at the bottom (numbers denote bits from an original block, e.g. 58th bit from the original block is placed in the first square, the 50th in the second, and so on)

1	2	3	4	5	6	7	8
9	10	11	12	13	14	15	16
17	18	19	20	21	22	23	24
25	26	27	28	29	30	31	32
33	34	35	36	37	38	39	40
41	42	43	44	45	46	47	48
49	50	51	52	53	54	55	56
57	58	59	60	61	62	63	64

Fig. 6.10. Key preparation (shaded region denotes parity bits)

57	49	41	33	25	17	9
1	58	50	42	34	26	18
10	2	59	51	43	35	27
19	11	3	60	52	44	36
63	55	47	39	31	23	15
7	62	54	46	38	30	22
14	6	61	53	45	37	29
21	13	5	28	20	12	4

14	17	11	24	1	5	3	28
15	6	21	10	23	19	12	4
26	8	16	7	27	20	13	2
41	52	31	37	47	55	30	40
51	45	33	48	44	49	39	56
34	53	46	42	50	36	29	32

Fig. 6.11. Permutations A (top) and B (bottom) of a key

Left (circular) shifting															
round	1	2	3	4	5	6	7	8	9	10	11	12	13	14	15	16
rotations	1	1	2	2	2	2	2	2	1	2	2	2	2	2	2	1

Fig. 6.12. Left shifting of a key

32	1	2	3	4	5
4	5	6	7	8	9
8	9	10	11	12	13
12	13	14	15	16	17
16	17	18	19	20	21
20	21	22	23	24	25
24	25	26	27	28	29
28	29	30	31	32	1

16	7	20	21	29	12	28	17
1	15	23	26	5	18	31	10
2	8	24	14	32	27	3	9
19	13	30	6	22	11	4	25

Fig. 6.13. Expansion permutation (top), where the shaded region denotes duplicated bits, and permutation (bottom)

To understand the nature of S-boxes, i.e. the mapping of the inner four bits, consider the following. A cipher that uses n bits of input and produces n bits of output must ensure a unique mapping if it is to be invertible. With 2^n possible outputs, there are $2^n!$ possible permutations of these outputs (if one wants a reversible mapping, each input block should be transformed to exactly one output block and vice versa). This means that 2^n inputs can be transformed in $2^n!$ ways. For small values of n it is not hard to find the permutation that presents the mapping, but as n increases, the statistical analysis becomes harder and harder. For sufficiently large n, it is not feasible.

Finally, decryption uses the same algorithm as encryption. The only difference is that sub-keys are applied in the reverse order, which enables mapping of a ciphertext to the corresponding plaintext.

DES had to be replaced a few years ago because of increased computing power (Moore's law). It became vulnerable to already mentioned brute force attacks. DES effectively uses only 56-bit keys and trying to obtain a plaintext from a ciphertext requires (in the worst case) 2^{56} DES runs, which is the number of available keys with 56 bits. Considering the current state of technology, this is not enough.

To improve its security, one might use DES twice, consecutively, with two different keys. This variant is called Double DES (2DES). The first key is used on the plaintext block, while the output of this first stage presents the input to the second run of DES with the second key. This apparently increases the number of required DES operations to attack the cipher to 2^{112}. This number

S-BOX 1															
14	4	13	1	2	15	11	8	3	10	6	12	5	9	0	7
0	15	7	4	14	2	13	1	10	6	12	11	9	5	3	8
4	1	14	8	13	6	2	11	15	12	9	7	3	10	5	0
15	12	8	2	4	9	1	7	5	11	3	14	10	0	6	13

S-BOX 2															
15	1	8	14	6	11	3	4	9	7	2	13	12	0	5	10
3	13	4	7	15	2	8	14	12	0	1	10	6	9	11	5
0	14	7	11	10	4	13	1	5	8	12	6	9	3	2	15
13	8	10	1	3	15	4	2	11	6	7	12	0	5	14	9

S-BOX 3															
10	0	9	14	6	3	15	5	1	13	12	7	11	4	2	8
13	7	0	9	3	4	6	10	2	8	5	14	12	11	15	1
13	6	4	9	8	15	3	0	11	1	2	12	5	10	14	7
1	10	13	0	6	9	8	7	4	15	14	3	11	5	2	12

S-BOX 4															
7	13	14	3	0	6	9	10	1	2	8	5	11	12	4	15
13	8	11	5	6	15	0	3	4	7	2	12	1	10	14	9
10	6	9	0	12	11	7	13	15	1	3	14	5	2	8	4
3	15	0	6	10	1	13	8	9	4	5	11	12	7	2	14

S-BOX 5															
2	12	4	1	7	10	11	6	8	5	3	15	13	0	14	9
14	11	2	12	4	7	13	1	5	0	15	10	3	9	8	6
4	2	1	11	10	13	7	8	15	9	12	5	6	3	0	14
11	8	12	7	1	14	2	13	6	15	0	9	10	4	5	3

S-BOX 6															
12	1	10	15	9	2	6	8	0	13	3	4	14	7	5	11
10	15	4	2	7	12	9	5	6	1	13	14	0	11	3	8
9	14	15	5	2	8	12	3	7	0	4	10	1	13	11	6
4	3	2	12	9	5	15	10	11	14	1	7	6	0	8	13

S-BOX 7															
4	11	2	14	15	0	8	13	3	12	9	7	5	10	6	1
13	0	11	7	4	9	1	10	14	3	5	12	2	15	8	6
1	4	11	13	12	3	7	14	10	15	6	8	0	5	9	2
6	11	13	8	1	4	10	7	9	5	0	15	14	2	3	12

S-BOX 8															
13	2	8	4	6	15	11	1	10	9	3	14	5	0	12	7
1	15	13	8	10	3	7	4	12	5	6	11	0	14	9	2
7	11	4	1	9	12	14	2	0	6	10	13	15	3	5	8
2	1	14	7	4	10	8	13	15	12	9	0	3	5	6	11

Fig. 6.14. The structure of S-boxes

of operations is for the worst case scenario, while the average case scenario requires one half of the above operations.

Let the two keys be denoted K_1 and K_2, let P stand for plaintext and C for ciphertext. 2DES operations E (encryption) and D (decryption) go as follows:

$$C = E_{K_2}(E_{K_1}(P)), P = D_{K_1}(D_{K_2}(C)).$$

The cautious reader would probably wonder whether this transformation is not equal to a single DES run with some key E_{K_3}. Indeed, this is a serious question, but in 1992 Campbell and Wiener proved that this fear is not justified [51]. Thus 2DES is strong, since using two different keys does not map to a single DES application. 2DES would be fine as a replacement for ordinary DES, if there did not exist another problem. This is meet-in-the-middle attack. The principle of this attack was first described in [91] and the attack goes as follows.

First recall that $C = E_{K_2}(E_{K_1}(P))$, therefore $E_{K_1}(P) = X = D_{K_2}(C)$. Now, given a pair (P, C), do the following [323]:

1. Encrypt P for all 2^{56} possible values of K_1 to obtain X and store the results in a table.
2. Sort the results in the table by X.
3. Decrypt C using 2^{56} possible values of K_2 and check each decryption immediately against the above table.
4. If there is a match, take a new pair (P', C') and check the key against this pair.
5. If there is another match, accept the keys. Otherwise, go to step 3 and continue with the rest of possible values for K_2.

What is the logic behind this attack? For any P there are 2^{64} possible C values. Further, there are 2^{48} keys per ciphertext on average, which is obtained by dividing 2^{112} keys by 2^{64} ciphertexts. Thus the number of false keys in case of the first match is roughly 2^{48}. When the second match is found, the false rate is $2^{48}/2^{64} = 2^{-16}$. Therefore, the probability that the key in question is not the right one is 2^{-16}, which can be neglected [323]. This means that an attack on 2DES does not require 2^{112} operations (worst case), but a number of operations that is roughly of the same order as for DES.

This ends the discussion of traditional crypto-systems and is continued by a description of two of the most important representatives of public-key cryptosystems: the RSA algorithm and the Diffie-Hellman key exchange. They will be the subject of detailed discussion in the next subsection, covering the principles of their functioning together with related computational complexity facts. Their complexity is not exceeding polynomial complexity (meaning the computation is tractable) for encryption. But for decryption it does not exceed polynomial time complexity only if one knows the appropriate key. Otherwise getting plaintext from ciphertext is computationally hard.

6.2.4 RSA Algorithm

The RSA algorithm starts with the generation of keys. By this process, the public key and the corresponding private key are computed as follows [236]:

1. Generate two large random and distinct primes p and q of roughly the same size.[7]
2. Compute modulus $n = pq$ and $\phi(n) = (p-1)(q-1)$.
3. Select a random integer e from the open interval $(1, \phi(n))$, such that $\gcd(e, \phi(n))=1$.
4. Use the extended Euclidean algorithm to compute the unique integer d from the open interval $(1, \phi(n))$, such that $ed \equiv_{\phi(n)} 1$.

The public key presents the pair (n, e), while d is the private key (e is the encryption and d the decryption exponent). To perform encryption, encrypt a message m by computing $c = m^e \bmod n$ (m is represented as an integer m in the interval $[0, n\text{-}1]$). To decrypt this message, compute $m = c^d \bmod n$.

To see that the desired properties of RSA exist, one can use Euler's theorem. Another form of Euler's theorem that is relevant to RSA, and can be obtained directly from equation 6.4, is as follows ($n = pq$, p and q are primes, k is an arbitrary integer, and m is a message such that $0 \le m \le (n-1)$)[323]:

$$m^{k\phi(n)+1} = m^{k(p-q)(q-1)+1} \equiv_n m. \tag{6.5}$$

The exponent in the above congruence reveals that there can be a split into two parts, where the exponentiation with the first part provides encryption, while further exponentiation with the second part results in recovery of the plaintext:

$$m^{ed} = m \bmod n.$$

Therefore to obtain an appropriate pair of keys (e for encryption and d for decryption), the following relationship has to be used:

$$ed = k\phi(n) + 1, \tag{6.6}$$

or equivalently

$$ed \equiv_{\phi(n)} 1 \text{ and } d \equiv_{\phi(n)} e^{-1}.$$

In order for the inverse to exist, d (and consequently e) has to be prime to $\phi(n)$.

An example with small values for parameters follows. First, key generation has to be performed. Let us choose the primes $p = 29$ and $q = 23$, and compute

---

[7]Testing primality used to be done exclusively by stochastic algorithms until recently [320], when three Indian mathematicians discovered a deterministic algorithm with polynomial time complexity [5]. Despite this, probabilistic tests are still more efficient for practical applications.

$n = pq = 667$, and $\phi(n) = (p-1)(q-1) = 616$. Next, we choose $e = 613$, which is (and has to be) prime to $\phi(n)$. By the extended Euclidean algorithm we find $d = 205$ such that $ed \equiv_{\phi(n)} 1$, which can be easily checked. The public key presents the pair $(n = 667, e = 613)$, while the private key is $d = 205$.

Now suppose a simple plaintext "asimpletest" has to be encrypted. Firstly, the characters have to be coded. Let us do this coding by assigning 0 to "a", 1 to "b", and so on, which results in the following coded plaintext 0, 18, 8, 12, 15, 11, 4, 19, 4, 18, 19 (commas and spaces are inserted for clarity only and are not encoded). Suppose further that each character is encrypted separately. Thus the following exponentiations modulo 667 have to be performed: $0^{613}, 18^{613}, 8^{613}, 12^{613}, 15^{613}, 11^{613}, 4^{613}, 19^{613}, 4^{613}, 18^{613}, 19^{613}$. The result is the ciphertext 0, 39, 142, 215, 617, 222, 469, 60, 469, 39, 60. To produce plaintext, decryption is performed by exponentiation of the above numbers, where the exponent presents the deciphering key: $0^{205}, 39^{205}, 142^{205}, \dots$ The result is, as expected, the plaintext: $0, 18, 8, \dots$

In the above example we performed encryption on a character by character basis. The proper approach would be concatenation of coded values that result in one large integer. It should be emphasized that the resulting large integer has to be smaller than the modulus, which poses limitations on provision of authentication and confidentiality with RSA. Of course, if the resulting large integer exceeds the modulus, it can be split and each part encrypted separately. This explanation should also help to understand why hashing of the plaintext is performed before it is signed.

6.2.5 Diffie-Hellman Key Agreement

The protocol is based on the assumption of the computational intractability of discrete logarithms, i.e. given a prime p, a generator α of $\mathbb{Z}_p^*$, and an element $\beta \in \mathbb{Z}_p^*$, it should be infeasible to compute x, $0 < x \le p-2$, such that $\alpha^x \equiv_p \beta$. The protocol goes as follows [236]:

1. Entities A and B agree on two public values: prime p and generator α of $\mathbb{Z}_p^*$, $2 \le \alpha \le p-2$.
2. Entity A chooses a random secret x from the closed interval $[1, p-2]$, while B does the same to obtain secret y.
3. A sends $\alpha^x \bmod p$ to B and B sends $\alpha^y \bmod p$ to A.
4. A computes $K = (\alpha^y)^x \bmod p$ and obtains the shared secret key, while B obtains it by computing $K = (\alpha^x)^y \bmod p$.

Variables x and y are referred to as private keys, while α^x and α^y are referred to as public keys. But an inherent danger exists with the basic DH, because it does not provide authentication. An already mentioned attack, which is called man-in-the-middle, goes as follows (all operations are $\bmod p$):

1. An attacker intercepts α^x and α^y.
2. The attacker uses fake x' and fake y' and sends $\alpha^{x'}$ to B and $\alpha^{y'}$ to A.

3. The calculated two session keys are $K_1 = (\alpha^y)^{x'}$ and $K_2 = (\alpha^{y'})^x$ and they enable the messages between A and B to be to relayed and read.

The above vulnerability is due to lack of authentication, because the public keys are not authenticated. While in this case the vulnerability is evident, this is far from being the case with the majority of other security protocols. To find even subtle flaws in cryptographic protocols, one should use formal methods.

6.3 Formal Methods

Cryptographic protocols play an important role in ISs security, because they present means by which security services are realized. Put another way - security in networked information systems depends heavily on protocols that use cryptographic primitives, i.e. cryptographic protocols. To provide assurance that a particular security service is realized once the protocol runs from its initial state to the final state, formal techniques are used.

Although cryptographic protocols consist typically of only few message exchanges, practice has shown that their design is all but a trivial technical issue. Numerous protocols that were believed for years to be secure have flaws, e.g. Needham-Schroeder protocol [254], and many of them were (or still are) standards. The latest examples are WEP [282], BCY [72], and TLS [191].

It is strongly advised to use protocols that have a sound reputation in the literature. However, there is always a chance of being forced to tailor existing solutions to particular needs, to deal with slightly different roles or assumptions, or to invent a completely new protocol. In this case, formal verification of sensitive software and hardware parts is a must.

Because formal methods require extensive knowledge and investment in terms of human resources and time, they are applied to the most critical subparts of ISs. But formal methods are no panacea - passing a formal verification method does not provide watertight evidence that a designed system is bug-free. Nevertheless, they are very useful to improve security of ISs.

6.3.1 Overview of Formal Methods

Formal methods provide strict and rigid means for evaluating protocols by excluding intuitive approaches during the design of protocols (and systems in general).[8] Intuition alone is a bad dowry for a protocol required to withstand various kinds of attacks in reality.

Formal methods can be divided into a number of groups, like model-based ones (e.g. language **Z** [321]), logic-based ones (e.g. Hoare logic [92]), process algebras (e.g. LOTOS [224]), and pure grammars (e.g. Rüppel's grammar [300]

---

[8]Formal methods are proposed to be used even for high level concepts in e-business operations and processes, e.g. electronic contract and obligations [140].

and its derivative SAFL [337]). There is another group based on logic with a notable example being logic BAN [48].

BAN logic has a strict syntax and proof derivation rules. It served as a basis for many other formalisms in the field of security, and its most successful successor is GNY logic [134]. The main improvement of the latter logic is that it uses message extensions, which enable different levels of trust between principals to be dealt with, i.e. principals can communicate their beliefs and thus reason about them. Another useful technique in the same field is SvO logic [330]. Nevertheless, BAN remains among the most successful formal methods in security engineering.

Currently, the most popular method in the area of software engineering is becoming Unified Modeling Language (UML) [262]. Its importance is growing in the field of systems analysis and design [200]. This is a graphic notation based language, which is not a true formal method per se. But UML is being expanded and slowly incorporating pure formal techniques - one such example is Object Constraint Language (OCL) [191]. Focusing on security, UML is evolving into UMLsec [191] and will be discussed in subsection 6.3.4.

6.3.2 Introduction to Logic BAN

BAN has a proven success record, it is mature, and it has been around for more than a decade. It is a relatively intuitive formalism and suitable for presenting the basic idea and application of formal methods. Thus it will serve to introduce formal methods within the methodology of this book.[9]

BAN logic is focused on proving the authentication properties of cryptographic protocols. It relies on cryptographically transformed messages, where proper use of cryptography assures integrity and freshness of exchanged messages. This is the basis for achieving authentication. The proof process starts with conversion of a protocol into an idealized form. Then assumptions at the initial state are given. Logical formulas are attached to these statements. In line with transformation rules and the run of a protocol, formulas are obtained which state beliefs of involved parties at the end of a protocol.

BAN provides answers to the following questions: What is actually achieved in terms of authentication when the protocol runs from its initial to the final state? Which are the exact assumptions that are required by a protocol - is the initial set of assumptions sufficient? Are there redundancies in the protocol? BAN logic does not address other problems that are typically related to protocols, e.g. dead-locks, which may lead to denial of service. Therefore formal verification of ordinary protocol properties is assured by applying other formal techniques, e.g. Spin and the like [156].

---

[9]This introduction extends the original paper [47] by complete derivation of one of its protocol examples. The original paper is freely available on the Web at HP site with the URL http://gatekeeper.research.compaq.com/pub/DEC/SRC/research-reports/abstracts/src-rr-039.html.

BAN logic distinguishes *principals, encryption keys* and *statements*. Statements present messages exchanged between communicating entities. Symbols A, B, S denote specific principals, K_{AB}, K_{AS}, K_{BS} denote specific symmetric keys, $K_A/K_A^{-1}, K_B/K_B^{-1}, K_C/K_C^{-1}$ denote specific public/private keys. Further, N_A, N_B and N_C denote specific statements, and symbols P, Q, R denote principals in general, and X, Y denote statements in general. Finally, T denotes a timestamp.

Cryptographic protocols are usually presented in so-called bit-string notation, which implies coding procedure. The general form is $A \to B : message$, which means that the principal A sends the *message* that is received by the principal B. Thus $A \to B : \{m\}_{K_{AB}}$ denotes message m encrypted with symmetric key K_{AB} that is sent from A to B.

The following subset of the basic constructs will be needed:

- $P \models X$: *P believes X*, which means that the principal P takes X for granted and acts accordingly.
- $P \triangleleft X$: *P sees X*, which means that P has received a message containig X, and can read or repeat it (after eventual decryption).
- $P \mid\sim X$: *P once said X*, which means that P at some time sent a message containing X, but it is not known whether this happened long ago or during the current run of the protocol (however, it is known that P believed X when he sent the message).
- $P \mid\Rightarrow X$: *P has jurisdiction over X*, which means that P is an authority on X and should be trusted on this matter.
- $\sharp(X)$: The formula X is *fresh*, i.e. it has not been sent in any message before the current run of the protocol (X is, or contains, a timestamp, a random number, or sequence number).
- $P \overset{K}{\leftrightarrow} Q$: P and Q use the shared secret key K to communicate, which may be known only to principals trusted by P and Q.
- $\{X\}_K$: This notation represents X, encrypted under the key K.

Further, the following subset of BAN logical postulates will be needed:

- The message meaning postulate is related to the interpretation of the messages (encrypted ones):

$$\frac{P \models Q \overset{K}{\leftrightarrow} P, P \triangleleft \{X\}_K}{P \models Q \mid\sim X} \tag{6.7}$$

- The nonce-verification postulate expresses the check of a message to verify if it is recent - if this is the case, the sender still believes in it:

$$\frac{P \models \sharp(X), P \models Q \mid\sim X}{P \models Q \models X} \tag{6.8}$$

- The jurisdiction postulate states that if principal P believes that principal Q has jurisdiction over X, then P trusts Q on the truth of statement X:

$$\frac{P \models Q \Mapsto X, P \models Q \models X}{P \models X} \tag{6.9}$$

- Composition and separation of statements with the operator $\models$ (P believes a set of statements iff P believes each individual statement):

$$\frac{P \models X, P \models Y}{P \models (X, Y)} \qquad \frac{P \models (X, Y)}{P \models X} \qquad \frac{P \models Q \models (X, Y)}{P \models Q \models X} \tag{6.10}$$

- A logical extension of the last part of the above postulate leads to a similar postulate for the operator $\mapsto$:

$$\frac{P \models Q \mapsto (X, Y)}{P \models Q \mapsto X} \tag{6.11}$$

- If a principal sees a (composite) formula and knows the keys, then this principal also sees its components:

$$\frac{P \triangleleft (X, Y)}{P \triangleleft X} \qquad \frac{P \models Q \overset{K}{\leftrightarrow} P, P \triangleleft \{X\}_K}{P \triangleleft X} \tag{6.12}$$

- A postulate about freshness of a message states that if a part of a formula is known to be fresh, then the entire formula must be fresh:

$$\frac{P \models \sharp(X)}{P \models \sharp(X, Y)} \tag{6.13}$$

- A postulate about commutativity is needed for symmetric keys:

$$\frac{P \models R \overset{K}{\leftrightarrow} R'}{P \models R' \overset{K}{\leftrightarrow} R} \qquad \frac{P \models Q \models R \overset{K}{\leftrightarrow} R'}{P \models Q \models R' \overset{K}{\leftrightarrow} R} \tag{6.14}$$

BAN logic uses only universal quantifiers, which can be in the majority of cases treated implicitly (an explicit treatment is required for complex delegation statements). Finally, the time is also treated implicitly and there are only two epochs: present and past.

And when do we know that formal goals of authentication have been achieved? When the derivation of final beliefs results in the following statements, formal goals of authentication have been achieved (these statements represent a subset of all beliefs, but they are sufficient for the introduction):

$$A \models A \overset{K}{\leftrightarrow} B \quad B \models A \overset{K}{\leftrightarrow} B \quad A \models B \models A \overset{K}{\leftrightarrow} B \quad B \models A \models A \overset{K}{\leftrightarrow} B \tag{6.15}$$

With the presented formal apparatus, the Wide-mouthed-frog protocol will be analyzed. The protocol is based on symmetric cryptography, it uses a server for authentication, which is trusted by principals, and synchronized clocks. The complete run consists of only two steps:

1. $A \rightarrow S : A, \{T_A, B, K_{AB}\}_{K_{AS}}$
2. $S \rightarrow B : \{T_S, A, K_{AB}\}_{K_{BS}}$

Bit-string notation can be ambiguous and is not suitable for formal analysis. Thus it has to be transformed into idealized form. Each message is written as a formula, where those parts are omitted that do not contribute to the beliefs of the recipient. This includes parts that are not encrypted or otherwise transformed. BAN authors suggest as a rough guide for idealization that a real message m can be interpreted as a formula X if the recipient, after the receipt of m, may deduce that the sender must have believed X when she sent it.

The idealization of the protocol "Wide-mouthed-frog" is as follows:

1. $A \rightarrow S : \{T_A, (A \overset{K_{AB}}{\leftrightarrow} B)\}_{K_{AS}}$
2. $S \rightarrow B : \{T_S, A \models (A \overset{K_{AB}}{\leftrightarrow} B)\}_{K_{BS}}$

These are the assumptions for the protocol:

$A \models (A \overset{K_{AS}}{\leftrightarrow} S) \quad B \models (B \overset{K_{BS}}{\leftrightarrow} S)$
$S \models (A \overset{K_{AS}}{\leftrightarrow} S) \quad S \models (B \overset{K_{BS}}{\leftrightarrow} S)$
$A \models (A \overset{K_{AB}}{\leftrightarrow} B) \quad B \models (A \mapsto A \overset{K_{AB}}{\leftrightarrow} B)$
$S \models \sharp(T_A) \qquad B \models \sharp(T_S)$
$B \models (S \mapsto A \models A \overset{K_{AB}}{\leftrightarrow} B)$

By use of 6.12, one result of the analysis of the first step is:

$$\frac{S \models (A \overset{K_{AS}}{\leftrightarrow} S), \quad S \triangleleft \{T_A, A \overset{K_{AB}}{\leftrightarrow} B\}_{K_{AS}}}{S \triangleleft (T_A, A \overset{K_{AB}}{\leftrightarrow} B)} \tag{6.16}$$

Because of 6.12 the following also holds true after the first step:

$$\frac{S \triangleleft (T_A, A \overset{K_{AB}}{\leftrightarrow} B)}{S \triangleleft (T_A)} \qquad \frac{S \triangleleft (T_A, A \overset{K_{AB}}{\leftrightarrow} B)}{S \triangleleft (A \overset{K_{AB}}{\leftrightarrow} B)} \tag{6.17}$$

Using the above assumptions and 6.13 one obtains:

$$\frac{S \models \sharp(T_A)}{S \models \sharp(T_A, A \overset{K_{AB}}{\leftrightarrow} B)} \tag{6.18}$$

Using again the assumptions, together with 6.12 and 6.7 one can derive:

$$\frac{S \models (A \overset{K_{AS}}{\leftrightarrow} S), \ S \triangleleft \{(T_A, A \overset{K_{AB}}{\leftrightarrow} B)\}_{K_{AS}}}{S \models A \mapsto (T_A, A \overset{K_{AB}}{\leftrightarrow} B)} \tag{6.19}$$

Using the last two results, and taking into account 6.8, we obtain beliefs after the first step:

$$\frac{S \models \sharp(T_A, A \stackrel{K_{AB}}{\leftrightarrow} B), \ S \models A \mid\!\sim (T_A, A \stackrel{K_{AB}}{\leftrightarrow} B)}{S \models A \models (T_A, A \stackrel{K_{AB}}{\leftrightarrow} B)} \tag{6.20}$$

After the exchange of the first message and by use of 6.10 we can write:

$$\frac{S \models A \models (T_A, A \stackrel{K_{AB}}{\leftrightarrow} B)}{S \models A \models (A \stackrel{K_{AB}}{\leftrightarrow} B)} \tag{6.21}$$

The analysis of the second step starts with the assumption (B believes that key K_{BS} is known only to the server S) and application of 6.7:

$$\frac{B \models (S \stackrel{K_{BS}}{\leftrightarrow} B), \quad B \triangleleft \{T_S, A \stackrel{K_{AB}}{\leftrightarrow} B\}_{K_{BS}}}{B \models S \mid\!\sim (T_S, A \models A \stackrel{K_{AB}}{\leftrightarrow} B)} \tag{6.22}$$

Similarly to the analysis of the first message, we take into account the assumption and 6.13:

$$\frac{B \models \sharp(T_S)}{B \models \sharp(T_S, A \models A \stackrel{K_{AB}}{\leftrightarrow} B)} \tag{6.23}$$

Using the last two results and applying 6.8 one can obtain:

$$\frac{B \models \sharp(T_S, A \models A \stackrel{K_{AB}}{\leftrightarrow} B), \quad B \models S \mid\!\sim (T_S, A \models A \stackrel{K_{AB}}{\leftrightarrow} B)}{B \models S \models (T_S, A \models A \stackrel{K_{AB}}{\leftrightarrow} B)} \tag{6.24}$$

Because of 6.10 we know that if a principal believes in a set of statements then she believes each individual statement:

$$\frac{B \models S \models (T_S, A \models A \stackrel{K_{AB}}{\leftrightarrow} B)}{B \models S \models (A \models A \stackrel{K_{AB}}{\leftrightarrow} B)} \tag{6.25}$$

Using 6.25, the assumption about jurisdiction of principal S, and 6.9 one can derive:

$$\frac{B \models (S \mapsto A \models A \stackrel{K_{AB}}{\leftrightarrow} B), \ B \models S \models (A \models A \stackrel{K_{AB}}{\leftrightarrow} B)}{B \models A \models A \stackrel{K_{AB}}{\leftrightarrow} B} \tag{6.26}$$

Using the last result, the assumptions, and 6.9 it can be derived:

$$\frac{B \models (A \mapsto A \stackrel{K_{AB}}{\leftrightarrow} B), \ B \models A \models A \stackrel{K_{AB}}{\leftrightarrow} B}{B \models (A \stackrel{K_{AB}}{\leftrightarrow} B)} \tag{6.27}$$

These results present the final beliefs of the principals. It can be seen that the formal goals of authentication are achieved:

$$A \models (A \overset{K_{AB}}{\leftrightarrow} B) \qquad B \models A \models (A \overset{K_{AB}}{\leftrightarrow} B)$$

$$S \models A \models (A \overset{K_{AB}}{\leftrightarrow} B) \qquad B \models (A \overset{K_{AB}}{\leftrightarrow} B)$$

One of the first remarkable successes of BAN logic was analysis of the X.509 protocol (CCITT 87). This protocol is based on asymmetric cryptography and intended to provide mutual authentication with optional exchange of a secret. Classical representation of the protocol goes as follows (T is a time stamp, N is a nonce, X parameters, Y secret data, e.g. session keys):

1. $A \rightarrow B : A, \{T_A, N_A, B, X_A, \{Y_A\}_{K_B}\}_{K_A^{-1}}$
2. $B \rightarrow A : B, \{T_B, N_B, A, N_A, X_B, \{Y_B\}_{K_A}\}_{K_B^{-1}}$
3. $A \rightarrow B : A, \{N_B\}_{K_A^{-1}}$

Using BAN analysis, the following beliefs are derived [47]:

$$B \models A \models X_A \qquad A \models B \models X_B \qquad B \models A \models N_B$$

Based on the derived beliefs, authors of BAN logic conclude:

- It was the intention of the authors of the standard to protect Y_A in Y_B, because they are the most intensively processed elements. But the analyzed protocol does not result in beliefs $B \models A \models Y_A$ and $A \models B \models Y_B$, although Y_A in Y_B are sent in digitally signed messages.
- It is not explicitly evident that the sender is aware of the contents of these data, therefore an attacker can remove the signature and simply sign these data using her key. The solution is, if a sender signs Y_A and Y_B before encrypting them with the recipient's key.
- The standard suggests that checking T_A is optional, which is a problem, as we cannot obtain the beliefs from 6.15.
- The protocol has some redundancy - identical beliefs can be achieved only either T_B or N_A.
- The purpose of the third message is to provide assurance to principal B that principal A has generated the first message recently. N_B should be sufficient to link the third and the first messages, because N_A logically links the first two messages, while N_B logically links the second two messages. However, N_B alone does not link logically the last two messages.

Before getting to details of an attack, the following should be known:

- The standard allows use of three variations, where the first variation consists of only the first message, the second of the first two messages and the last of all three messages.
- The reason for optional checking of timestamps is most likely a wish to obtain a generally applicable protocol that would not require a synchronized time base, thus random numbers should provide sufficient means to ensure freshness, if checked.

- The protocol steps do not necessarily include the secret content (session key), but, if present, the standard allows $Y_A = Y_B$.

Based on discovered weaknesses, an attack on the protocol can be constructed. Assume that an attacker C attacks the variation with all three steps [47, 164]. The nonce N_B will be used to falsely convince B that she is communicating with A. C starts with a replay:

$$C \to B : A, \{T_A, N_A, B, X_A, \{Y_A\}_{K_B}\}_{K_A^{-1}}$$

Because it is not required that B checks the timestamp T_A, B will respond with the following packet:

$$B \to C : B, \{T_B, N_B, A, N_A, X_B, \{Y_B\}_{K_A}\}_{K_B^{-1}}$$

Principal B thus believes that she is communicating with A and includes a random value N_B. This enables the attacker to continue a masquerade against A and she challenges A to start authentication. A responds:

$$A \to C : A, \{T_A', N_A', C, X_A', \{Y_A'\}_{K_C}\}_{K_A^{-1}}$$

Principal C sends a reply to A, where she uses random number N_B that was generated by B:

$$C \to A : C, \{T_C, N_B, A, N_A', X_C, \{Y_C\}_{K_A}\}_{K_C^{-1}}$$

A then replies to C, signs the exact message that is needed by C to mislead B that the first message was recently sent by A, and that this is not a reply:

$$A \to C : A, \{N_B\}_{K_A^{-1}}$$

This is what C needs to successfully attack the protocol and (falsely) convince B of being A.

Another possibility to attack secret content of communication between A in B goes as follows (the variant with the first two steps of the protocol is used) [164, 47]. A sends a message M to B (e.g. a database query), which is of a secret nature and encrypted with the asymmetric key:

$$A \to B : A, \{T_A, N_A, B, N_B, X_A, \{Y_A\}_{K_B}\}_{K_A^{-1}}$$

C catches the message and constructs a new one by taking X_A and $\{Y_A\}_{K_B}$ directly from the previous message:

$$C \to B : C, \{T_C, N_C, B, N_B, X_A, \{Y_A\}_{K_B}\}_{K_C^{-1}}$$

B receives the message, decrypts it, checks it all except the freshness, and believes that it is coming from C. Therefore B constructs a response and sends it to C. C can now use this response to recover the contents of the database query, generated by A in the first step. The response $\{Y_A\}_{K_C}$ is encrypted now with the public key of C, which C can easily decrypt.

6.3.3 Language Z Overview

Language **Z** was developed at Oxford University in the late eighties. Two decades after its introduction it still remains an important formal method [321]. It is based on set theory and first order logic, i.e. it has mathematical semantics, while its syntax is standardized as well - **Z** has been recognized as international standard by ISO [179].

Z is a typed language. Using schemas, models are constructed that cover static and dynamic properties of systems. Once a system is formalized, errors can be discovered, the system can be rigorously analyzed, and sometimes its critical properties can be proved. This significantly reduces a possibility of false or buggy implementations, and contributes to the strength of proper transformations into executable code.

Specification in **Z** consists mainly of schemas, which are divided into two parts: declarations and predicates. The first part serves to define variables and their types. The second part puts logical constraints on these variables through predicates.

$$
\begin{array}{|l}
\hline
\textit{Schema} \\
\hline
\textit{declarations} \\
\hline
\textit{predicates} \\
\hline
\end{array}
$$

Besides schemas, square brackets are used to define basic types:

$[type]$

Axiomatic definitions are given in a modified schema notation, which has no upper and bottom lines:

$$
\begin{array}{|l}
\textit{MaxSize} : \mathbb{N} \\
\hline
\textit{MaxSize} \leq 1024 \\
\end{array}
$$

This axiomatic definition states that the maximal size (of something) is denoted by a natural number, which is smaller or equal to 1024.

For the generic definitions, another kind of modified schema is used with a double upper line:

$$
\begin{array}{|l}
\hline\hline
[\textit{SchemaSecond}] \\
\textit{Second} : A \times A \to A \\
\hline
\forall\, a, b : A \bullet \textit{Second}(a, b) = b \\
\hline
\end{array}
$$

This generic definition states that the operation *Second*, which takes as an input an ordered pair of elements, outputs the second element of this pair.

In order to model the dynamic behavior of systems, input variables are decorated with a question mark, and output variables are decorated with an exclamation mark. In the below example, the remainder from the division of the input by 10 is calculated and given on the output:

```
┌─ ModOperation ──────────────────────────────────
│  in?, out! : ℤ
├─────────────────────────────────────────────────
│  out! = in? mod 10
└─────────────────────────────────────────────────
```

Input and output variables are not enough for modeling of systems, and internal variables have to be used. For these variables, their pre-operation state has no decoration. For their post-operation state, we use apostrophes. If the schema name is prepended with Δ, this denotes a new schema that is a conjunction of an original before-schema and the derived after-schema.

Let *Family* schema denote the fact that each family consists of at least one member, and the number of members in a family is given by the cardinality[10] of set *familyMembers* - this is assured with two predicates. Variable *familyMembers* is a set with elements of type *Person*, while *numberOfMembers* variable belongs to natural numbers.

```
┌─ Family ─────────────────────────────────────────
│  familyMembers : ℙ Person
│  numberOfMembers : ℕ
├─────────────────────────────────────────────────
│  familyMembers ≠ ∅
│  numberOfMembers = #familyMembers
└─────────────────────────────────────────────────
```

Suppose some change has happened in a family, then post-operation states of variables will have to be used.

```
┌─ ΔFamily ────────────────────────────────────────
│  familyMembers, familyMembers' : ℙ Person
│  numberOfMembers, numberOfMembers' : ℕ
├─────────────────────────────────────────────────
│  familyMembers ≠ ∅
│  familyMembers' ≠ ∅
│  numberOfMembers = #familyMembers
│  numberOfMembers' = #familyMembers'
└─────────────────────────────────────────────────
```

But if no change actually occurred to the family during some operation, the post-operation state of variables remains unchanged, which is denoted by prepended symbol Ξ to the name of schema:

```
┌─ Ξ Family ───────────────────────────────────────
│  ΔFamily
├─────────────────────────────────────────────────
│  familyMembers = familyMembers'
│  numberOfMembers = numberOfMembers'
└─────────────────────────────────────────────────
```

---

[10]Cardinality means the number of elements in a set, and its operator is #.

A simple specification of an automaton that assigns nonces to packets follows. It will be proved that the operation of this automaton preserves uniqueness of the assigned nonces. Before being able to do this, renaming, hiding and composition of schemas have to be given.

Schema renaming means renaming local variables. More precisely, if free occurrences of x in *SchemaOne* are replaced by u, this operation is denoted by $SchemaOne[u/x]$.

$$\begin{array}{|l}\hline \_SchemaOne_____ \\ x, y : \mathbb{Z} \\ A : \mathbb{P}\,\mathbb{Z} \\ \hline x \in A \Rightarrow y \in A \land y > x \\ \hline \end{array}$$

Now let us form *SchemaTwo* by replacing x with u in *SchemaOne* (this operation is written as $SchemaTwo \,\widehat{=}\, SchemaOne[u/x]$, where operator $\widehat{=}$ denotes schema definition):

$$\begin{array}{|l}\hline \_SchemaTwo_____ \\ u, y : \mathbb{Z} \\ A : \mathbb{P}\,\mathbb{Z} \\ \hline u \in A \Rightarrow y \in A \land y > u \\ \hline \end{array}$$

Hiding a variable in *SchemaOne* results in *SchemaThree* (this operation is denoted by $SchemaThree \,\widehat{=}\, SchemaOne \setminus (x)$):

$$\begin{array}{|l}\hline \_SchemaThree_____ \\ y : \mathbb{Z} \\ A : \mathbb{P}\,\mathbb{Z} \\ \hline \exists x : \mathbb{Z} \bullet (x \in A \Rightarrow y \in A \land y > x) \\ \hline \end{array}$$

With hiding, a variable is removed from the declaration part and expressed with an existential quantifier in the predicate part. This operation often enables simplification of schemas, as will be shown in the next example.

To relate after-state variables of one schema to before-state variables of another schema, schema composition is used. The base name of related variables is preserved (this is the name of variables without decorations), while input and output variables remain unaffected. The procedure to form a composition of schemas *SchemaA* and *SchemaB* goes as follows [93]:[11]

1. Form $SchemaA[s^+/s']$, which means renaming the after-state variables in *SchemaA* to something new.

---

[11] This explanation is derived from Z - An Introduction to Formal Methods, written by A. Diller. ©1994 John Wiley & Sons Ltd. Reproduced with permission.

2. Form $SchemaB[s^+/s]$, which means renaming of before state variables in $SchemaB$ into the same new name as used in step 1.
3. Form the conjunction of the renamed schemas, i.e. $SchemaA[s^+/s'] \wedge SchemaB[s^+/s]$.
4. Hide the new variable s^+ from steps 1 and 2; the result is schema composition $SchemaA \mathbin{\substack{\circ\\\circ}} SchemaB$ (operator $\mathbin{\substack{\circ\\\circ}}$ denotes composition).

Suppose there exist schemas $SchemaA$ and $SchemaB$:

```
┌─ SchemaA ──────────────────────────────────────────────
│ x?, s, s', y! : ℕ
├────────────────────────────────────────────────────────
│ s' = s + x?
│ y! = 2 * s
└────────────────────────────────────────────────────────
```

```
┌─ SchemaB ──────────────────────────────────────────────
│ x?, s, s' : ℕ
├────────────────────────────────────────────────────────
│ s < x?
│ s' = s
└────────────────────────────────────────────────────────
```

After renaming (steps 1 and 2) the conjunction is formed:

```
┌─ ConjunctionOfRenamedSchemas ──────────────────────────
│ x?, s, s⁺, s', y! : ℕ
├────────────────────────────────────────────────────────
│ s⁺ = s + x?
│ y! = 2 * s
│ s⁺ < x?
│ s' = s⁺
└────────────────────────────────────────────────────────
```

In the last step s^+ is hidden:

```
┌─ SchemaComposition ────────────────────────────────────
│ x?, s, s', y! : ℕ
├────────────────────────────────────────────────────────
│ ∃ s⁺ : ℕ • (s⁺ = s + x? ∧
│ y! = 2 * s ∧
│ s⁺ < x? ∧
│ s' = s⁺)
└────────────────────────────────────────────────────────
```

The result of composition can be often simplified - in the above case s^+ can be completely eliminated:[12]

---

[12] This is possible due to the syntactic equivalence rule $P[t/y] \dashv\vdash \exists y : Y \bullet P \wedge y = t$, where t is a term of the same type as variable y and variable y can occur free in formula P (operator $\dashv\vdash$ denotes syntactic equivalence). In our case

```
┌─ FinalSchemaComposition ─────────────────────────────
│ x?, s, s', y! : ℕ
├──────────────────────────────────────────────────────
│ s' = s + x?
│ y! = 2 * s
│ s' < x?
└──────────────────────────────────────────────────────
```

Finally, the specification of an automaton for the unique assignment of nonces can be given [235]:

```
┌─ Nonce ──────────────────────────────────────────────
│ assigned : ℙ ℕ
└──────────────────────────────────────────────────────
```

```
┌─ Initialization ─────────────────────────────────────
│ Nonce
├──────────────────────────────────────────────────────
│ assigned = ∅
└──────────────────────────────────────────────────────
```

```
┌─ NewNonce ───────────────────────────────────────────
│ ΔNonce
│ nonce₁! : ℕ
├──────────────────────────────────────────────────────
│ nonce₁! ∉ assigned
│ assigned' = assigned ∪ {nonce₁!}
└──────────────────────────────────────────────────────
```

Now the automaton is run for two consecutive runs:

$$TwoConsecutiveNonces \; \widehat{=} \; NewNonce \; _{9}^{\circ} \; NewNonce[nonce_2!/nonce_1!]$$

The above operation, denoted by schema $TwoConsecutiveNonces$, preserves uniqueness of assigned nonces. The proof goes as follows:

$$assigned' = assigned \cup \{nonce_1!\} \cup \{nonce_2!\} \; \wedge$$
$$nonce_2! \notin assigned \cup \{nonce_1!\} \Rightarrow nonce_1! \neq nonce_2!$$

The advantage of **Z** is its standardization, and long and proven record of applications. Moreover, many tools exist for computer supported manipulations, ranging from type checkers like ZTC [363] to automated proof derivation tools like Z-Eves [235].

An excellent introduction to **Z** (and formal methods in general) is given in [93]. A specific formalism that is based on **Z** and belongs to the same field of application as logic BAN can be found in [38].

$$\exists \, s^+ : \mathbb{N} \bullet \underbrace{s^+ = s + x? \wedge y! = 2 * s \wedge s^+ < x?}_{P} \wedge s^+ = s'$$

and equivalently

$$s' = s + x? \wedge y! = 2 * s \wedge s' < x?.$$

6.3.4 Emerging Formal Methods

Among emerging formal methods, the two most notable examples are formalism based on Abstract State Machines (ASMs) [39] and formalism based on UML, i.e. UMLsec [191].

ASMs are grounded on the premise that any algorithm can be abstracted by natural reflection through corresponding ASM.[13] There always exists a gap between formal specification and its realization. ASMs are intended to narrow this gap, by tying abstraction to the level of algorithms. Security services can be (conditionally) seen as algorithms, thus ASMs are applicable to assure security and one such attempt can be found in [26].

With regards to UMLsec, it explores the possibility of UML extensions. The main premises of this approach are that UML has a large base, the professional community is familiar with it, and it deals with systems from the preferred point of view - through objects and exchange of messages between these objects. Thus UMLsec extends UML in a way that enables analysis of security services issues. In order to obtain a true formal basis, UMLsec introduces UML machines that enable formal semantics. This in turn is extended to secrecy (i.e. confidentiality), integrity, authenticity, freshness, and secure information flow (i.e. access control).

Both the above approaches are promising. But how successful they will be remains open question, especially taking into account that a large basis of established formal methods has existed for years. Besides, it is more and more evident that the human factor plays a crucial role in ISs security and privacy. Hence the emphasis in the future is expected to be on the field of methodologies for qualitative and quantitative support of human factor management.

6.4 Socio-Technical Systems Modeling and Simulation

Management of ISs security and privacy has evolved into a multi-disciplinary area that covers IT and human resources management. Now the question is how to improve decision making in this field. Formal methods are focused on technology and have not been intended to support the complex interplay between IT and human factor. Because of its complexity, this interplay can be often effectively dealt with only through computer simulations.

With models, which are abstractions of real world phenomena, only relevant elements and their relationships of the problem domain are considered. They are then transformed to the model domain, solved there, and the results transformed back to the original domain. Without such abstractions, solutions to a large number of problems would remain unknown. Due to the fact that many systems in reality are highly non-linear, simulations are almost unavoidable in the majority of cases, because exact analytical solutions

---

[13]One kind of generalized machine is TM.

cannot be obtained. Thanks to advances in computing science, we have the possibility of analyzing such systems using simulations.

It is the intention of this section to provide an insight into the evolving research of supporting management of ISs security and privacy through the use of computer simulations. The methodologies as such are mature, but their application to ISs security and privacy is rather new.

6.4.1 Business Dynamics[14]

A methodology that enables to address human factor in ISs is business dynamics [326]. It evolved from systems dynamics [122], which in turn had its origins in the field of engineering. From there the basic ideas have been tailored to the needs of management sciences. Business dynamics addresses people, processes, and material and information flows by exposing the importance of feedback loops. According to business dynamics, feedback loops are the major driver of systems' behavior.

Another premise of business dynamics is that all the diversity of complex behavior emerges through interactions of the following basic patterns:

- exponential growth, which arises from a positive feedback loop;
- a goal seeking pattern, which arises from a negative feedback loop;
- oscillation, which arises from a goal seeking pattern, where time delays are present in the negative loop;
- S-shaped growth, which arises from interaction of a positive feedback loop that prevails at the beginning, then becomes dominated and stabilized by a negative feedback loop;
- S-shaped growth with overshoot, which is derived from S-shaped growth, but delays are taking place in the negative feedback loop;
- overshoot and collapse, which is derived from S-shaped growth structure with an additional negative feedback loop that drives the system back towards initial conditions, and away from the stabilization point of S-shaped growth.

In business dynamics, the modeling consists of two phases. It starts with a qualitative (graphical) representation of the system. The model is formed with iterations by identifying the relevant variables, the nature of these variables and the links between them that form feed-back loops, also called causal loops. Therefore, these graphical models are called causal loop diagrams. Regarding the links - they have positive polarity if an increase of causal variable results in an increase of the consecutive variable. If the output variable is decreased by an increase of input variable, the polarity is negative. Among the variables, there is a distinct set called levels or accumulators, which play a special role in the system. They are the source of inertia, and they constitute a kind of

---

[14]This subsection is based on work published in [343].

primitive memory within the system, an aggregate of past events. Additionally, they serve as absorbers, and decouple inflows from outflows (flows or rates are another important kind of variable that are coupled with levels). Thus when a certain variable has the above mentioned properties, it has to be addressed explicitly as a level.

Causal loop diagrams provide a holistic view of the system, which enables a better understanding of the basic principles of its functioning. They serve for further upgrade into quantitative models. In quantitative models concrete relationships between variables are defined by appropriate equations. These equations often contain translation parameters or scaling factors to tune the system so that it behaves in a way that closely reflects the real system.

An example model for the area of security policies will be given that will provide a basic insight into security policy management related issues. The model needs to include essential variables, such as threats, perception of threats, intensity of security related tasks and security policy levels.

We start the modeling with human perception and threats. Human perceptions are often modeled as adaptive learning processes with exponential smoothing, also called adaptive expectations.[15] It follows from the literature that adaptive expectations mostly outperform other methods for forecasting [227].

Belief about threats is modeled as a stock variable, because perception is a state of mind which remains unchanged unless there is a reason to change it. In our case this reason is the discrepancy between real and perceived values.

Threats (THR) are a challenging issue that requires much additional work. But for the purpose of our model we will simplify it. Threats will appear at a given rate and having once appeared, they will remain on the scene for a certain period of time, when a program patch is published. It is assumed that all organizations will install this patch immediately. Risks then cease, when another cycle begins with the set of newly discovered vulnerabilities in software.

The second basic variable is perceived risk (PR), which denotes the number of threats that employees believe in. The discrepancy between PR and THR drives the rate of adaptation, i.e. change in perceived risk (CPR). Certainly, internal accident frequency (IAF) is influenced by PR - the higher the perception of threats, the more intensive the efforts of the personnel to block them.

Next, we have to address means in the hands of the management. This is security policy, modeled with security policy level (SPL). SPL, which is driven independently by corrective intensity (CI), is another external factor that drives CPR. Additionally, CPR is driven by real adjustment time (RAT)

---

[15]In adaptive expectations, the rate of change in a perceived value X^* is given by a first order, linear differential equation $dX^*/dt = (X - X^*)/D$, where X is the reported input variable (current value), while D is a time constant, called adjustment time.

that is further divided into intrinsic adjustment time (IAT) and length of normal operation (LNO). The reason is that RAT depends on particular circumstances. Let us assume a longer period without breaches. Now when a new breach happens, expectations are based on past experiences, and people are likely to perceive this event as an isolated one. It is the opposite situation if one experiences attack after attack for a longer period of time. This will lead a person to assume a similar frequency of breaches when the next strike takes place, even if this one belongs to the beginning of a period with a smaller frequency of breaches.

Finally, there are two delays that model the fact that security policy level and discrepancy are subject to delayed information. There is also the plausibility level (PL), which serves to compensate for simplified threats modeling. PL serves to model a fact that two ISs are not likely to be attacked at the same time. The model is presented in Fig. 6.15.

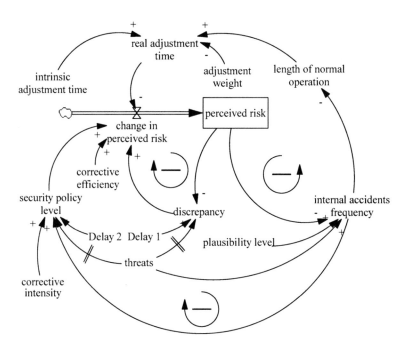

Fig. 6.15. A simple model for security policy management

The model can also be analyzed from the loops perspective. There are three balancing loops.[16] The upper left loop is the loop of perceived risk (PR, discrepancy, CPR). There is a trust loop in the upper right corner (PR,

---

[16]Balancing loops drive the system to a certain stable state. Their counterparts, reinforcement loops, drive the system away from any stable state.

IAF, LNO, RAT, CPR). It represents the trust of employees in the system according to experienced operational patterns that influence RAT. The third is the adjustment loop (PR, IAF, SPL, CPR), positioned at the bottom, and it models adjustment of perceived risk caused by the management through SPL.

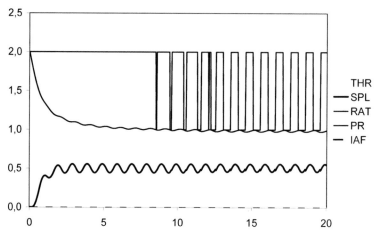

Fig. 6.16. System behavior with initial values (the unit on the horizontal axis is day, and the units on the vertical axis are accident/day for THR, tasks/day for SPL, day for RAT, accident/day for PR, and accident/day for IAF)

The basic premise of the model is that breaches should decline, if threats are properly perceived. This requires their timely and punctual perception in terms of their quantity and nature.

Let us simulate this model using deterministic approach (i.e. without stochastic variables) to better illustrate the main patterns and behavior of the system. As emphasized, the generator of the whole behavior are threats that are modeled with a narrow pulse sequence. The period for all simulations is 20 days. Attacks appear every day with a frequency one per day. Further, factors and parameters are set to initial values. This means PR is set to 2, while all other variables are set to 1.

The simulation reveals that, using initial conditions, there is a transition period of approximately eight days before the system reaches equilibrium. This is the time needed for the human factor to adjust PR to THR. One can also note a lightly oscillating security policy level, which can be neglected in this case. But in general, oscillations are undesirable, because permanently changing orders lead to resistant behavior of employees. The situation is presented in Fig. 6.16.

What happens if there is a delayed propagation of information about successful breaches, i.e. if we delay the inputs to discrepancy and SPL (see Fig.

6.17)? In this case, delays increase the rate of successful breaches. The system reaches equilibrium again after approximately 8 days. In the meantime there are stronger oscillations of SPL, which disappear after this period. This means that the system is over sensitive in terms of reaction at the beginning due to strong change in PR.

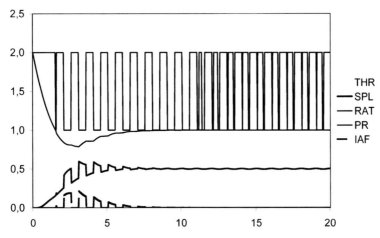

Fig. 6.17. System behavior with increased values of information delays (delay 1 and delay 2)

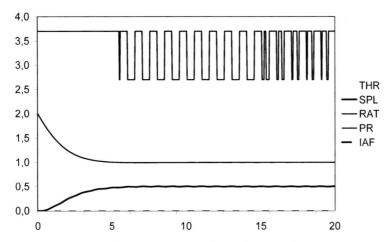

Fig. 6.18. System behavior after enlarging IAT values

Now what happens when employees adapt slowly to changes? This requires high values for RAT (see Fig. 6.18). It is anticipated that this will reduce the initial over sensitivity of the system and the simulation approves this expectation.

Finally, let the security manager investigate the influence of increased corrective intensity and, consequently, SPL. Put another way, suppose that security manager tries to eliminate further successful attacks by appropriate driving of SPL. The simulation shows that it pays off to implicitly signal initial values for threats that are slightly higher than the real ones (see Fig. 6.19). Practically all oscillations are eliminated and the system is gradually driven from its initial conditions to a desired state (IAF has small values and its dashed line is not noticeable in the diagrams, except in the diagram 6.17).

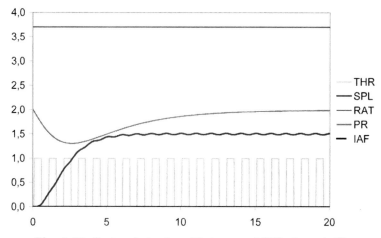

Fig. 6.19. System behavior with increased SPL through CI

It should be emphasized that the scientific relevance of the above model is far from being proved. There are still many open issues to be addressed before sound models will be obtained that are general enough to accommodate the diverse real life situations that organizations are facing. Open issues include modeling of risk related factors as given in Fig. 2.2, various kinds of interactions of users, standardized basis for formal description and evaluation of security policies, etc.

Some promising attempts at deploying business dynamics in security area already exist, e.g. [136, 137, 12]. But generally, such applications are at their early stage. Nevertheless, even at this they can be useful for demonstrations and security awareness activities.

6.4.2 Agent Technologies

Agents are active software objects that perceive their environment through sensors and act upon it through effectors. When agents are able to move from one computing environment to another, they become mobile agents. In addition, if agents are able to perform a number of functions or activities without external intervention and over an extended time, they are referred to as autonomous agents. Further evolution leads to intelligent agents that are able to act autonomously, to express negotiation capabilities and to exhibit interoperability [329, 142].

In recent years we have been facing intensive standardization in the field of intelligent agents that is led by FIPA. Its standardization can be divided into three categories. The first is about agent management, targeting coexistence and cooperation of agents. It covers communication and the discovery of each others capabilities. The second is concentrated on communication language and communication details. The third is agent-software integration with non-agents based environments.

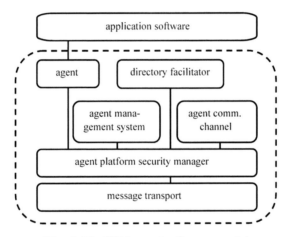

Fig. 6.20. FIPA agent reference model

FIPA has standardized an agent reference model that is given in Fig. 6.20 [124]. This model shows how a typical agent platform looks like. The directory facilitator is an agent that stores descriptions of other agents and their services (capabilities). The agent management system manages creation, deletion, suspension, resumption and migration of agents. The agent communication channel is an agent for routing messages between platforms. The agent platform security manager maintains security policy, provides transport level security and takes care of auditing.

The above model in its basic form, or slight modifications of it, can be found at the heart of many agent platforms. Agent platforms are software environments, which enable a user to create agent communities, define their properties, initiate their interaction, and control and monitor them. All this is usually possible on a high level through graphical user interfaces, without the need to be a skilled programmer. Many agent platforms now exist, e.g. [75], and even quality free distributions with eminent history track that goes back to the legendary Santa Fe Institute research of complex systems [83].

For socio-technical systems simulations, business dynamics and agent technologies can be seen as complementary methodologies. They are both modeling techniques, enabling experiments with the system, where these cannot be performed within real systems for various reasons, e.g. where such experiments would be too costly, dangerous or the like.

While business dynamics deals with systems at the level of aggregates and global causal dependencies, agent based modeling deals with systems at the level of its atomic ingredients, i.e. active individual entities (objects) that follow their own patterns of behavior and interact one with another. This is a significant improvement, because agents provide an insight into the dynamics of the system at micro level. They enable study of important phenomena that is not possible with business dynamics, e.g. emergence and self-organization.

On the macro level, when the number of agents is sufficiently large, statistical aggregates emerge that lead to behavior patterns, the same as those in business dynamics (assuming, of course, that the same phenomenon is being properly modeled and simulated). In some cases agent models may be harder to develop, less efficient or not even suitable at all. In such cases, one should stick with business dynamics.

Business dynamics and agents based simulations are generic counterparts, which also holds true for their application to management of ISs security and privacy. Independent modeling of the same problem by the two approaches can further support the appropriateness and soundness of a model.

A comparative study of business dynamics and agents technologies is presented in a quality paper written by Borshchev and Filippov [36]. The paper also gives concrete hints how to remodel typical business dynamics structures by deploying agent technologies.

In the rest of this appendix, the latest research attempts to use agent technologies for the management of ISs security and privacy will be presented [341, 342]. In this particular case the focus will be on trust, which plays an important role in ISs security, and also in societies in general [127]. Trust is a complex phenomenon, and dealing with it requires the inclusion of knowledge from other fields of science, most notably psychology [273]. Besides rationality there are additional factors that have to be taken into account: irrationality, context dependence, action binding, temporal dynamics, feed-back dependence, and trust differentiation [341].

For the formal treatment, *trust can be defined as a relationship between agents A and B denoted by $\omega_{A,B}$, which means agent's A attitude towards agent B*. This relationship can specify trusted, untrusted or undecided attitude.

Social interactions have to be formally addressed next. They comprise *propagated trust in a society with n agents, which is defined by a trust matrix M, where elements $w_{i,j}$ denote attitude of i-th agent towards j-th agent, and have values 1, 0 or -1 to denote trusting, undecided and not trusting relationships. If a relation is not defined, it is denoted by "-".* The latter means a relation, where an agent is not aware of existence of another agent. Note that $w_{i,j} = " - "$ does not imply that $w_{j,i} = " - "$.

In the last step, a trust function is introduced. Now trust is computed by using the agents own trust values and values obtained from society. Further, an agent's trust depends on the context, which is defined by time and consequences of actions of agents, i.e. their deeds. Let t denote time, t^+ its next incremented value, and let $\delta_{i,j}$ denote a deed of the i-th agent related to the j-th agent. Then *trust is defined as a dynamic function, where input variables include the i-th agent's own trust, trust of other members in society, time, and deeds of agents:*

$$w_{i,j}(t^+) = f_i(w_{1,j}(t, \delta_{1,j}, \delta_{2,j}, ..., \delta_{n,j}), ..., w_{n,j}(t, \delta_{1,j}, \delta_{2,j}, ..., \delta_{n,j})),$$

where

$$n \in \mathbb{N}, i, j \in [1, n], i \neq j \text{ and } w_{i,j} \neq " - ".$$

The last condition means that the diagonal elements and undefined relations are excluded from the calculation.

For a general society, the trust matrix is given below on the left, while on the right side there is a matrix for a society for which the corresponding directed graph is given in Fig.6.21:

$$\mathbf{M} = \begin{bmatrix} w_{11} & w_{12} & \dots & w_{1n} \\ w_{21} & w_{22} & \dots & w_{2n} \\ \vdots & & \ddots & \\ w_{n1} & w_{n2} & \dots & w_{nn} \end{bmatrix} \qquad \begin{bmatrix} 1 & 1 & -1 \\ -1 & 1 & 1 \\ 0 & 1 & 1 \end{bmatrix}$$

Assuming that an agent trusts herself, it follows that all diagonal elements in trust matrixes are equal to 1. Further, rows represent a given agent's trust towards other agents, while columns represent trust of the community towards a particular agent (columns present so-called trust vectors).

With this apparatus it is now possible to build models and perform simulations. One possible simulation procedure goes as follows (below, a fully connected society means a society in which each agent knows all other agents, while in a fragmented society agents do not know all other agents):

1. Set $t \leftarrow 0$ and define trust functions $w_{i,j}$ for each agent.
2. Define the initial trust matrix $\mathbf{M}$.
3. Increment time: $t \leftarrow t + 1$.
4. Perform trust calculations to obtain new values $w_{i,j}$ in the trust matrix $\mathbf{M}$ for current time t:

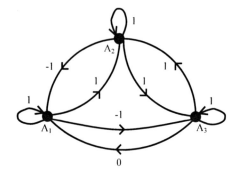

Fig. 6.21. A model society with trust values

a) In the case of a fully connected society: For every trust vector and its associated $\omega_{i,j}$, where $j = const.$, perform calculations, defined for a particular i, and all operands $\omega_{i,j}, i \neq j$, to obtain the resulting $\omega_{i,j}$.

b) In the case of a fragmented society: For every trust vector and the associated $\omega_{i,j}$, where $j = const.$, perform calculations, defined for a particular i, and only those operands $\omega_{i,j}, i \neq j$ that are not marked with a dash "-", to obtain the resulting $\omega_{i,j}$. If the basic $\omega_{i,j} = $ " $-$ ", leave it unchanged and continue with the next element from a trust vector.

5. If the values in the trust matrix $\mathbf{M}$ are still changing, go to step 3, otherwise end the procedure.

The remaining details of the above approach to formal treatment of trust, which is still in its early stages, can be found in [341, 342]. With regard to other approaches for formal treatment of trust, a reader is advised to look at [188], while an extensive overview of existing methodologies is given in [139].

Scientifically sound simulation has to obey the following basic rules: the model has to be fully documented, the assumptions and data used for simulation have to be given explicitly, the results have to fit the behavior of a real life phenomenon (behavior tests), and simulations have to be repeatable under the same conditions. Important additional steps include proper model boundaries, structure assessment, extreme conditions tests, sensitivity analysis, and discovery of errors arising from numerical computations [326].

And when all these criteria are met, the question arises whether the model is now validated. But such questions are not sensible, because "no models are valid or verifiable in the sense of establishing their truth" [326]. Therefore the sensible question is only whether a model is useful or not.

To paraphrase this all - the only truth about a model is its usefulness.

7

Further Reading

It is common in the literature for the reader to be recommended to expand knowledge in the field by a large number of additional titles. Practical experience shows that the reader rarely does this. If this happens, selection is focused.

Therefore further suggested reading covers the most complementary and influential titles that this book is related to:

- Burrows M., Abadi M., Needham R.: Logic of Authentication. SRC Research Report No. 39, Digital Equipment Corporation, (1989)
- Denning D. E.: Cryptography and Data Security. Addison Wesley, Boston, (1982)
- Diller A.: Z – An Introduction to Formal Methods. John Wiley & Sons, Chichester, (1994)
- International Standards Organization: Information Technology - Code of Practice for Information Security Management, ISO 17799, Geneva, (2000)[1]
- International Standards Organization: Information Technology - Guidelines for the Management of IT Security. Parts 1 through 5, ISO, Geneva, (1996, 1997, 1998, 2000)
- Kendall K.E., Kendall J.E.: Systems Analysis and Design. Prentice Hall, Upper Saddle River, (1999)
- Laudon K. C., Laudon J. P.: Management Information Systems - Organization and Technology. Prentice Hall, Upper Saddle River, (2003)
- Menezes A.J., van Oorschot P.C., Vanstone S.A.: Handbook of Applied Cryptography. CRC Press, New York, (2001)
- Powers M. D.: The Internet Legal Guide. John Wiley & Sons, New York, (2002)
- Schneier B.: Applied Cryptography. John Wiley & Sons, New York, (1996)

---

[1]At the time of publication of this book a new version of this standard has been released.

- Stallings W.: Cryptography and Network Security. Prentice Hall, Upper Saddle River, (2003)
- Sterman J.: Business Dynamics - Systems Thinking for a Complex World. McGraw Hill, New York, (2000)
- Tanenbaum A.S.: Computer networks. Prentice Hall, Upper Saddle River, (1996)

Finally, the career of every professional has been built on a limited set of titles that present the basis of her or his knowledge in related field(s). It is not uncommon that these books shape the professional's vocabulary, and sometimes even philosophy. Thus it is fair to authors of the above titles (and readers of this book) to state these works explicitly.

8
Listing of the Simulation Model

A complete list of equations that are used in simulations described in sub-section 6.4.1 is given below. The model has been simulated with $Vensim^{TM}$ package with the simulation increment set to 0.03125 days with a total duration of 20 days:

- adjustment weight = 1
  units: dimensionless
- change in perceived risk = (discrepancy + corrective efficiency * security policy level)/real adjustment time
  units: accident/(day*day)
- corrective efficiency = 1
  units: accident/task
- corrective intensity = 1
  units: task/accident
- delay 1 = 1
  units: day
- delay 2 = 1
  units: day
- discrepancy = SMOOTH3(threats, Delay 1) - perceived risk
  units: accident/day
- internal accidents frequency = IF THEN ELSE(RANDOM UNIFORM(0, 1, 0) ≥ plausibility level, MAX((threats - perceived risk), 0), 0)
  units: accident/day
- intrinsic adjustment time = 1
  units: day
- length of normal operation = IF THEN ELSE(internal accidents frequency > 0, 0 , 1)
  units: day
- perceived risk = INTEG (change in perceived risk, 2)
  units: accident/day

- plausibility level = 0
  units: dimensionless
- real adjustment time = intrinsic adjustment time + (length of normal operation/adjustment weight)
  units: day
- security policy level = corrective intensity * (SMOOTH3(threats, Delay 2) + internal accidents frequency)
  units: task/day
- threats = PULSE TRAIN(0.1, 0.5, 1, 20)
  units: accident/day

References

1. Abadi M., Needham R.: Prudent Engineering Practice for Cryptographic Protocols. SRC Research Report No. 125, Digital Corporation, Palo Alto (1994)
2. Aberdeen Group: Evaluating the Cost of Ownership for Digital Certificate Projects. Aberdeen Group, Boston, (1998)
3. Adams C., Farrell S.: Internet X.509 Public Key Infrastructure Certificate Management Protocols. IETF RFC 2510, Reston, (1999)
4. Adams C., Gilchrist J.: The CAST-256 Encryption Algorithm. IETF RFC 2612, Reston, (1999)
5. Agrawal M., Kayal N., Saxena N.: Primes Is in P. Preprint, (2002), http://www.cse.iitk.ac.in/primality.pdf
6. Ajtai M., Dwork C.: A Public-Key Cryptosystem with Worst-Case / Average-Case Equivalence. Proceedings of the 29th ACM STOC, ACM, New York (1997)
7. Aljifri H., Sanchez D. N.: International Legal Aspects of Cryptography. Computers & Security, Vol. 22, No. 3, pp. 196–203, Elsevier, (2003)
8. Alliance for Telecommunications Industry Solutions: ATIS Telecom Glossary 2000, ATIS Committee T1A1, Ref. T1.523-2001, NIST, Gaithersburg, (2001), http://www.atis.org/tg2k
9. Alvarez G., Petrović S.: A New Taxonomy of Web Attacks Suitable for Efficient Encoding. Computers & Security, Vol. 22, No. 5, pp. 435-449, Elsevier, (2003)
10. American National Standards Institute: Financial Institution Key Management (Wholesale). Standard X9.17, Washington D.C., (1985)
11. Amoroso E.G.: Fundamentals of Computer Security Technology. Prentice Hall, Upper Saddle River, (1994)
12. Anderson D. et al.: Preliminary System Dynamics Maps of the Insider Cyber Threat Problem. John Wiley & Sons, Proceedings of the 22nd Conference of the SDS, Oxford, (2004)
13. Anderson R. J.: Whither Cryptography. Information Management & Computer Security, Vol. 2, No. 5, pp. 13–20, Emerald, (1994)
14. Anderson R.J., Kuhn M.: Tamper Resistance - a Cautionary Note. Proceedings of the Second USENIX Workshop on Electronic Commerce, pp. 1–11, Oakland, (1996)
15. Anderson R.J.: Security Engineering. John Wiley & Sons, New York, (2001)
16. Annoni M., Javornik T., Kandus G., Mohorčič M., Švigelj A., Trček D., Hu Y.F., Maral G., Ferro E.: Service Efficient Network Interconnection Via Satellite. John Wiley & Sons, New York, (2001)

17. Aslam T.: A Taxonomy of Security Faults in the UNIX Operating System. Purdue University, M.Sc. Thesis, Lafayette, (1995)
18. Association of Chief Police Officers: Good Practice Guide for Computer Based Evidence. Computer Crime Group, London, (2003)
19. Ayoade J. O., Kosuge T.: Breakthrough in Privacy Concerns and Lawful Access Conflicts. Telematics and Informatics, Vol. 19, No. 4, pp. 273–289, Elsevier, (2002)
20. Baker & Mc Kenzie: Global E-Commerce Law. Baker & Mc Kenzie, Chicago, (2002), http://www.bmck.com/ecommerce/intlegis-t.htm
21. Baldwin R., Rivest R.: The RC5, RC5-CBC, RC5-CBC-Pad, and RC5-CTS Algorithms. IETF RFC 2040, Reston, (1996)
22. Barrett N.: Penetration and Social Engineering - Hacking the Weakest Link. Information Security Technical Report, Vol. 8, No. 4. pp. 56–64, Elsevier, (2003)
23. Bartel M., Boyer J., Fox B., LaMacchia B., Simon B.: XML-Signature Syntax and Processing. W3C REC-xmldsig-core-20020212, Cambridge / Sophia Antipolis / Kanagawa, (2002), http://www.w3.org/TR/2002/REC-xmldsig-core-20020212
24. Bell D.E., LaPadula L.J.: Secure Computer Systems - Mathematical Foundations. Mitre Corp., ESD-TR-73-278, Washington D.C., (1973)
25. Bell D.E., LaPadula L.J.: Secure computer System. MITRE, Technical Report, MTR-2997, Bedford, (1976)
26. Bella G., Riccobene E.: A Realistic Environment for Crypto-Protocol Analyses by ASMs. Proc. of Workshop on Abstract State Machines, pp. 127–138, Magdeburg, (1998)
27. Bergkamp L.: EU Data Protection Policy. Computer Law & Security, Vol. 18, No. 1. pp. 31–47, Elsevier, (2002)
28. Berinato S.: Calculated Risk. CSO Online, December 2002, CXO Media Inc., Framingham, (2002), http://www.csoonline.com/read/120902/calculate.html
29. Berners-Lee T., Fielding R., Masinter L.: Uniform Resource Identifiers (URI) - Generic Syntax. IETF RFC 2396, Reston, (1998)
30. Bishop M., Bailey D.: A Critical Analysis of Vulnerability Taxonomies. University of California at Davis, TR CSE-96-11, Davis, (1996)
31. Black E.P. (editor): Dictionary of Algorithms and Data Structures. NIST, Washington D.C., (2005), http://www.nist.gov/dads
32. Blum M., Micali S.: How to Generate Cryptographically Strong Sequences of Pseudo-Random Bits. Journal on Computing, Vol. 13., No. 4., pp. 850–864, SIAM, (1984)
33. Blum L., Blum M., Shub M.: A Simple Unpredictable Pseudo-Random Number Generator. Journal on Computing, Vol. 15, No. 2, pp. 364–383, SIAM, (1986)
34. Blyth A., Cunliffe D., Sutherland I.: Security Analysis of XML Usage and XML Parsing. Computers & Security, Vol. 22, No. 6, pp. 494–505, Elsevier, (2003)
35. Boer B., Bosselaers A.: Collisions for the Compress Functions of MD5. Eurocrypt '93, Lecture Notes in Computer Science, Vol. 773, pp. 294–304, Springer Verlag, Heidelberg, (1993)
36. Borshchev A., Filippov A.: From System Dynamics and Discrete Event to Practical Agent Based Modelling - Reasons, Techniques, Tools. John Wiley & Sons, Proceedings of the 22nd Conference of the SDS, Oxford, (2004)
37. Bosak J., Bray T., Connolly D., Maler E., Nicol G., Sperberg-McQueen C., Wood L., Clark J. (editors): Guide to the W3C XML Specification DTD, Ver-

sion 2.1. W3C DTD Specification Version 2.1, Cambridge / Sophia Antipolis / Kanagawa, (1998), http://www.w3.org/XML/1998/06/xmlspec-report-v21.htm#AEN49

38. Boyd C.: Security Architectures Using formal Methods. IEEE Journal on Selected Areas in Communications, Vol. 11, No. 3, pp. 694–701, IEEE, (1993)

39. Börger E.: The Origins and the Development of the ASM Method for High Level System Design and Analysis. Journal of Universal Computer Science, Vol. 8, No. 1, pp. 2–74, Graz, (2002)

40. Bray T., Paoli J., Sperberg-McQueen C.M., Maler E., Yergeau F. (editors): Extensible Markup Language (XML) 1.1. W3C REC-xml11-20040204, Cambridge / Sophia Antipolis / Kanagawa, (2004), http://www.w3.org/TR/xml11/

41. Brewer D.F.C., Nash M.J.: The Chinese Wall Security Policy. Proceedings of IEEE Symposium on Research in Security & Privacy, pp. 206–214, New York, (1989)

42. Brezinski D., Killalea T.: Guidelines for Evidence Collection and Archiving. IETF RFC 3227, Reston, (2002)

43. British Standards Institute: Code of Practice For Information Security Management. BSI, BS 7799, London, (1999)

44. British Standards Institute: Information Security Management Systems. BSI, BS 7799-2, London, (2002)

45. Broder J.F.: Risk Analysis - The Security Survey. Butterworth - Heinemann, Woburn, (2000)

46. Bundesahmt für Sicherheit in der Informationstechnik: IT Baseline Protection Manual. BSI, Bonn, (2003), http://www.bsi.bund.de/english/gshb/manual/index.htm

47. Burrows M., Abadi M., Needham R.: Logic of Authentication. SRC Research Report Number 39, Digital Equipment Corporation - DEC, (1989), http://gatekeeper.research.compaq.com/pub/DEC/SRC/research-reports/abstracts/src-rr-039.html

48. Burrows M., Abadi M., Needham R.: Logic of Authentication. ACM Transactions on Computer Systems, Vol. 8, No. 1, pp. 18–36, ACM, New York, (1990)

49. Buzzard K.: Adequate Security - What Exactly Do You Mean? Computer Law & Security, Vol. 19, No. 5, pp. 406–410, Elsevier, (2003)

50. Callas J., Donnerhacke L., Finney H., Thayer R.: OpenPGP Message Format. IETF RFC 2440, Reston, (1998)

51. Campbell K., Wiener M.: Proof That DES is Not a Group. Proceedings of the Crypto 1992, Springer Verlag, Heidelberg, (1992)

52. Cantor S., Kemp J., Philpott R., Maler E. (editors): Assertions and Protocols for the OASIS Security Assertion Markup Language v 2.0. OASIS saml-core-2.0-os, Billerica, (2005), http://docs.oasis-open.org/security/saml/v2.0/

53. Carey P., Russel C.: Data Protection - Security/Data Security - The Key to Privacy. Computer Law & Security Report, Vol. 18, No. 2, pp. 112–113, Elsevier, (2002)

54. Center for Democracy & Technology: Anti-Spyware Legislation on Fast Track Through House. Center for Democracy & Technology, Washington D.C., (2004), http://www.cdt.org/privacy/spyware/

55. CERT/CC: CERT/CC Advisories. CERT, Pittsburgh, (2005), http://www.cert.org/advisories/

56. Chadwick D.W., Otenko A.: The PERMIS X.509 Role Based Privilege Management Infrastructure. Proceedings of the 7th ACM Symposium on Access Control Models and Technologies, pp. 135–140, Monterey, (2002)
57. Chadwick D.W., Mundy D., New J.: Experiences of Using PKI to Access a Hospital Information System by High Street Opticians. Computer Communications, Vol. 26, No. 16, pp. 1893–1903, Elsevier, (2003)
58. Charvat J.: Project Management Methodologies - Selecting, Implementing, and Supporting Methodologies and Processes for Projects. John Wiley & Sons, New York, (2003)
59. Chase N.: XML Primer Plus. SAMS Publishing, Indianapolis, (2003)
60. Chaum D.: Blind Signatures for Untraceable Payments. Advances in Cryptology, Proceedings of the ACM Crypto '82, pp. 199–203, New York, (1983)
61. Chaum D.: Security Without Identification - Transaction Systems to Make the big Brother Obsolete. Communications of the ACM, Vol. 28, No. 10, pp. 1030–1044, New York, (1985)
62. Chaum D., Fiat A., Naor M.: Untraceable Electronic Cash. Proceedings of Crypto '88, pp. 319–327, Springer Verlag, (1990)
63. Chaum D.: Online Cash Checks. Proceedings of Eurocrypt '89, pp. 288–293, Springer Verlag, (1990)
64. Cheswick W.R., Bellovin S.M.: Firewalls and Internet Security. Addison-Wesley, Reading, (1994)
65. Chirillo J., Blaul S.: Implementing Biometric Security. John Wiley & Sons, Indianapolis, (2003)
66. Christensen E., Curbera F., Meredith G., Weerawarana S.: Web Services Description Language (WSDL) v 1.1. W3C 2001/NOTE-wsdl-20010315, Cambridge / Sophia Antipolis / Kanagawa, (2001), http://www.w3.org/TR/2001/NOTE-wsdl-20010315
67. Clark D.D., Wilson D.R.: A Comparison of Commercial and Military Computer Security Policies. Proceedings of IEEE Symposium on Research in Security & Privacy, New York, (1987)
68. Clark J., DeRose S.: XML Path Language (XPath) v 1.0. W3C REC-xpath-19991116, Cambridge / Sophia Antipolis / Kanagawa, (1999), http://www.w3.org/TR/1999/REC-xpath-19991116
69. Clark J.: XSL Transformations (XSLT) v 1.0. W3C REC-xslt-19991116, Cambridge / Sophia Antipolis / Kanagawa, (1999), http://www.w3.org/TR/1999/REC-xslt-19991116
70. Clement L., Hatley A., von Riegen C., Rogers T. (editors): UDDI v 3.0.2. OASIS, Billerica, (2004), http://uddi.org/pubs/uddi-v3.0.2-20041019.htm
71. COBIT Steering Committee: Overview. Information Systems Audit and Control Foundation, Rolling Meadows, (1998)
72. Coffey T., Dojen R., Flanaga T.: Formal Verification - An Imperative Step in the Design of Security Protocols. Computer Networks, Vol. 2003, No. 43, pp. 601–618, Elsevier, (2003)
73. Cohen F.B.: Information System Attacks: A Preliminary Classification Scheme. Computers & Security, Vol. 16, No. 1, pp. 29–46, Elsevier, (1997)
74. Coles R.S., Moulton R.: Operationalizing IT Risk Management. Computers & Security, Vol. 22, No. 6, pp. 487–493, Elsevier, (2003)
75. Collis J., Ndumu D.: The Zeus Agent Building Toolkit. Parts 1 through 4, British Telecom, London, (1999)

76. Coloyannides M.: Society Cannot Function Without Privacy. Security & Privacy, Vol. 2, No. 3, pp. 84–86, IEEE, (2003)
77. Corell L.C.: Brainstorming Reinvented - A Corporate Communications Guide to Ideation. SAGE Publications, Thousand Oaks, (2004)
78. Council of Europe: On the Protection of Personal Data Used for Employment. Recommendation No. R (89) 2, Strasbourg, (1989), http://cm.coe.int/ta/rec/1989/89r2.htm
79. Council of Europe: CyberCrime Convention. ETS No. 185, Budapest, (2001), http://conventions.coe.int/Treaty/EN/Treaties/Html/185.htm
80. Crannor L.F. (editor): P3P Guiding Principles. W3C Recommendation NOTE-P3P10-principles-19980721, Cambridge / Sophia Antipolis / Kanagawa, (2002), http://www.w3.org/TR/1998/NOTE-P3P10-principles-19980721
81. Crocker D.H.: Standard for the Format of ARPA Internet Text Messages. IETF RFC 822, Reston, (1982)
82. Culley A.: Computer Forensics - Past, Present and Future. Information Security Technical Report, Vol. 8, No. 2, pp. 32–36, Elsevier, (2003)
83. Daniels M.: Integrating Simulation Technologies With Swarm. Agent Simulation - Applications, Models, and Tools Conference, Chicago, (1999), http://www.santafe.edu/ mgd/anl/anlchicago.html
84. David J.: Incident Response. Network Security, Vol. 2003, No. 9. pp. 17–19, Elsevier, (2003)
85. Denning D. E.: Cryptography and Data Security. Addison Wesley, Boston, (1982)
86. Denning D.E., Brandstad D.K.: A Taxonomy for Key Escrow Encryption Systems. Communications of the ACM, Vol. 39, No. 3, pp. 34–40, ACM, (1996)
87. Denning D. E.: Information Warfare and Security. Addison Wesley, Boston, (1999)
88. Der-Chyuan L., Jiang-Lung L.: Steganographic Method for Secure Communications. Computers & Security, Vol. 21, No. 5, pp. 449–460, Elsevier, (2002)
89. Devargas M.: Survival is Not Compulsory. Computers & Security, Vol. 18, No. 1, pp. 35–46, Elsevier, (1999)
90. Diffie W., Hellman M.: New Directions in Cryptography. Transactions on Information Theory, Vol. 22, No. 6, pp. 644–654, New York, (1976)
91. Diffie W., Hellman M.: Exhaustive Cryptanalysis of the NBS Data Encryption Standard. Computer, Vol. 10, No. 6, pp. 74–84, IEEE, (1977)
92. Dijkstra E.W., Scholten C.S.: Predicate Calculus and Program Semantics. Springer Verlag, Heidelberg, (1990)
93. Diller A.: Z – An Introduction to Formal Methods. John Wiley & Sons, Chichester, (1994)
94. Dobbertin H.: The Status of MD5 After a Recent Attack. CryptoBytes, Vol. 2, No. 3, pp. 1–6, RSA Labs, Redwood City, (1996)
95. Dournaee B.: XML Security. McGraw-Hill, New York, (2002)
96. Du W., Mathur A.P.: Categorization of Software Errors That Lead to Security Breaches. Proceedings of the 21st National Information Systems Security Conference, p. ?, Arlington, (1998)
97. Du W., Mathur A.P.: Testing the Software Vulnerability Using Environment Perturbation. Proceedings of the International Conference on Dependable Systems and Networks, pp. 603–612, New York, (2000)
98. Eastlake D.E., Niles K.: Secure XML - The New Syntax for Signatures and Encryption. Addison Wesley, Boston, (2003)

99. Editorial: Port Scanning Legal in US. Network Security, Vol. 2001, No. 1, p. 2, Elsevier, (2001)

100. Editorial: 17 Ways to Crack Passwords. Network Security, Vol. 2003, No. 8, pp. 1–2, Elsevier, (2003)

101. Electronic Privacy Information Center: Privacy Law Sourcebook. EPIC, Washington D.C., (2001)

102. ElGamal T.: A Public Key Cryptosystem and a Signature Scheme Based on Discrete Logarithms. IEEE Transactions on Information Theory, Vol. 31, No. 4, pp. 469–472, IEEE, (1985)

103. Ellison C., Frantz B., Lampson B., Rivest R., Thomas B., Ylonnen T.: SPKI Certificate Theory. IETF RFC 2693, Reston, (1999)

104. European Commission: Data Protection Directive, 95/64/EC. Official Journal of the European Communities, L 281, 23/11/1995, Brussels, (1995)

105. European Commission: Telecommunications Data Protection Directive, 97/66/EC. Official Journal of the European Communities, L 024, 30/1/1998, Brussels, (1998)

106. European Commission: Setting up a Community Regime for the Control of Exports of Dual-use Items and Technology. Official Journal of the European Communities, L 159, 30/06/2000, Brussels, (2000)

107. European Commission: Amending Regulation with Regard to Intra-Community Transfers and Exports of Dual-use Items and Technology. Official Journal of the European Communities, L 336, 30/12/2000, Brussels, (2000)

108. European Commission: A Community Framework for Electronic Signatures, 1999/93/EC. Official Journal of the European Communities, L 013, 19/01/2000, Brussels, (2000)

109. European Commission: Amending Regulation With Regard to the List of Controlled Dual-use Items and Technology When Exported. Official Journal of the European Communities, L 065, 07/03/2001, Brussels, (2001)

110. European Commission: Directive on the Harmonization of Certain Aspects of Copyright and Related Rights in the Information Society. Official Journal of the European Communities, L 167/10, 22/6/2001, Brussels, (2001)

111. European Commission: Privacy and Electronic Communications Directive, 02/58/EC. Official Journal of the European Communities, L201, 31/7/2002, Brussels, (2002)

112. European Telecommunications Standards Institute: Baseline Security Standards - Features and Mechanisms. Security Techniques Advisory Group, Standard DTR/NA-002608, Sophia Antipolis, (1996)

113. Evans J.R., Olson D.L.: Simulation and Risk Analysis. Prentice Hall, Upper Saddle River, (1998)

114. Fallside D.C., Walmsley P. (editors): XML Schema - Primer. W3C REC-xmlschema-0-20041028, Cambridge / Sophia Antipolis / Kanagawa, (2004), http://www.w3.org/TR/xmlschema-0/

115. Farmer D.: Striking a Balance Between Security and Privacy. Card Technology Today, Vol. 14, No. 3, pp. 11–12, Elsevier, (2002)

116. Farrel S., Housley R.: An Internet Attribute Certificate Profile for Authorization. IETF RFC 3281, Reston, (2002)

117. Feistel H.: Cryptography and Computer Privacy. Scientific American, Scientific American, Vol. 228, No. 5, pp. 15–23, New York, (1973)

118. Fenn C., Shooter R., Allan K.: IT Security Outsourcing. Computer Law & Security, Vol. 18, No. 2, pp. 109–111, Elsevier, (2002)

119. Fielding R. et al.: Hypertext Transfer Protocol - HTTP v 1.1. RFC 2616, IETF, Reston, (1999)
120. Florio L., Wierenga K.: Eduroam, Providing Mobility for Roaming Users. Proceedings of EUNIS '05 Conference, p. ?, Manchester, (2005)
121. Forrester J.: Industrial Dynamics - A Major Breakthrough for Decision Makers. Harvard Business Review, Vol. 36, No. 4, pp. 37–66, Cambridge, (1958)
122. Forrester J.: Industrial Dynamics. MIT Press, Cambridge, (1961)
123. Forte D.: Biometrics - Future Abuses. Computer Fraud & Security, Vol. 2003, No. 10, pp. 12–14, Elsevier, (2004)
124. Foundation for Intellignet Agents: FIPA Agent Management Specification. FIPA SC00023J, Geneva, (2002)
125. Freed N., Borenstein N.: Multipurpose Internet Mail Extensions, part 1. IETF RFC 2045, Reston, (1996)
126. Freier, A.O., et al.: Secure Sockets Layer Protocol (version 3). Netscape Corp., Mountain View, (1996), http://wp.netscape.com/eng/ssl3/index.html
127. Fukuyama F.: Trust - The Social Virtues and the Creation of Prosperity. Free Press, New York, (1996)
128. Fumy W.: From Common Criteria to Elliptic Curves. ISO Bulletin, Vol. 2000, No. 6, pp. 20–25, ISO, (2000)
129. Fung R.A., Farn K.J., Lin A.C.: A Study on the Certification of the Information Security Management Systems. Computer Standards & Interfaces, Vol. 2003, No. 25, pp. 447–461, Elsevier, (2003)
130. Geer D.: Risk Management is Still Where the Money Is. Computer, Vol. 36, No. 12, pp. 129–131, IEEE, (2003)
131. Geihs K.: Middleware Challenges Ahead, IEEE Computer, Volume 34, No. 6, pp. 24–31, IEEE, Washington D.C., (2001)
132. Gerberick D.: Developing E-business Trust. Security, Vol. 38, No. 9, pp. 37–40, ?, (2001)
133. Goldreich O.: Cryptography and Cryptographic Protocols. Distributed Computing, Vol. 16, No. 2–3, pp. 177–199, Springer Verlag, (2003)
134. Gong L., Needham R., Yahalom R.: Reasoning About Belief in Cryptographic Protocols. Proceedings of the IEEE Symposium on Research in Security and Privacy, pp. 234–248, Oakland, (1990)
135. Gonzales J. M. et al.: Key Recovery for the Commercial Environment. International Journal on Information Security, Vol. 1, No. 3, pp. 161–174, Springer Verlag, Heidelberg, (2002)
136. Gonzalez J.J., Sawicka A.: A Framework for Human Factors in Information Security. Proceedings of the WSEAS Conference on Security, HW/SW Codesign, E-Commerce and Computer Networks, Rio de Janeiro, (2002)
137. Gonzalez J.J. (editor): From Modeling to Managing Security - A System Dynamics Approach. Høyskole Forlaget AS, Kristiansand, (2003)
138. Government of Canada - Communications Security Establishment: Canadian Handbook on Information Technology Security. Government of Canada, Ottawa, (1998)
139. Grandison T., Sloman M.: A Survey of Trust in Internet Applications. IEEE Communications Surveys, Vol. 2000, No. 4, pp. 2–13, IEEE, (2000)
140. Grimm R., Ochsenschläger P.: Binding Telecooperation – A Formal Model for Electronic Commerce. Computer Networks, Vol. 2001, No. 37, pp. 171–193, Elsevier, (2001)

141. Grosso P., Maler E., Marsh J., Walsh N. (editors): XPointer Framework. W3C REC-xptr-framework-20030325, Cambridge / Sophia Antipolis / Kanagawa, (2003), http://www.w3.org/TR/2003/REC-xptr-framework-20030325
142. Guessoum Z., Briot J.P.: From Active Objects to Autonomous Agents. IEEE Concurrency, Vol. 7, No. 3, pp. 68–76, IEEE, (1999)
143. Gunara-Chen G.: The Art of Intrusion Testing. Information Security Technical Report, Vol. 8, No. 4, pp. 6–13, Elsevier, (2003)
144. Gupta J.N.D., Sharma S.K. (editors): Intelligent enterprises of the 21st century. Idea Group Inc., Hershey, (2004)
145. Gutman P.: PKI Is Not Dead, Just Resting. IEEE Computer, Vol. 35, No. 8, pp. 41–49, New York, (2002)
146. Haas H., Brown A. (editors): Web Services Glossary. W3C NOTE-ws-gloss-20040211, Cambridge / Sophia Antipolis / Kanagawa, (2004), http://www.w3.org/TR/2004/NOTE-ws-gloss-20040211/#securitymechanism
147. Haller N.M.: The S/Key One-Time Password System. Proceedings of the ISOC SNDSS, pp. 151–157, San Diego, (1994)
148. Halliday D. et al.: EU Update: Baker & McKenzies Regular Article Tracking Developments in EU Law Relating to IP, IT & Telecommunications. Computer Law & Security Report, Vol. 19, No. 2, pp. 61–64, Elsevier, (2003)
149. Hansen M., Kohntopp K., Pfitzmann A.: The Open Source Approach - Opportunities and Limitations With Respect to Security and Privacy. Computers & Security, Vol. 21, No. 5, pp. 461–471, Elsevier, (2002)
150. Harkins D., Carel D.: The Internet Key Exchange (IKE). IETF RFC 2409, Reston, (1998)
151. Hearn J.: Does CC Paradigm Have a Future? Security & Privacy, Vol. 2004, No. 1, pp. 64–65, IEEE, (2004)
152. Hendry M.: Smart Card Security and Applications. Artech House, Norwood, (1997)
153. Hinde S.: Privacy Legislation - A Comparison of the US and EU Approaches. Computers & Security, Vol. 22, No. 5, pp. 378–387, Elsevier, (2003)
154. Hinde S.: Careless About Privacy. Computers & Security, Vol. 22, No. 4, pp. 284–288, Elsevier, (2003)
155. Hirsch F., Philpott R., Maler E. (editors): Security and Privacy Considerations for the OASIS Security Assertion Markup Language (SAML) v 2.0. OASIS saml-sec-consider-2.0-os, Billerica, (2005), http://docs.oasis-open.org/security/saml/v2.0/
156. Holzmann J.G.: Design and Validation of Computer Protocols. Prentice Hall, London, (1991)
157. Hopcroft J.E., Ullman J.D.: Introduction to Automata Theory, Languages and Computation. Addison Wesley, Boston, (1979)
158. Hollins B.: Brainstorming Products for the Long-term Future. Creativity and Innovation Management, Vol. 8, No. 4, pp. 286–293, Blackwell Publishing, Oxford, (1999)
159. Housley R. et al.: Internet X.509 Public Key Infrastructure Certificate and CRL Profile. IETF RFC 2459, Reston, (1999)
160. Housley R., Hoffman P.: Internet X.509 Public Key Infrastructure Operational Protocols - FTP and HTTP. IETF RFC 2585, Reston, (1999)
161. Hoyle D.: ISO 9000 Quality Systems Handbook. Butterworth-Heinemann, Oxford, (1998)

162. Hunter P.: Quantum Cryptography Latest - Promises to Boost Security Within a Decade but Won't End the Arms Race. Computer Fraud & Security, Vol. 2002, No. 3, pp. 14–15, Elsevier, (2002)
163. Hwang J., Wu K., Liu D.: Access Control With Role Attribute Certificates. Computer Standards & Interfaces, Vol. 22, No. 1, pp. 43–53, Elsevier, (2000)
164. I'Anson C., Mitchell C.: Security Defects in CCITT Recommendation X.509. ACM SIGCOMM, Vol. 20, No. 2, pp. 30–40, New York, (1990)
165. Imamura T., Dillaway B., Simon E.: XML Encryption Syntax and Processing. W3C REC-xmlenc-core-20021210, Cambridge / Sophia Antipolis / Kanagawa, (2002), http://www.w3.org/TR/2002/REC-xmlenc-core-20021210/
166. International Labor Organization: Protection of Workers Personal Data. ILO Code of Practice, ILO, Geneva, (1997)
167. International Standards Organization: Information Processing - Text and Office Systems - Standard Generalized Markup Language (SGML). ISO 8879, Geneva, (1986)
168. International Standards Organization: Information Processing Systems - Open Systems Interconnection - Basic Reference Model, Security Architecture, part 2. ISO 7498-2, Geneva, (1989)
169. International Standards Organization: Information Processing Systems - Open Systems Interconnection - Basic Reference Model - The Basic Model. ISO 7498-1, Geneva, (1994)
170. International Standards Organization: Banking and Related Financial Services - Information Security Guidelines. TC 68 / SC 2, ISO 13569, Geneva, (1997)
171. International Standards Organization: IT / 8-bit Single-byte Coded Graphic Character Sets / Part 1: Latin Alphabet No. 1. ISO/IEC 8859-1, Geneva, (1998)
172. International Standards Organization: Common Criteria, Security Techniques - Evaluation Criteria for IT Security. IS 15408, parts 1 through 3. Geneva, (1999)
173. International Standards Organization: IT - Management of Information and Communications Technology Security, Part 1: Concepts and Models for Information and Communications Technology Security Management. ISO / IEC 13335-1, Geneva, (2004)
174. International Standards Organization: IT - Guidelines for the Management of IT Security, Part 2: Managing and Planning. ISO / IEC TR 13335-2, Geneva, (1997)
175. International Standards Organization: IT - Guidelines for the Management of IT Security, Part 3: Techniques for the Management of IT Security. ISO / IEC TR 13335-3, Geneva, (1998)
176. International Standards Organization: IT - Guidelines for the Management of IT Security, Part 4: Selection of Safeguards. ISO / IEC TR 13335-4, Geneva, (2000)
177. International Standards Organization: IT - Guidelines for the Management of IT Security, Part 5: Management Guidance on Network Security. ISO / IEC TR 13335-5, Geneva, (2001)
178. International Standards Organization: IT - Code of Practice for Information Security Management. ISO 17799, Geneva, (2000)
179. International Standards Organization: IT – Z Formal Specification Notation – Syntax, Type System and Semantics. ISO / IEC 13568, Geneva, (2002)
180. International Standards Organization: IT - Security techniques - Hash-functions - Part 3: Dedicated Hash Functions. ISO 10118-3, Geneva, (2003)

181. International Standards Organization: Identification Cards - Integrated Circuit Cards With Contacts. ISO 7816 1 through 6, Geneva, (1998–2004)
182. International Standards Organization: Identification Cards - Contactless Integrated Circuit Cards. ISO 10536 1 through 6, Geneva, (1996–2000)
183. Internet Security Systems: X-Force Web Archives. ISS, Atlanta, (2005), http://xforce.iss.net/
184. ITU-T: IT - Open Systems Interconnection - The Directory: Overview of Concepts, Models and Services. Recommendation X.500, Geneva, (1997)
185. ITU-T: IT - Open Systems Interconnection - The Directory - Public Key and Attribute Certificate Frameworks. X.509 v4, Geneva, (2000)
186. Jaweed S.: Could There Ever be a Unitary Digital Certificate? Information Security Journal, Vol. 8, No. 3, pp. 36–44, Elsevier, (2003)
187. Joint Research Centre, PricewaterhouseCooopers: Final Report - GUIDES. Deliverable D5.2, (2002), http://eprivacyforum.jrc.it
188. Jøsang A.: A Logic for Uncertain Probabilities. International Journal of Uncertainty, Fuzziness and Knowledge-Based Systems, Vol. 9, No. 3, pp. 279–311, World Scientific Publishing Company, New York, (2001)
189. Jurišič A., Menezes A.: Elliptic Curves and Cryptography. Dr. Dobb's Journal, Vol. 1997, No. 264, pp. 26–37, CMP Media, (1997)
190. Jutla D.N., Bodorik P.: Sociotechnical Architecture for Online Privacy. Security & Privacy, Vol. 4, No. 2, pp. 29–39, IEEE, (2005)
191. Jürjens J.: Secure Systems Development with UML. Springer Verlag, Heidelberg, (2004)
192. Kalakota R., Robinson M., Tapscott D.: e-Business 2.0 - Roadmap for Success. Addison-Wesley, Reading, (2000)
193. Kaler C. (editor): Web Services Security (WS-Security), v 1.0. IBM, Cambridge / Sophia Antipolis / Kanagawa, (2002), http://www-106.ibm.com/developerworks/webservices/library/ws-secure
194. Kaliski B.: Certification Request Syntax - PKCS #10. IETF RFC 2314, Reston, (1998)
195. Kalin T., Kandus G., Trček D., Novak R., Sušelj M.: Smart-card and IP-based Infrastructure for a Health-care Information System in Slovenia. Proceedings of the INET 2000 - The internet global summit, Internet Society, Yokohama, (2000)
196. Katzenbeisser S., Petitcolas A.P.F.: Information Hiding Techniques for Steganography and Digital Watermarking. Artech house, Boston, (2000)
197. Keller S.S.: NIST-Recommended Random Number Generator Based on ANSI X9.31, Appendix A.2.4 Using the 3-Key Triple DES and AES Algorithms. NIST, Washington D.C., (2005)
198. Kemmerer R.A., Vigna G.: Intrusion Detection - A Brief History and Overview. Security & Privacy, Vol. 35, No. 5, pp. 27–30, IEEE, (2002)
199. Kemp G.: Auditing - The Future of IT Security. Computer Fraud & Security, Vol. 2001, No. 10, pp. 15–18, Elsevier, (2001)
200. Kendall K.E., Kendall J.E.: Systems Analysis and Design. Prentice Hall, Upper Saddle River, (1999)
201. Kenneally E.: The Byte Stops Here - Duty and Liability for Negligent Internet Security. IEEE Computer Security Journal, Vol. 16, No. 4, pp. 1–26, IEEE, (2000)
202. Kent S., Atkinson R.: Security Architecture for the Internet Protocol. IETF RFC 2401, Reston, (1998)

203. Kent S., Atkinson R.: IP Authentication Header (AH). IETF RFC 2402, Reston, (1998)

204. Kent S., Atkinson R.: IP Encapsulating Security Payload (ESP). IETF RFC 2406, Reston, (1998)

205. King S.: Threats and Solutions to Web Services Security. Network Security, Vol. 2003, No. 9, pp. 8–12, Elsevier (2003)

206. Kocher P.C., Jaffe J., Jun B.: Differential Power Analysis. Proceedings of the 19th Annual International Cryptology Conference on Advances in Cryptology, Lecture Notes In Computer Science, Vol. 1666, pp. 388–397, Springer Verlag, Heidelberg, (1999)

207. Koops   B.   J.:   Crypto   Law   Survey.   Tilburg,   (2004), http://rechten.uvt.nl/koops/cryptolaw/

208. Krawczyk, H.: SKEME - A Versatile Secure Key Exchange Mechanism for Internet. IEEE Proceedings of the 1996 Symposium on Network and Distributed Systems Security, pp. 114–127, San Diego, (1996)

209. Krawczyk H., Bellare M., Canetti R.: HMAC – Keyed-Hashing for Message Authentication. IETF RFC 2104, Reston, (1997)

210. Krsul I.: Software Vulnerability Analysis. Purdue University, PhD Thesis, Lafayette, (1998)

211. Krutz R.L., Vines R.D.: The CISSP Preparation Guide - Mastering the Ten Domains of Computer Security. John Wiley & Sons, New York, (2001)

212. Lamport L.: Password Authentication with Insecure Communication. Communications of ACM, Vol. 24, No. 11, pp. 770–772, ACM, (1981)

213. Lampson B.: Computer Security in the Real World. Computer, Vol. 37, No. 6, pp. 37–46, IEEE, (2004)

214. Lancaster S.: Public Key Infrastructure - A Micro and Macro Analysis. Computer Standards & Interfaces, Vol. 25. No. 5, pp. 437–446, Elsevier, (2003)

215. Landwehr C.E. et al.: A Taxonomy of Computer Program Security Flaws. ACM Computing Surveys, Vol. 26, No. 3, pp. 211–254, New York, (1994)

216. Laudon K. C., Laudon J. P.: Management Information Systems. Prentice Hall, Upper Saddle River, (2003)

217. Leach J.: Improving User Security Behavior. Computers & Security, Vol. 22, No. 8, pp. 685–692, Elsevier, (2003)

218. Le Hors A., Le Hegaret P., Wood L., Nicol G., Robie J., Champion M., Byrne S. (editors): Document Object Model (DOM) Level 3 Core Specification v 1.0. W3C REC-DOM-Level-3-Core-20040407, Cambridge / Sophia Antipolis / Kanagawa, (2004), http://www.w3.org/TR/2004/REC-DOM-Level-3-Core-20040407

219. Lesk M.: Micropayments - An Idea Whose Time Has Passed Twice? Computers & Security, Vol. 3, No. 1, pp. 61–63, Elsevier, (2004)

220. Lie H., Bos B.: Cascading Style Sheets, level 1. W3C REC-CSS1-19990111, Cambridge / Sophia Antipolis / Kanagawa, (1999), http://www.w3.org/TR/1999/REC-CSS1-19990111

221. Liu S., Silverman M.: A Practical Guide to Biometric Security Technology. IT Pro, Vol. 3, No. 1, pp. 27–32, IEEE, (2001)

222. Lobo C.: Security Log Management. Network Security, Vol. 2003, No. 11, pp. 6–9, Elsevier, (2003)

223. Locard E.: Manuel de technique policiére. Payot, Paris, (1934)

224. Logrippo L., Melanchuk T., Wors R.J.D.: The Algebraic Specification Language LOTOS. ACM SIGSOFT Software Engineering Notes, Vol. 15, No. 4, pp. 59–66, ACM, (1990)

225. Lopez J., Oppliger R., Pernul G.: Authentication and Authorization Infrastructures - A Comparative Survey. Computers & Security, Vol. 23, No. 7, pp. 578–590, Elsevier, (2004)

226. Madson C., Glenn R.: The Use of HMAC-MD5 within ESP and AH. IETF RFC 2403, Reston, (1998)

227. Makridakis S., et al.: The Forecasting Accuracy of Major Time Series Methods. John Wiley & Sons, Chichester, (1986)

228. Manny H. C.: Personal Privacy - Transatlantic Perspective. Computer Law & Security, Vol. 19, No. 1, pp. 4–10, Elsevier, (2003)

229. Marchesini J., Smith S.W., Zhao M.: Keyjacking - The Surprising Insecurity of Client-Side SSL. Computers & Security, Vol. 24, No. 2, pp. 109–123, Elsevier, (2005)

230. MasterCard Cardholder Solutions: Secure Electronic Payment Protocol. Draft standards, parts 1 through 4, St. Louis, (1995), http://www.x5.net/faqs/crypto/q140.html

231. Maughan D., Schertler M., Schneider M., Turner J.: Internet Security Association and Key Management Protocol (ISAKMP). IETF RFC 2408, Reston, (1998)

232. May C.: Dynamic Corporate Culture Lies at the Heart of Effective Security Strategy. Computer Fraud & Security, Vol. 2003, No. 5, pp. 10–13, Elsevier, (2003)

233. McClure S., Scambray J, Kurtz G.: Hacking Exposed. McGraw-Hill, New York, (2003)

234. Mead N. R.: Who Is Liable for Insecure Systems? IEEE Computer, Vol. 37, No. 7, pp. 27–34, IEEE, (2004)

235. Meisels I., Saaltink M.: The Z/EVES Reference Manual. ORA TR-97-5493-03d, Ottawa, (1997)

236. Menezes A.J., van Oorschot P.C., Vanstone S.A.: Handbook of Applied Cryptography. CRC Press, New York, (2001)

237. Meunchinger E. N.: Information Privacy Regulation: The EU Model and the French Model. Computer Law & Security Report, Vol. 17, No. 6, pp. 390–394, Elsevier, (2001)

238. Mills D.L.: Network Time Protocol (Version 3) Specification. IETF RFC 1305, Reston, (1992)

239. Miller R.: US to EU on Software Patents: "We sold out, you should too". NewsForge, (2004), http://trends.newsforge.com/trends/04/06/09/.

240. MITRE Corp.: Common Vulnerabilities and Exposures Database. MITRE, Washington D.C., (2005), http://cvs.mitre.org

241. Mockapetris P.: Domain Names - Concepts and Facilities. IETF RFC 1034, Reston, (1987)

242. Moses T. (editor): eXtensible Access Control Markup Language (XACML) v 2.0. OASIS Access_control-xacml-2.0-core-spec-cd-04, Billerica, (2004), http://docs.oasis-open.org/xacml/access_control-xacml-2.0-core-spec-cd-04.pdf

243. Mulej M., Likar B.: Increasing the Capacity of Companies to Absorb Inventions from Research Organizations and Encouraging People to Innovate. Cybernetics and Systems, Vol. 36, No. 5, pp. 491–512, Taylor and Francis, (2005)

244. Myers M., Akney R., Malpani A., Gaperin S., Adams C.: X.509 Internet Public Key Infrastructure Online Certificate Status Protocol - OCSP. IETF RFC 2560, Reston, (1999)
245. Nagappan R., Skoczylas R., Sriganesh R.P.: Developing Java Web Services. John Wiley & Sons, Indianapolis, (2003)
246. National Bureau of Standards: Data Encryption Standard. FIPS PUB 46, Washington D.C., (1977)
247. National Infrastructure Security Co-ordination Centre: Understanding Firewalls. NISCC Technical Note 10/04, rev. 2, London, (2005)
248. National Institute of Standards and Technology: Digital Signature Standard - DSS. FIPS 186, Washington D.C., (1994)
249. National Institute of Standards and Technology: An Introduction to Computer Security. NIST Special Publication 800-12, Washington D.C., (1996)
250. National Institute of Standards and Technology: Data Encryption Standard. FIPS PUB 46-3, Washington D.C., (1999)
251. National Institute of Standards and Technology: Advanced Encryption Standard. FIPS PUB 197, Washington D.C., (2001)
252. National Institute of Standards and Technology: Secure Hash Signature Standard. FIPS PUB 180-2, Washingotn D.C., (2002)
253. National Institute of Standards and Technology / SEMATECH: e-Handbook of Statistical Methods. NIST / SEMATECH, Gaithersburg / Austin, (2005), http://www.itl.nist.gov/div898/handbook/
254. Needham R.M., Schroeder M.D.: Using Encryption for Authentication in Large Networks of Computers. Communications of the ACM, Vol. 21, No. 12, pp. 993–999, ACM, (1978)
255. Network World: Executive Guide to Wireless Security. Network World Inc., Southborough, (2005)
256. Neumann B.C., T'so T.: Kerberos - An Authentication Service for Computer Networks. IEEE Comm. Magazine, Vol. 32, No. 9, pp. 33–38, IEEE, (1994)
257. Nguyen P, Stern J.: Cryptanalysis of the Ajtai-Dwork Cryptosystem. Proceedings of Crypto '98, Lecture Notes in Computer Science, Vol. 1462, pp. 223–242, Springer Verlag, Heidelberg, (1998)
258. Nichols R.K., Lekkas P.C.: Wireless Security - Models, Threats, and Solutions. McGraw-Hill, New York, (2002)
259. Niss H.: Application to Application Web Services - Interactive Web Services. Course materials, IT University of Copenhagen, Copenhagen, (2004), http://www.itu.dk/courses/IWSJ/E2004/slides/app2app.pdf
260. Northcutt S.: Network Intrusion Detection. New Riders Publishing, Indianapolis, (2002)
261. Novak, R.: Side-Channel Attack on Substitution Blocks. Proceedings of the Int. Conference on Applied Cryptography and Network Security 2003, Lecture Notes in Computer Science, Vol. 2846, pp. 307–318, Springer-Verlag, Heidelberg, (2003)
262. Object Management Group: Unified Modeling Language. OMG Specification v 1.5, OMG, Needham, (2003)
263. Odlyzko A.M.: The Case Against Micropayments. Proceedings of Financial Cryptography 03, Lecture Notes on Computer Science, No. 2742, pp. 77–83, Springer Verlag, Heidelberg, (2003)
264. Organization for Economic Co-operation and Development: Guidelines for Cryptography Policy. OECD, Paris, (1997)

265. Organization for Economic Co-operation and Development: Implementing The OECD "Privacy Guidelines" In The Electronic Environment: Focus On The Internet. DSTI/ICCP/REG(97)6/FINAL, OECD, Paris, (1998)

266. Orman H.: The OAKLEY Key Determination Protocol. IETF RFC 2412, Reston, (1998)

267. Palmer T.: PKI Needs Good Standards? Information Security Technical Report, Vol. 8, No. 3, pp. 6–13, Elsevier, (2003)

268. Parameswaran M., et al.: P2P Networking - An Information Sharing Alternative. IEEE Computer, Vol. 34, No. 7, pp. 31–37, IEEE, (2001)

269. Pelton J.N.: Wireless and Satellite Telecommunications. Prentice Hall, Upper Saddle River, (1995)

270. Pemble M.: Balancing the Security Budget. Computer Fraud & Security, Vol. 3, No. 10, pp. 8–11, Elsevier, (2003)

271. Pernul G.: Information Systems Security: Scope, State-of-the-art and Evaluation of Techniques. International Journal of Information Management, Vol. 15. No. 3, pp. 242–256, Elsevier, (1995)

272. Peyravian M., Roginsky A., Žunić N.: Non-PKI Methods for Public Key Distribution. Computers & Security, Vol. 2004, No. 23, pp. 97–103, Elsevier, (2004)

273. Piaget J.: Judgment and Reasoning in the Child. Routledge, London, (1999)

274. Piper D.: The Internet IP Security Domain of Interpretation for ISAKMP. IETF RFC 2407, Reston, (1998)

275. Piper F.: Some Trends in Research in Cryptography and Security Mechanisms. Computers & Security, Vol. 22, No. 1, pp. 22–25, Elsevier, (2003)

276. Pisa Consortium: Privacy Incorporate Software Agent. (2005), http://pet-pisa.openspace.nl

277. Postel J.B.: User Datagram Protocol (UDP). IETF RFC 768, Reston, (1981)

278. Postel J.B.: Internet Protocol (IP). IETF RFC 791, Reston, (1981)

279. Postel J.B. (editor): Transmission Control Protocol (TCP). IETF RFC 793, Reston, (1981)

280. Postel J.B.: Simple Mail Transfer Protocol. IETF RFC 821, Reston, (1982)

281. Postel J.B., Reynolds J.: File Transfer Protocol. IETF RFC 959, Reston, (1985)

282. Potter B.: Wireless Security policies. Network Security, Vol. 2003, No. 10, pp. 10–12, Elsevier, (2003)

283. Pounder C.: The Emergence of a Comprehensive Obligation Towards Computer Security. Computers & Security, Vol. 21., No. 4., pp. 328–332, Elsevier, (2002)

284. Powers M. D.: The Internet Legal Guide. John Wiley & Sons, New York, (2002)

285. Prasad N., Rugieri M.: Technology Trends in Wireless Communications. Artceh House, London, (2003)

286. Priami C.: Preface to the Special Issue on Security in Global Computing. International Journal on Information Security, Vol. 2, No. 3-4, p. 125, Springer Verlag, (2004)

287. Ramsdell B. (editor): S/MIME Version 3 Message Specification. IETF RFC 2633, Reston, (1999)

288. Räpple M.: Sicherheitskonzepte für das Internet. dpunkt-Verlag, Heidelberg, (2001)

289. Regan K.: Wireless LAN Security - Things You Should Know About WLAN Security. Network Security, Vol. 03, No. 1, pp. 7–9, Elsevier, (2003)

290. Reid C.R., Floyd S.A.: Extending the Risk Analysis Model to Include Market-Insurance. Computers & Security, Vol. 20, No. 4, pp. 331–339, Elsevier, (2001)

291. Reiser H., Volker G.: A Honeynet within the German Network - Experiences and Results. Lecture Notes in Informatics, Vol. 46, pp. 113–128, Springer Verlag, Heidelberg, (2004)

292. Rivest R.L., Shamir A., Adleman L.M.: A Method for Obtaining Digital Signatures and Public-Key Cryptosystems. Communications of the ACM, Vol. 21, No. 2, pp. 120–126, ACM, (1978)

293. Rivest R.: The MD5 Message Digest Algorithm. RFC 1321, IETF, Reston, (1992)

294. Rivest R., Shamir A.: PayWord and MicroMint - Two Simple Micropayment Schemes. Lecture Notes In Computer Science, Vol. 1189, pp. 69–87, Springer Verlag, Heidelberg, (1996)

295. Rivest R.: The Case Against Regulating Encryption Technology. Scientific American, Vol. 10, No. 10, pp. 88–89, New York, (1998)

296. Rivest R.L.: Can We Eliminate Revocation Lists? Proceedings of Financial Cryptography 98, Lecture Notes in Computer Science, Vol. 1465, pp. 178–183, Springer Verlag, Heidelberg, (1998)

297. Roe M.: CA Requirements. PASSWORD Project R. 2.5 document. Cambridge, (1993)

298. Roesh M. et al.: Snort^{TM}Users Manual. The Snort Project, (2004), http://www.snort.org

299. RSA Laboratories: The RSA Laboratories' Frequently Asked Questions About Today's Cryptography, v 4.1. RSA Security Inc, Bedford, (2000)

300. Rüppel R.A.: A Formal Approach to Security Architectures. Proceedings of Eurocrypt 91, pp. 387–398, Brighton, (1991)

301. Sammes T., Jankinson B.: Forensic Computing - A Practitioners Guide. Springer Verlag, Heidelberg, (2000)

302. SANS institute: SANS/FBI Top 20 Vulnerabilities List. SANS, Bethesda, (2005), http://www.sans.org/resources/

303. Saxby S.: New Copyright Regulations Make Their Debut. Computer Law & Security Report, Vol. 19, No. 2, p. 443, Elsevier, (2003)

304. Saxby S.: EU Gets Tough on Intellectual Property Piracy. Computer Law & Security, Vol. 20, No. 3, p. 163, Elsevier, (2004)

305. Schneier B.: Description of a New Variable-Length Key, 64-Bit Block Cipher. Proceedings of Fast Software Encryption '93, pp. 191–204, Springer Verlag, Heidelberg, (1994)

306. Schneier B.: Applied Cryptography. John Wiley & Sons, New York, (1996)

307. Schneier B.: Secrets and Lies - Digital Security in a Networked World. John Wiley & Sons, New York, (2000)

308. Schneier B.: Regulating Cryptography. Crypto-Gram Newsletter, Vol. 4, No. 09/01, p. ?, Counterpane Inc., Mountain View, (2001), http://www.schneier.com/crypto-gram-0109a.html#5

309. Schneier B.: Hacking the Business Climate for Network Security. Computer, Vol. 37, No. 4, pp. 87–89, IEEE, (2004)

310. Schneier B.: SHA-1 Broken. Crypto-gram Newsletter, Vol. 8, No. 03/05, p. ?, Counterpane Internet Security, Mountain View, (2005), http://www.schneier.com/crypto-gram-0503.html#1

311. Schultz E.: Security views. Computers & Security, Vol. 21, No. 4, pp. 293–302, Elsevier, (2002)

312. Schultz E.: The Gap Between Cryptography and Information Security. Computers & Security, Vol. 21, No. 8, pp. 674–676, Elsevier, (2002)

313. Schultz E.: Security Views. Computers & Security, Vol. 21, No. 8, pp. 677–688, Elsevier, (2002)
314. Schultz E.: Security Views. Computers & Security, Vol. 22, No. 7, pp. 559–569, Elsevier, (2003)
315. Schwartau W.: Information Warfare. Thunder's Mouth Press, New York, (1996)
316. Security Focus: Bugtraq Archives. Symantec corporation, Cupertino, (2005), http://www.securityfocus.com/
317. Shannon C.E.: A Mathematical Theory of Communication. Bell Systems Technical Journal, Vol. 27, No. ? / No. ?, pp. 379–423 / pp. 623–656, ?, (1948)
318. Sharpe A., Russel C.: Employee Monitoring. Computer Law & Security, Vol. 19, No. 5, pp. 411–415, Elsevier, (2003)
319. Shooman M.L.: Reliability of Computer Systems and Networks. John Wiley & Sons, New York, (2002)
320. Solovay R., Strassen V.: A Fast Monte-Carlo Test for Primality. SIAM Journal on Computing, Vol. 1977, No. 6, pp. 84–85, Philadelphia, (1977)
321. Spivey M. J.: The Z Notation - A Reference Manual. Prentice-Hall, London, (1989)
322. Srisuresh P., Holdrege M.: IP Network Address Translator (NAT) Terminology and Considerations. IETF RFC 2663, Reston, (1999)
323. Stallings W.: Cryptography and Network Security. Prentice Hall, Upper Saddle River, (2003)
324. Steinke G.: Data Privacy Approaches From US and EU Perspectives. Telematics and Informatics, Vol. 19, No. 2, pp. 193–200, Elsevier, (2000)
325. Stephenson P.: Applying Forensic Techniques to Information System Risk Management. Computer Fraud & Security, Vol. 2003, No. 12, pp. 17–19, Elsevier, (2003)
326. Sterman J.: Business Dynamics - Systems Thinking for a Complex World. McGraw Hill, New York, (2000)
327. Stewart J.: Spam & Sobig – Arm in Arm. Network Security, Vol. 3, No. 10. pp. 12–16, Elsevier, (2003)
328. Stool C.: The Cuckoo's Egg. Pocket Books, New York, (1990)
329. Stuart R., Norvig P.: Artificial Intelligence – A Modern Approach. Prentice Hall, New York, (1995)
330. Syverson P., van Oorschot P.: On Unifying Some Cryptographic Protocol Logic. IEEE Proceedings of the Symposium on Security & Privacy, pp. 14–28, Oakland, (1994)
331. Tanenbaum A.S.: Computer Networks. Prentice Hall, Upper Saddle River, (1996)
332. The Institute of Electrical and Electronics Engineers: Standards for Information Technology - Telecommunications and Information Exchange between Systems - Local and Metropolitan Area Network - Specific Requirements - Part 11 / Wireless LAN Medium Access Control (MAC) and Physical Layer (PHY) Specifications. IEEE 802.11, Piscataway, (1999), http://grouper.ieee.org/groups/802/11/main.html
333. Tittel E., Chapple M., Stewart J.M.: CISSP - Certified Information Systems Security Professional Study Guide. Cybex, Alameda, (2003)
334. Torrubia A. et al.: Cryptography Regulations for E-commerce and Digital Rights Management. Computers & Security, Vol. 20, No. 8, pp. 724–738, Elsevier, (2010)

335. Trček D.: Organization of Certification Authorities in a Global Network. Computer Security Journal, Vol. 10, No. 1. pp. 71–81, Computer Security Institute, (1994)

336. Trček D., Klobučar T., Jerman B.B., Bračun F.: CA-Browsing System – A Supporting Application for Global Security Services. IEEE Proceedings of the ISOC Symposium on Network and Distributed System Security, pp. 123–128, San Diego, (1994)

337. Trček D., Jerman B.B.: Formal Language for Security Services Base Modeling and Analysis. Computer Communications, Vol. 18, No. 12, pp. 921–928, Elsevier, (1995)

338. Trček D., Jerman B.B.: Certification Authorities in a Global Network - Procedures and Guidelines for a PKI. Australian Computer Journal, Vol. 29, No. 2, pp. 41–47, Sydney, (1997)

339. Trček D.: Minimizing the Risk of Electronic Document Forgery. Computer Standards & Interfaces, Vol. 19, No. 2, pp. 161–167, Elsevier, (1998)

340. Trček D., Novak R., Kandus G., Sušelj M.: Slovene Smart-card and IP Based Health-care Information System Infrastructure. International Journal of Medical Informatics, Vol. 61. No. 1, pp. 33–43, Elsevier, (2001)

341. Trček D.: Towards Trust Management Standardization. Computer Standards and Interfaces, Vol. 26, No. 6, pp. 543–548, Elsevier, (2004)

342. Trček D.: Trust Formalization - From Taxonomy to Modeling and Simulation Framework. Proceedings of the IASTED International Conference on Software Engineering, pp. 297–302, Acta Press, Innsbruck, (2004)

343. Trček D.: Business Dynamics Supported Security Policy Management. Proceedings of the 22nd Conference of the SDS, John Wiley & Sons, Oxford, (2004)

344. Trosow S.: Digital Millenium Copyright Act - Does Canada Really Need It? University of Toronto Information Rights Salon, (2003), http://www.fis.utoronto.ca/research/inforights/SamuelTrosow.htm

345. UK Government: UK Government Gateway. UK Government, (2005), http://www.gateway.gov.uk/

346. UN Commission on International Trade Law - UNCITRAL: Model Law on Electronic Commerce. UNCITRAL, Vienna, (1996), http://www.uncitral.org/english/texts/elect-com/ecommerceindex.htm

347. UN Commission on International Trade Law: Model Law on Digital Signatures. UNCITRAL, Vienna, (2001), http://www.uncitral.org/english/texts/elect-com/ecommerceindex.htm

348. Ungureanu V.: Formal Support for Certificate Management Policies. Computers & Security, Vol. 23, No. 4, pp. 300–311, Elsevier, (2004)

349. US Department of Defense: Trusted Computer System Evaluation Criteria. DoD, standard CSC-STD-00l-83, Washington D.C., (1983)

350. US Department of Justice: Electronic Crime Scene Investigation - A Guide for First Responders. NCJ-187736, Washington D.C., (2001)

351. US Government: e-Authentication Gateway, Washington D.C., (2005), http://www.cio.gov/eauthentication/

352. US Senate / House of Representatives: Digital Millennium Copyright Act - DMCA. US Senate / House of Representatives, Washington D.C., (1998), http://www.copyright.gov/legislation/dmca.pdf

353. US Senate / House of Representatives: Controlling the Assault of Non-Solicited Pornography and Marketing Act of 2003 - CAN-SPAM Act of 2003, US Senate, Washington D.C., (2003), http://www.spamlaws.com/federal/108s877.html

354. Van de Hof S.: Digital Signature Law Survey. Tilburg, (2004), http://rechten.uvt.nl/simone/DS-LAWSU.htm
355. Wack J., Cutler K., Pole J.: Guidelines on Firewalls and Firewall Policy, NIST Special Publication 800-41, Gaithersburg, (2002)
356. Weinberg N.: Digital Dough Fails to Rise. Network World, 04/12/99, Southborough, (1999), http://www.nwfusion.com/news/1999/0412dough.html
357. Wilson P.: "Top-down" versus "Bottom-up" - Different Approaches to Security. Network Security, Vol. 2003, No. 12, pp. 17–19, Elsevier, (2003)
358. Wirtz B.: Biometric System Security - part 1. Biometric Technology Today, Vol. 11, No. 2, pp. 6–8, Elsevier, (2003)
359. Wirtz B.: Biometric System Security - part 2. Biometric Technology Today, Vol. 11, No. 3, pp. 8–9, Elsevier, (2003)
360. Wolfe-Wilson J., Wolfe B.H.: Management Strategies for Implementing Forensic Security Measures. Information Security Technical Report, Vol. 8, No. 2, pp. 55–64, Elsevier, (2003)
361. World Intellectual Property Organization: Primer On E-commerce and Intellectual Property Issues. WIPO, Geneva, (2000)
362. World Wide Web Consortium: Simple Object Access Protocol. W3C Recommendations TR 20030624, Parts 0, 1 and 2, Cambridge / Sophia Antipolis / Kanagawa, (2003), http://www.w3.org/TR/soap/
363. Xiaoping J.: ZTC – A Type Checker for Z Notation. User's Guide, Chicago, (1998)
364. Xuejia L, Massey J.L.: A Proposal for a New Block Encryption Standard. EUROCRYPT '90, pp. 389–404, Springer Verlag, Heidelberg, (1991)
365. Young K.: Overcoming PKI Obstacles. eWeek, January 4, CNET Networks Inc., (2001), http://www.zdnet.com/

Index

About the Author

Dr. Denis Trček has been involved in the field of computer networks and IS security and privacy for almost fifteen years.

He has taken part in various European research and application projects, as well as domestic projects in government, banking and insurance sectors. His bibliography includes over one hundred titles, including contributions to books published by John Wiley & Sons, Springer Verlag and Idea Group Inc.

D. Trček has served (and still serves) as a member of various international boards, from editorial to professional ones, and he is also a member of IEEE.

He is inventor of a family of light-weight cryptographic protocols for authentication and key exchange (patent pending).

Breinigsville, PA USA
23 September 2010
245807BV00010B/74/P